SEARCHING
FOR
SPIDERMAN

Ally Chumley is a writer and investigative journalist with a background in education and research. She is the author of dozens of books in the education sphere, where she has been published by Macmillan, Blake Education, John Wiley and many others. Ally is based on the Mid North Coast of New South Wales, not far from the town where William Tyrrell went missing.

SEARCHING

FOR

SPIDERMAN

The disappearance of three-year-old
WILLIAM TYRRELL

ALLY CHUMLEY

Hardie Grant

BOOKS

Published in 2020 by Hardie Grant Books,
an imprint of Hardie Grant Publishing

Hardie Grant Books (Melbourne)
Building 1, 658 Church Street
Richmond, Victoria 3121

Hardie Grant Books (London)
5th & 6th Floors
52–54 Southwark Street
London SE1 1UN

hardiegrantbooks.com

 A catalogue record for this
NATIONAL
LIBRARY
OF AUSTRALIA
book is available from the
National Library of Australia

Searching for Spiderman
ISBN 978 1 74379 606 1

10 9 8 7 6 5 4 3 2 1

Cover design by Josh Durham, Design by Committee
Cover image by Nadezhda1906/Bigstock.com
Diagrams and illustrations by Ally Chumley
Typeset in 10.75/16 pt Sabon LT Std by Kirby Jones
Printed in Australia by Griffin Press, part of Ovato, an Accredited
ISO AS/NZS 14001 Environmental Management System printer

FSC
www.fsc.org
MIX
Paper from
responsible sources
FSC® C009448

The paper this book is printed on is certified against the Forest
Stewardship Council® Standards. Griffin Press holds FSC® chain
of custody certification SGS-COC-005088. FSC® promotes
environmentally responsible, socially beneficial and economically
viable management of the world's forests.

To Kendall – a big heart, broken

CONTENTS

AUTHOR'S NOTE

Lots of people could claim a special connection with William Tyrrell's story. It's no more mine than it is yours. My own search for Spiderman began simply because he disappeared from my figurative backyard – I've lived a stone's throw from Kendall for most of my life. The tragedy hit us full force and, in absentia, William soon became Australia's favourite little boy. Like others, I kept on top of developments in the case. And being a researcher, I took notes. Driven by a need to understand this baffling disappearance, I compiled an extensive dossier.

Then, out of the blue, someone I knew was sensationally named a person of interest. Stunned at this shocking twist, I offered my help and was catapulted straight into the deep end. In 2014, I was a textbook author working from home, but by 2015, I'd made a necessary leap into investigative journalism.

I would spend more than five years on the case, interviewing, researching, compiling evidence and attending all three sittings of the inquest at the NSW State Coroner's Court in 2019 and 2020. I was able to get my hands on court documents that helped me draw all the threads of William's story together. I dug deep because I wanted you to hear the full story. The material in this book is entirely factual. The conclusions I draw from those facts are my own. In this book, you'll hear family members, witnesses and investigators speak in their own words, apart from a few instances of reconstructed dialogue. Non-publication orders require me to use pseudonyms to protect the identities of certain people. But their testimony invites you to look behind the veil of secrecy that has shrouded this investigation.

Although I promise a good deal of new insight, certain facts have necessarily been left out of this book. I had to ensure that the investigation was not compromised by untimely revelations. The need to bring the perpetrators to justice must never be trumped by the need to know.

The more devoted Marvel fans out there will have noticed that a hyphen is missing from 'Spiderman'. It might seem trivial, but I decided to reshape the legendary name in this way for the purposes of this book. In the Australian consciousness, the names William Tyrrell and Spiderman have become one, but it just didn't seem right to turn this dear little boy into a trademark. So you won't see the official spelling anywhere in this account.

ACKNOWLEDGEMENTS

I extend my sincere thanks to my partner in true crime, Andy Chumley. Special thanks to Lewis and Curtis for your patience in waiting for me all this time. You never complained. I am deeply indebted to Catherine for her vital assistance, so much so that I'll use her real name – thanks, Fuzz. You really did go above and beyond and I'm very grateful. Thanks also to Delilah for casting her expert eyes over the manuscript, to Jo for her unfailing support and to my dear Mum and Dad for imparting to me their love of words and their outrage at injustice. I'd like to thank the people who graciously permitted me to chat with them – William's family members, police from Strike Force Rosann and the people of Kendall and the Camden Haven. You've been generous and patient. I'm especially thankful to the team at Hardie Grant for permitting me to write this book. I'd always hoped William's story would be told by a local.

LIST OF KEY FIGURES

William's birth family

Brendan Collins – William's birth father

Karlie Tyrrell – William's birth mother

Natalie Collins – William's paternal grandmother; mother of
Brendan Collins

William's foster family

Nathan Thomas – William's foster father

Anna Wyndham – William's foster mother

Lindsay Tyrrell – William's older sister (foster daughter of Anna
and Nathan)

Phillip Wyndham – William's foster grandfather (known by the
children as 'Opa')

Nancy Wyndham – William's foster grandmother (known by the
children as 'Nana')

Organisations and their representatives

FACS – Family and Community Services (NSW Department of
Communities and Justice)

Young Hope – the Salvation Army's Out of Home Care
Organisation

Captain Michelle White – Young Hope Program Director

Ben Atwood – Young Hope Program Case Worker

Judicial figures and legal representatives

Harriet Grahame DSC – Deputy NSW State Coroner
Gerard Craddock SC – counsel assisting the Coroner
Margaret Cunneen – barrister for Gary Jubelin
Robin Bhalla – barrister for NSW Police
Michelle Swift – barrister for Brendan Collins
Peter O'Brien – barrister for Bill Spedding

Law enforcement officers

Detective Chief Inspector Gary Jubelin
Detective Chief Inspector David Laidlaw
Detective Senior Sergeant Mark Dukes
Detective Sergeant Laura Beacroft
Senior Constable Chris Rowley
Senior Constable Daniel Dring
Senior Constable Wendy Hudson
Senior Constable Robert Dingle

Selected persons of interest

Bill Spedding
Danny Parish
Derek Nichols
Dooley Northam
Frank Abbott
Geoffrey Owen
Paul Bickford
Paul Savage
Ray Porter
Robert Donohoe
Steve Arter
Tony Jones

Selected key witnesses

Jeffrey (pseudonym) – protected
    witness
Mr Ribbon (pseudonym) –
    protected witness
Ronald Chapman
Tanya (pseudonym) – protected
    witness

The little boy lost in the lonely fen,
Led by the wand'ring light,
Began to cry, but God ever nigh,
Appeared like his father in white.

William Blake

PROLOGUE

'Shh. Quiet!' Kay held up one hand, head tilted against the wind. 'I heard something.' The party of four shuffled forward, listening intently. A young man she'd met just that evening started his dog in the direction Kay was pointing, but the reeds were too thick to penetrate. The dog signalled that way. The handler brought her up short. The dog insisted. He relented and followed her lead. The searchers trudged in the greenish mud, stagnant water swallowing their gumboots. Torchlight threw strange shadows over the swamp. A rhythm asserted itself. *Call out, stop, listen, move forward.*

'Listen. Did you hear that?' Kay's voice was an urgent whisper. But the only sounds were other searchers' voices at the edge of the pine forest. She stood in limbo, body tentative, mind racing on instinct. Then a faint whimper came, and the spell was broken. Impulsively, Kay dropped to her knees in the slush and forced herself through the thick bushes choking the swamp's shallows.

'He's in there,' Kay's teenage son said, crashing past her, arms shielding his face from spiked, broken branches. He tore through the barrier that rescuers said was impossible for a toddler to breach. Looking down at the boggy tangle of reeds, he gasped. Kay caught up with him, then time stood still. There, with his mouth and nose just an inch clear of the water, lay a little boy, huddled against the cold. Kay's heart leapt and hot tears sprang up. She didn't remember making the guttural sound that prompted a commotion from somewhere behind her. A scattering of torch beams flashed between the pines on the verge of the marshland.

'What's going on? You got him?' A brief pause, scuffling noises, then the answer rang out.

'We've got him!' A human chain carried the limp little body to the roadside. Kay peered into the boy's pale face. He was little more than a baby. His eyes were loosely closed. A thin t-shirt clung to his chest, soaked and stained green with algae. Tender arms and legs were bloodied with scratches. Kay whispered a word to little Tyler: 'Mummy'. He made a small response. Small, but a sure sign of life. She breathed out a long sigh and stroked the dog's head.

Tyler Kennedy was found alive by volunteers untrained and uninvited. Kay and her son were among them – two good Samaritans with no connection to the child. I had gone on the search for Tyler Kennedy myself that night – a confronting experience that left its mark on me, despite the positive outcome.

News of the Johns River operation spread across the state. Journalists publicly chided the local command for getting it wrong; police admitted as much. They shouldn't have called off the search at nightfall. Factors of danger multiply for searchers after dark. But they also become graver threats to a lost child. It's a balancing act. They throw every resource into a rescue, ever alert that they're risking lives. Abandoning a search for a missing child is a tough call. A tough call made easier when it's not your child.

At 1.15 in the morning Amanda Kennedy heard her son had been found. At that moment, time ceased to be important again. She'd suffocated watching the clock for fifteen hours, imagining every breath she took was one taken from her little boy. She could feel the advance of each precious minute lessening his chances of survival. Two-year-old Tyler went missing around 10.30 on a Friday morning, a time and day that superstitious folks in the Camden Haven now consider cursed. Because, the following year, again at around 10.30 on a Friday morning, another toddler would disappear from a spot just up the highway. This one would be wearing a Spiderman suit.

1

DÉJÀ VU

I was driving home from Laurieton and a story was unfolding on local radio. Kendall was abuzz with activity. A little boy had wandered off from his grandmother's house. That time again: 10.30 in the morning. It was 12 September 2014, a Friday.

I was concerned but confident. Children lost in the bush are findable. No need to panic. September's warmer than May and this boy was older than Tyler, and missing from a house, not a forty-acre farm. News channels sang the praises of locals who'd once again turned out in force to get the job done. It'd just be a matter of time and William Tyrrell would be back in safe arms.

I drove through Kendall. It's on the way back to Comboyne, my home town. Two patrol cars turned off the main drag, heading to the showground. Police had set up a command post there. I saw a scattering of vigilant locals on the corner, and a little swell of pride rose.

'The kid's lucky he got himself lost in the right place.' I always talk to myself when I'm driving, and living in Comboyne, I do a lot of it. Reliving the Johns River search for Tyler Kennedy, I rehearsed the scenes to come: exhilaration when the good news came, a breathless outpouring of gratitude from the boy's parents.

When the Pacific Highway brings you up this way, you get your bearings from a trio of mountains – North, Middle and South Brother. It was the Birpai people who'd first imagined these majestic peaks as watchful brothers, although a moderately distinguished sea captain called Cook would claim the credit for naming them. But he didn't get to enjoy it for long because as he sailed around the Pacific naming things, some Hawaiians took his name a bit too literally. They lit a fire, roasted him up and ate him.

The three Brothers preside over the blue waterways of the region, home to valuable fisheries and oyster farms. Osprey hunt overhead; cormorants down below. Creeks snake through croplands with dairy farms at their feet. South Brother rises from the swampy lowlands of Moorland and Johns River. West of the highway is Middle Brother, the largest of the siblings. And the village of Kendall fends off the mountain's encroaching forests.

You go east to find the river's mouth, where North Brother looms over Laurieton. This is where you do banking, visit the doctor and treat yourself and the pelicans to fish and chips. North Brother's lookout offers spectacular views of the Camden Haven River's inlet. It's a straight channel linking mountain and sea. Rumours say its unusual geography attracts covens of witches who conduct secret rites on the summit after dark. If they do, I've never seen them. In North Brother's shadow, on the shores of Queens Lake, is Lakewood, where they sell life's essentials – groceries, fuel and lottery tickets.

The hamlet of Comboyne is a good thirty minutes away, up an unsealed mountain road. Winding through state forest, the Lorne Road is a hazardous climb. Timber jinkers, cattle trucks and speeding milk tankers make it interesting. At the top, the land flattens out to a plateau seven hundred metres above sea level. It's cool, often foggy – the perfect escape in summer. On its emerald fields and iron-rich, red soil, Comboyne grows cattle, avocadoes and blueberries. And privet, tobacco and lantana. Despite being confirmed coasties for decades, my husband and I rented a farmhouse there the year before Kendall first heard the name of William Tyrrell.

That Friday afternoon, I mowed the orchard and the guinea fowl followed me, picking up the insects I'd disturbed. I thought about the missing boy as I dealt with an injured chook. I sprayed purple antiseptic around a cut on her head. I wondered if William might be hurt as well as lost. When birds see a red patch they'll viciously peck at the spot until they kill the unfortunate creature. You need to disguise the blood with a different colour.

I came inside and checked the news. I was surprised the little boy hadn't yet been found and resolved to join the search in the morning. I collected the eggs and fed Banjo, our poultry-friendly cat. Then, with rare and fortuitous forward planning, I made chicken soup.

Curiosity and empathy kept William Tyrrell's plight before me that night. The familiar grip of worry tightened as I looked at state forest maps. All that dark green conjured up horrors involving my kids. We'd lost our three-year-old son in Settlement City shopping centre once and I'd momentarily glimpsed my worst fear. I don't recommend it. But we'd found him quickly and the panic was over. Euphoria sedated us into the belief that our children's safety depends only on our vigilance. A strong cuppa soon saw me recover. But now, with William, as with Tyler, I'd see the sweet face of my own child superimposed on every image of that little boy lost. To banish the spectre, I sat at my keyboard issuing online pleas. 'Keep looking!' I reposted updates on Facebook and scanned the headlines.

Saturday dawned and my husband and children awoke with change-of-season colds. At seven and six years old, the boys needed me at home. I couldn't get down to Kendall after all. I fed the chooks some kitchen scraps and the family some chicken soup – synergistic recycling. I telephoned a friend from Kendall. Gossip was simmering already. That person – whom I decline to name – was a rich source of material for this book. He knows everyone living within a fifty-kilometre radius.

There was plenty of activity online. I looked for good news. None had come, not yet. Television updates were broadcast live from the scene. It was strange to see people I knew fronting the cameras, Kendall's humble surrounds in the background. They looked awkward, some furtive, most bewildered. No one risked a one-finger salute for the cameras, not even the kids. Quiet little Kendall was in the spotlight for all the wrong reasons.

*

At day three, William Tyrrell still hadn't been found. A jolt of pain at the news made me realise the Johns River incident was still raw. 'Not again,' I thought. The relief of rescue had temporarily overwritten my memory of the sickening fear that had torn at my stomach the year before. But now it was back. Standing in my kitchen I freshly remembered when Tyler Kennedy went missing, how I imagined it was my child out there in the dark bushland. I felt I owed something to his parents – penance for their suffering. Was their bad fortune the cost of my good fortune to have my kids safe at home?

Searching on that unusually cold May night, I remember being scared to peer into dark places, fearful of seeing things that couldn't be unseen. But fear gave way to a greater worry – never finding him, never knowing what happened. How could his parents learn to live with that? So I'd forced myself to prod at mounds of earth and leaves and peer down steep dam banks, frustrated yet relieved that my watery torch beam never illuminated a body. In the days after Tyler's rescue, sheer jubilation had banished those memories. But now, William Tyrrell's disappearance forcefully revived the urgency and dread. Searching for a lost child is best described by a forgivable cliché – every parent's worst nightmare.

Later that afternoon I logged off Facebook and drove over to the general store. It's the bush telegraph exchange around Comboyne village. Fears for William Tyrrell had crept up the mountain overnight. My optimism faltered as I talked with locals alert to dangers on their own properties: creeks, dams, well-holes, snakes, wild dogs, hidden drop-offs in the bush. We stood outside the shop and shared what we knew. It was busy for a Sunday. Someone wondered if William could have made it to the railway line. Or the river. Another person mentioned the temperature was 13.2 degrees in Kendall overnight. I went into the shop to buy bread. A knot of locals had formed around the dairy freezer and I was drawn into another conversation, leading nowhere.

Back at home, my disquieting thoughts grew. Without warrant, I began second-guessing the leaders of the search operation. They'd made multiple passes over the ground where Tyler Kennedy lay, and they'd missed him. *I'd missed him.* If Kay's son hadn't pushed into that place – the place I'd abandoned – Tyler would have surely drowned or perished from hypothermia. But the online chatter surrounding William Tyrrell's disappearance disagreed with me. There was unbounded confidence, faith in the dogs, choppers, expert ground searchers and the State Emergency Service (SES). I never questioned their commitment, but my faith wavered when I considered the vastness of the search area and the proximity of the river.

Police consult the authoritative *National land search operations manual* (2010) when enacting searches. But that weighty tome doesn't fill you with hope. It discusses survivability in clinical terms heartbreaking to read when you apply it to a child of three-and-a-half: 'Survivors often fail to accomplish simple tasks in a logical order, thus hindering, delaying or even preventing their own rescue. This is an effect of shock, affecting even the strong minded. As shock wears off, some will develop active attitudes. Those that do not will die unless rescued quickly.'[1] I wondered what that meant for William.

In devastating detail, the manual describes other factors affecting life expectancy: clothing, thirst, hunger, exhaustion, fear, loneliness and the all-important will to live. William was wearing a thin polyester Spiderman suit and open sandals. He had no food or water. He faced the terrifying situation of being lost. Or worse.

As the day closed, I succumbed to the family bug. I couldn't join the search and spread the virus, I told myself. So I heated up some chicken soup and searched from the sidelines. I printed colour maps and layouts of the neighbourhood, tracing in red texta a logical route William could have taken away from the house in just five short minutes. A red path of logic through all that green.

I mentally timed a walk down Benaroon Drive to its junction at Batar Creek Road. (If you pronounce 'Batar' like 'guitar', with the last syllable emphasised, you've got it about right.) Two or three minutes, perhaps? But how long for a toddler? Was he running? The SIX Maps online tool gave the distance from 48 Benaroon Drive to Batar Creek Road – just under two hundred metres.

I have some friends who live on that road, just before you hit the corrugations that rattle your teeth loose. I don't like going out there to visit them. There's dense bush between each driveway, winding, grinding trails that are barely drivable. Much of Batar Creek Road has eroded into deep ditches that catch the unwary visitor off-guard. Jagged rocks puncture the hard-baked soil and threaten to do the same to your tyres. There is nothing green at the roadside, just scrub thickly coated with orange dust.

I'd been down Benaroon Drive to a garage sale a few years earlier. It branches off to the right, ending in bushland. The dog-leg leads beyond number 48 to a rough track that takes you to Kendall Cemetery. It's four-wheel drive access only. Twenty-one houses make up the little estate of two streets – Benaroon Drive and Ellendale Crescent. They're set back from the road with frontages of twenty metres or more. Natural barriers of trees and bushes obscure the house fronts from view. It's quiet. Very quiet. In the cool, you can hear the throaty calls of doves, and in the heat of the day, the menacing caws of crows.

Tissues piled up and constant sneezing drove me away from the keyboard and into bed. The house was chilly for September. I put a chunk of tallowwood on the fire, then got under the covers. I wondered how long it would be before William's family faced the cameras. Probably no need. They'd find him today for sure. But a different narrative invaded my sleep. I dreamt about the search for Tyler Kennedy. He was wearing a Spiderman suit. There were different endings. He drowned in the river, he tumbled out of a climbing tree, he fell down a well-hole, he was entangled in reeds face down in the swamp. All of these endings took turns in my dream and, each time, he died.

Over the next few days, energy levels at my place waned, weakening my resolve to join the search. I never did get there. At the time, I couldn't quite explain why. I wasn't in great physical shape, I reasoned. What could I contribute that fitter, faster people couldn't? Still, I felt guilty for opting out. Later, I would realise what had stopped me. I'm just going to tell you straight: it was fear. I couldn't put myself out there. If I was a searcher, I'd be terrified of finding him. And of not finding him. The same old tussle. I couldn't face it again. The irony is I could never have predicted just how deep into the search for Spiderman I'd end up going.

*

On television, I watched the Mid North Coast's Police District Commander, Superintendent Paul Fehon make impassioned pleas to the public. He told us to come forward if we had any information about young William's whereabouts. As the updates went to air, I noticed Fehon kept calling him 'young William'. My Kendall friends found it endearing. I'm not sure what I thought about it, but now I catch myself using the same phrase. In my heart, and yours I imagine, the cruel fact of his tender age is what really hurts.

While the television news kept William's cheeky little face before the public, I rang Jen, a friend in Kendall. We arranged to meet up. On the phone, she said there was a backstory we weren't being told. So I headed down the mountain.

Arriving in Kendall, I parked in Comboyne Street, outside the post office. I spotted Jen across the road at the general store. She was with Trish, a woman I'd met earlier that year. The pair filled me in on the latest. A question was circulating around the village – why hadn't we seen William's parents? On the news we'd seen a woman representing the family. She was identified by her first name only: Nicole. Jen told me William's parents were from Sydney. They were visiting Kendall for the weekend. But neither Jen nor Trish knew them – they only knew his nana, who lived at Benaroon Drive.

I asked my friends over coffee what they thought had happened. We sat outdoors at Miss Nellie's café. Jen feigned a blank look, and Trish looked conflicted, as though she didn't want to talk about it. I didn't know her all that well. She was hard to read.

'What's the hush-hush backstory you mentioned on the phone?'

'Just tell her, Trish,' Jen prompted, adding sweetener to her coffee.

'William Tyrrell is a foster child.'

I assumed Trish was a friend of the foster family. I wish now that I'd asked her more questions that day, because I wouldn't get another chance to speak with her. But of course at the time, I had no intention of writing a book on the case. Over the next week I discovered there were others in Kendall who knew about William's foster status. His foster grandmother had told her friends and neighbours. It had been discussed quite casually around town.

Things unfolded in fast-forward online. Onlookers said this was an odd tale. What *has* happened to William Tyrrell? Theories ran way ahead of the Little Boy Lost scenario favoured by print and TV news. The mainstream narrative was clear: William was lost in thick bushland and a massive search effort was underway. Hopes of a live rescue gave way to a grim recovery mission.

Online, official reports only poured fuel on the fires of speculation. Armchair detectives scoured for new titbits to help them formulate their theories. I confess I was one of them. Drawn into local gossip and confused by the secrecy around William's family, I could think of nothing other than the case. I kept looking at the picture of the adorable little guy in his blue-checked shirt. His expression intrigued me – intrigued *us*. We fancied there was something in those eyes that made him special.

Social media groups and pages were popping up on Facebook like mushrooms after rain. I promptly joined them under my husband's name. Research told me most members would be middle-aged women. Intuition told me they'd share information more readily with a man. Sexist or not, I was right. My posts on Facebook were directed to locals on the search: 'He's out there. We found Tyler; we'll find William.'

But there was another compelling reason I stayed glued to social media that November. Like my Kendall friends, I'd come to believe we were looking at an abduction. The bush was too rugged, the timeframe too short for a toddler to travel far. It was becoming more and more patent that William wasn't in the bush.

*

The year before William vanished, I had volunteered to undertake a research project for a relative. Elaine Braun was sixty and had been adopted as an infant. She had hopes of finding her birth mother. Her new parents had been cruel; she recalled her adoptive mother reminding her that she was trash they'd 'picked up out of the gutter'.

Elaine had no knowledge of her history – nothing more than a name written on a birth certificate. My work in solving this puzzle was greatly complicated by the absence of any official records of the adoption. In the 1950s, Australia and New Zealand had a reciprocal agreement termed 'native adoption', whereby children were moved between countries without passing through official immigration channels. Unwed mothers could deliver their child at discreetly operated, private medical facilities, complete the bare minimum of paperwork and have an adoption handled for them without leaving much of a papertrail.

Online searches had yielded a list of more than three hundred hits containing the names of women across six Commonwealth countries. Electoral rolls, obituaries, cemetery records and births, deaths and marriage registers yielded addresses to attach to the names. I printed them out on pink copy paper. My mid-size bulldog clip barely enclosed the sheaf. People would look at that list and commiserate, noting the impossibility of the task. But I would correct them because I came to realise that it's highly likely that one of those names was the right one. I felt it was only a matter of time. If I worked systematically, I would come to find Elaine's mum.

I was about three-quarters of the way through the list when I did find her. Some meticulous soul had noted the woman's maiden name in her late husband's obituary, along with the married names of her daughters. The surnames were unusual, enabling me to find them on Facebook. I checked out some of their pictures and the physical resemblances were undeniable. The sight of what was evidently a tight-knit, loving family made me choke back tears. Then I saw a silver-haired little lady pictured posing with her family at a wedding. Comments told me this was Elaine's mother. As of just a week ago, she was alive. My discovery took a while to sink in. The woman was in her eighties when we found her and she lived in good health for some years after she was reunited with her eldest daughter. She'd kept Elaine's existence secret for more than sixty years.

The outcome of that research paid me in far better currency than dollars. Elaine was returned to her family. She went from being a lonely, abused adoptee to a much-loved sister of five. Her family are firmly a part of her life now, and they travel between Australia and New Zealand regularly to maintain that connection. Best of all, Elaine found she had been loved and wanted by her mother – desperately so. The adoption had been forced on Elaine's mother by her parents – keen to avoid a scandal in their small town. That research gave a broken woman the answers that allowed her to heal. Since then, my belief in the magic of methodical research has been unwavering.

A few months after I had completed my search on behalf of Elaine, I found something that galvanised me into decisive action on the William Tyrrell case. It was a familiar, stapled sheaf of pink copy paper among my documents – my list of Elaine's possible birth mothers. Around two hundred entries had been crossed out. Each time I'd picked up that list, it had been with a sense of excitement. On the first day of November 2014, I opened a fresh Word document and started compiling a new list. I noted all the names mentioned in connection with William's disappearance, the investigative efforts and social media chatter. Then I loaded my printer with pink paper.

Originally an English teacher by trade, I have worked in educational publishing since stepping out of the classroom to raise my children. I work from home, writing textbooks and classroom resources when I'm not tutoring students. After William disappeared, the rhythm of my days saw me working afternoons, leaving my nights free to investigate. His story began to keep me up later and later. I was noticing some bizarre connections between key people. The conundrums kept coming. Some nights, I'd be so caught up that it was only a brightening sky that told me I'd once again missed the opportunity for sleep.

To a city journo, Kendall could be mistaken for an irrelevant whistle-stop, but in fact it's a lively community with a proud heritage and a tight team of volunteers who keep finding innovative ways to put it on the map. It's heartbreaking that a small boy was lost here, of all places. Forevermore, Kendall's name will evoke the beautiful little face of an innocent child. The devastation the tragedy wreaked on the place was palpable. It was as if the heart of the town had stopped beating. I knew I needed to do something.

Family law in Australia provides that when children are deemed at risk of harm or neglect, the Department of Family and Community Services (FACS) steps in. Then, the Family Court makes determinations in the child's best interests – a worthy aim. But when the best interests of kids and parents clash – and they invariably do – tough decisions have to be made.

Before FACS was FACS, it was DOCS, the Department of Community Services. I've met many people who've had dealings with FACS. They've had children removed. Some have had them returned. Can I be honest with you? As a teacher, I used to have an aversion to meeting parents who'd lost their kids to a government department. Those families always unsettled me. The children came with so much baggage. I didn't want to involve myself in a mess. And I feared the parents would let me down, like they'd let their kids down. This was the tenor of my thinking back then. And yes, I am ashamed of that thinking.

The foster care system was a world away from my quiet little life on the farm. Despite my work finding Elaine Braun's birth mother, and even despite her miserable childhood as an adoptee, to me adoption felt very different from foster care. Adoption held promise. Its permanence felt hopeful and nurturing, while the temporary nature of foster care felt negative and desperate. The FACS system was a world I shied away from, until William Tyrrell softened my heart; broke it, in fact. He taught me that you can't look away from

12

the pain of others, from suffering families, from emotional need. It's gutless. So for his sake, for six years after he went missing, I made myself look.

In 2014, more than 18,000 children in New South Wales were unable to live with their families.[2] My café conversation with Jen and Trish had revealed that William Tyrrell and his sister Lindsay were among them. Soon, lots of other people knew this sensitive information. As the story of the missing foster child gained traction, FACS must have been growing worried. I imagine they realised that the loose lips of social media would probably sink their ship into the cold waters of public resentment before an official ruling could be made to suppress the truth about William Tyrrell's family circumstances.

Within days, we knew about William's birth parents, Karlie Tyrrell and Brendan Collins. Separated, both lived in the Sydney area. They had two other sons, known here by pseudonyms assigned by FACS. Francis was born in 2013 and Connor was born in 2014, just weeks before William disappeared. The chatter illustrated people's instinctive distaste for secrets, particularly those kept by government departments. Leaks abounded.

For a while, William's other set of parents remained shrouded. Non-publication orders require me to use pseudonyms, so I'm calling them Anna Wyndham and Nathan Thomas. The couple were married and lived on Sydney's North Shore. But soon enough people knew their home address, their workplaces, their friends. We saw pictures of them. We peeked at their holiday snaps. We knew they were renovating their house. Erasing digital footprints takes time and, in the interim, people took it upon themselves to spread what they'd uncovered.

In 2011, while Karlie Tyrrell was giving birth to baby William, Anna and Nathan were preparing to become foster carers for the first time. They'd been taking weekend classes. FACS gave them approval and two short assignments: an infant for a night and a pair of sibling babies on a two-night sleepover. Early in 2012, their initiation was complete. Anna and Nathan received Lindsay and, five weeks later, they would receive William Tyrrell.

*

In January 2015, a fresh story broke that spotlit the Camden Haven area once again. By then, we were getting used to media attention, but this new wave would really knock me off my feet. The police investigating William Tyrrell's disappearance were saying they had identified a person of interest. When the story broke, I was watching the news at home.

My audible shock brought my husband, Andy, into the room. We were completely floored to hear that a whitegoods repairer called Bill Spedding had been implicated. The thing is, we'd known Bill for some years. He and his wife, Margaret, were our next-door neighbours in 2008 and 2009 when we'd lived in a small complex of villas in Laurieton. And now, detectives were naming him publicly as a person of interest in the case I'd been closely following for months. I could not believe it.

I was immediately worried for the Speddings. My concerns weren't quelled when Superintendent Paul Fehon said on camera that Bill was not formally considered a suspect. Still, he was being publicly named and the damage couldn't be undone. Footage showed Bill trying to avoid the cameras, but he's quite tall and has a distinctive thatch of white hair. When Australia saw him sidling around vehicles and ducking for cover, he appeared furtive – and guilty. And that was the intended effect.

I'd became friendly with Margaret not long after we moved into the villa in 2008. She's a short lady in her sixties. Back then, she wore her reddish-blonde hair curly. I remember one day their little collie, Missy, didn't come home. I went out looking for her with Margaret and we couldn't find her, but she turned up of her own accord later that night. Some time after Andy and I moved out of the villa, Margaret came to our tuition centre seeking some after-school help for one of her grandsons. By this time, we were quite well known to each other. I always found her friendly.

Bill operated his whitegoods rental business from its headquarters in Wellington, in central New South Wales. Wellington is about a five-hour drive from the coast, and Bill would do this commute every second weekend. I don't recall him being around Laurieton very much in those days. I'd know when Bill was back from Wello because I'd see his now nationally recognisable white work van in the courtyard. He was quiet and reserved, usually attending to his business rather than socialising.

By late 2015, the Australian media was awash with details about Bill Spedding. And yet suppression orders prevented any reporting about William's foster family. It didn't seem fair. In response, people turned to social media. While undeniably fruitful in linking people and providing character sketches, online chatter is not a reliable repository of facts. When an inquest was ordered by the NSW Deputy State Coroner in 2018, documentary evidence finally became available. It was just what I needed.

The inquest yielded reports, police statements, verbal testimony, video and audio-recorded interviews that would fill many gaps in the picture I was building of William Tyrrell's family life. It gave me the opportunity to meet some of William's family face to face. These were people who had their worst nightmare come true, not once but twice. They lost Lindsay to FACS and, it seemed, William to Fate. Tragically, in due course, they would also lose their two remaining children to the custody of others.

2

FULL HOUSE

Four-and-a-half years after William Tyrrell vanished without a trace, the New South Wales Deputy State Coroner's inquest opened in Lidcombe. I travelled down to Sydney, ill-advisedly, on the Trainlink red-eye service. I couldn't help but feel a touch of drama catching that southbound train from Wauchope twenty minutes after midnight. The first station we passed through was Kendall.

The little town is rattled awake with marvellous regularity by the passage of the Trainlink service. Local night-owls set their watches by it. Throughout the journey, I didn't get much sleep, but my left leg did. I couldn't leave my seat because of a sprawling sleeper next to me. I didn't dare disturb him. He joined the train at Taree and fell asleep supernaturally fast, effectively locking me into position in my window seat.

Arriving in Sydney, I gingerly tested out my numb leg, alighted and caught a cab to the Lidcombe Coroner's Court. I learned on this trip that there isn't a single cab driver in Sydney who knows where to find it.

I'd never attended an inquest before. I felt guiltily excited, curious about the process. My ignorance about this strange court became immediately, embarrassingly apparent. So I set about educating myself. I spoke with veteran journalists and lawyers who explained that an inquest is not a trial, in any sense. There's no prosecutor, just a barrister in the role of counsel assisting the Coroner. 'Counsel assisting' leads the proceedings, presenting the brief of evidence that police have prepared for the Coroner.

The brief contains police reports, statements, video and audio files and transcripts, and documents describing material objects entered as exhibits – in William's case over 15,000 pieces of evidence and counting.[3] More than three thousand pages in all. Each section is called a 'tranche' – the French word for 'slice'.

At an inquest, there are no defendants, only witnesses. Counsel assisting questions them and presents the material that makes up the brief. Unlike in trials, the use of leading questions is permitted. The Coroner may ask questions, then the lawyers at the bar table are invited to ask questions on behalf of the parties they represent. The nuances can be frustrating for rookies like me who – at the time – didn't understand the philosophical underpinnings of justice.

In the William Tyrrell inquest, the first tranche of evidence was presented in March 2019. The second was heard over four weeks straddling August and September the same year. And the third and final tranche was unveiled in March 2020.

When the courtroom opened on 25 March 2019, I wondered if I'd get a seat. Every chair was reserved in the area where the detectives were sitting. One of those *Reserved* signs was moved by a sudden gust of serendipity as I passed by, so I took that spot. I watched a procession of people enter and gave some of them nicknames. I called Sydney lawyer Tracey Stevens 'Goldie', after the female lead in the popular Aussie cop show *Water Rats*. With their dark suits, crisp white blouses and curly, stylishly bobbed hair, the TV character and the real-life lawyer could be twins. Goldie's role was to assist counsel assisting the Coroner.

Next came two young detectives, one with a passing resemblance to Meghan, the self-demoted ex-Duchess of Sussex, and another woman I dubbed the School Prefect. Through my reading glasses the two women merged into a blurry blob of tan and black. I removed my specs and saw that the Duchess wore a name-tag. She was Detective Senior Constable Kristy Ford of the Homicide Squad. The School Prefect was a detective of the same rank, Vanessa Partridge, who I feel sure would've made an excellent student leader. Her jacket was like a school blazer, and she had a no-nonsense ponytail.

Last but not least, Colonel Mustard and Jack Reacher swept in and took their places in the front row. Detective Chief Inspector David Laidlaw had assumed command of the William Tyrrell investigation (known as Strike Force Rosann) after Detective Chief Inspector Gary Jubelin's ignominious exit in 2019. More on that fiasco later. I noticed Laidlaw walked with a slight limp. I wondered if he'd acquired it in the line of duty. Like his namesake from *Cluedo*, Colonel Mustard sported a military-style moustache. His manner reminded me of a British soldier who's found himself stuck behind enemy lines.

I spent some time studying the man I'd dubbed Jack Reacher. The first thing I noticed about Detective Senior Sergeant Mark Dukes was his wide white smile. I was afraid to expose my off-white teeth in his presence. He walked with the air of a seasoned FBI agent. But like his chief, Dukes looked like a man under siege. When Tom Cruise, who played Reacher in the franchise, discovered he was being cut, the tension of being told he was no longer right for the role showed up in his work. I felt Dukes was under pressure to prove himself.

In the front row of the birth family's camp sat Natalie Collins, William's grandmother, with William's father Brendan and Brendan's half-brother, Mitchell Moroney. I remembered seeing Natalie interviewed on television. When I saw Brendan Collins, known to his friends as 'Bones', I observed that he lives up to his nickname. He was whip-thin under his signature hoodie, with a wiry build. Brendan wore an expression that could be read as hostile or haunted – I couldn't decide which. His light brown hair grows in the same pattern at the hairline as little William's.

Conspicuously absent from the group was William's birth mother, Karlie Tyrrell. She wasn't scheduled to give evidence until the following week. But then, neither was Brendan, yet he was there. I found out later that relations had soured between Natalie, Brendan and Karlie. William's mother was emotionally shattered. Her closest confidante later told me Karlie couldn't face going through the evidence in court – evidence that in her view only pointed toward the likelihood of her son's suffering at the hands of a child killer.

Accompanying the family was someone I would come to know well over the course of the inquest. I didn't have to give her a nickname because I recognised her immediately after seeing her on *A Current Affair*. Allana Smith – a woman unconnected to either of William Tyrrell's families – won a case against FACS in August 2017 in the New South Wales Supreme Court. It lifted statutory restrictions that had prevented William's foster child status from being reported. Justice Paul Brereton ruled the matter was 'of legitimate public interest in the integrity of the foster care system'. Brereton said the public had been misled 'to think that William's carers were his parents'.[4]

Smith was sympathetic to William's birth family and threw her support behind them. She pointedly sat with the family in court each day, glaring across at FACS' reps and the foster parents. And when Allana Smith glares at you, it sticks. With a solid frame, a decent pair of guns and cropped hair, she looks like she could hold her own in a pub dust-up.

After her victory, Allana Smith was initially presented as the people's champion. Some journalists would take the moral high ground, telling Australia that FACS had concealed an important truth from us against the public interest. The protection of privacy came to be considered 'lying'. But, after the dust settled and in the absence of other William Tyrrell–related news, some sections of the media elected to turn on Smith and paint her as an interfering busybody.

The ruling to publicly acknowledge William's foster status must've come as a significant blow to his foster family. The question remains: was the disclosure indeed in the public interest?

*

Because they have so many kids on their books, FACS are empowered to accredit non-government organisations to administer foster care. One is the Salvation Army organisation Young Hope Out of Home Care. Directed by Captain Michelle White, Young Hope won a FACS contract in 2012 and within their case-managing portfolio were the Tyrrell children. This was an intersection of firsts – Young Hope's first FACS contract; Anna and Nathan's first tilt at foster care. Hope sprang eternal that year.

The term 'foster care' evokes a sense of impermanence. For kids under short-term orders, nothing is solid, dependable. They're removed from their parents because the goings-on in their house put them at risk. They wait for that house to become a home. Some get lucky. Their parents get themselves together, and home becomes a reality. Others grow up in transit, on a homeward-bound journey but never quite getting there. For many, short-term becomes long-term and they move from family to family, the dream of home never materialising. It's easy to see how foster kids become jaded. Many grow up believing that a 'forever home' is only for dogs adopted from the RSPCA.

For some families, though, foster care is the first stage of permanent adoption. Such was the situation of William and Lindsay. But there were roadblocks to overcome. The Tyrrell children knew their carers were not their birth parents, despite being infants when taken into care. The knowledge was sensed, rather than remembered, through seemingly little things that complicated daily life. They were aware their home lives were under scrutiny. A man called Ben visited them and they were taken to see people who called themselves their 'real Mum and Dad'. They had a different surname, a permanent and unwelcome reminder of their circumstances.

A source who'd worked with the Department of Family and Community Services walked me through the process FACS follow when they contact a family. He told me a meeting is called to discuss the situation that brought the family to the Department's attention. Note is taken of the way a parent dresses and presents themselves; whether they're affected by drugs or alcohol, overwrought by emotions or depressed, and importantly, whether they have support from extended family. A care plan is then developed, detailing potential risks to the child. It lists the steps parents must take to reduce or eliminate those risks.

I contemplated this as I sat in the courtroom that late-March morning. The Coroner still hadn't arrived, so I spent the time surveying the public gallery. Three people caught my attention. Assuming I'd read the seating arrangements correctly, they were on the birth family's side. I called two of them Top Knot and Rapunzel, names inspired only by their noteworthy hairstyles. The third woman I called Miss Marple, for her earnestness.

I immediately picked them as Websleuths members, a group of online amateur detectives and an occasional qualified expert. In making my own private investigations into William's case, the site was a source for unsubstantiated gossip, and occasionally, links to useful media stories. It's ironic that the owner named the site, by chance, in a way that perfectly captures its function. Members delight in spinning strange tales and theories, tying themselves up in knots and catching unsuspecting onlookers in a web from which even Spiderman couldn't extricate himself.

It was a pity I wasn't permitted to take a coffee into the courtroom. But don't let that stop you. I invite you to grab yourself a cuppa now, because I'm about to launch into what happened when the inquest finally got underway.

From the outset, seating arrangements mattered a great deal to some people. I was informed that I'd inadvertently 'sided' with the foster family by sitting in their area. When invited to side with the birth family instead, I pleaded neutrality and told them I was sitting in Switzerland. But the Swiss seats were few, so some days I would end up on the other side, near the foster family's camp.

A tap-tap on the door from chambers signalled the most significant arrival. Everyone dutifully stood. I was halfway to my feet when my laptop strap snagged on my oversized coat button. It pulled me up short. I froze in this awkwardly stooped position but was released when Deputy State Coroner Harriet Grahame bowed to the court.

The first thing I noticed about the Coroner was her alertness. It flashed, barely contained, in her eyes. Those astute orbs elevated Her Honour from a nondescript personage with collar-length, mousy hair and pale skin. In her black silks, with all due respect, she was like a well-trained terrier that's spotted a rabbit but isn't allowed to run after it. I didn't dare give Her Honour a nickname. I feel sure there lurks a law against it somewhere in the corridors of justice.

After the parties introduced themselves, the Coroner expressed her sincerest condolences to William's birth family and his foster carers for 'the heartache you have endured'. She called for the proceedings to begin and counsel assisting the Coroner, Gerard Craddock SC, made his opening address. I dubbed Mr Craddock 'The Boss'. No, he looks nothing like Bruce Springsteen. A grey-suited gentleman sporting some salt-and-pepper fuzz on his otherwise bald head, Mr Craddock's manner is as understated as his steel-framed glasses.

I named him after a school principal I'd worked under when I taught high school English.

Like my old boss, Mr Craddock is a man who weighs every word carefully. He uses details, and timing, to break the will of his opponents. He believes, I'm sure, that the pause is mightier than the word. Mr Craddock has delicate, white hands that flutter like a jazz-ballet spirit fingers gesture, but in slow motion. His quietly spoken manner held the court's attention far better than a more flamboyant performer could. But it felt like a performance nonetheless.

Mr Craddock called the first witness to the stand. The court officer ushered her to the box and called for silence as the oath was taken. Katherine Alexander is a senior practitioner with FACS. A stylish brunette of around fifty, her tone was officious. When she did permit herself to emote, it sounded patronising. Katherine Alexander had a bombshell to drop in court that day. She put it out there that William's birth parents had been responsible for a previous 'abduction'.

I would soon hear the backstory from William's grandmother Natalie Collins. Meanwhile, I watched Mr Craddock pausing to allow the full weight of this piece of intel to descend on the courtroom. If he was relishing his role as puppet-master, he was doing a good job of concealing it. The man is inscrutable.

Ms Alexander said William's family's involvement with FACS had been 'multigenerational'. FACS had intended for William to live with his sister in a permanent placement. This is their policy wherever possible because outcomes for siblings are always better when they're kept together, she said.

Thinking about the life experiences of foster children, I feel I'm being pulled below the surface of a murky pond. I get a physical reaction. My heart surges and I almost lose my breath. In the image my mind conjures, the parents have no faces, no identities. They are just blanks. No doubt, I leave them that way because I am reserving the right to judge them later, to lay the blame for their loss at their own feet. But whenever I picture the children in that image – they are my boys.

This day, in court, I listened. I permitted myself to imagine my two boys being separated from Andy and me, and from each other. It was almost too much to bear. As Katherine Alexander reported on her duties and routines, I filled in one of those blank parental faces with the gaunt countenance and haunted eyes of Brendan Collins. And tears came.

Ms Alexander told Mr Craddock that care plans had been filed for both William and Lindsay before they were born. I expected The Boss to force a pause here, but he didn't. It took me a while to get the hang of his impeccable timing. Final orders were made, although the birth parents had contested the temporary orders.

Considering the fact that two families were wrangling over the children, I found it remarkable there was no enmity recorded on William's case file. Katherine Alexander told the inquest 'if there was animosity, we would want it written down,' implying that if no written record of animosity existed, there was no animosity full stop. And not a soul I spoke to at the inquest believed that for an instant.

From talks with my FACS friend who'd briefed me before the inquest, I could see that anecdotal evidence abounds of foster carers being watched, followed and stalked on social media by birth families. The truth is, no one knows what efforts people may be making to find out where their kids are living. Mr Craddock asked Ms Alexander what happens if birth parents try to gather information from their children about the foster carers – names, addresses or other details that might identify them and their whereabouts. She replied that supervisors remain alert to such conversations, but if there are no indicators of such behaviour occurring, FACS assumes no safety concerns exist. Mr Craddock had addressed the elephant in the courtroom. Ms Alexander deftly produced a smoke bomb in the form of 'departmental policy'. And when the haze cleared, the elephant was gone.

According to Natalie and Brendan Collins, the birth parents did display open animosity toward the foster carers, as logic would tell us to expect. It was certainly on display at the inquest. The middle of the room was a veritable force field of electricity buzzing between the two camps. During a bathroom break, this fizz boiled over into a war of words between one of the foster carers' supporters and a keyboard warrior whom I won't embarrass here. The women butted heads over the meaning behind the glares and stares exchanged during that day's proceedings.

Ms Alexander admitted there had been plans for adoption, which would likely have extinguished any hope of a positive relationship between the foster and biological families. She also conceded the birth parents hadn't been formally made aware of plans to adopt the Tyrrell children before 12 September 2014. In an open adoption through the foster care system, both biological parents are required to give their consent.

Ms Alexander also explained that, in her professional experience, children do better in foster homes when they maintain contact with their birth families under FACS' supervision. The 'Safe Contact' rule governs the planning of visits, and if concerns exist, 'a series of scaled questions are used to determine the level of that concern.' Case workers report their observations during visits. They must be alert to potential threats to the safety of the children. With her scaled questions and written assessments, the net result of Ms Alexander's testimony was to make FACS look ultra-reasonable and eminently civilised.

Case worker Ben Atwood was tasked with transferring FACS' approval of the foster carers to Young Hope. As he testified, his bald head glistened with sweat, his eyes giving him the appearance of the proverbial possum in headlights. He was clearly nervous about giving answers to the Coroner. Atwood informed us that foster carers must endure a lengthy, invasive approval process involving hours of discussion, assessment and meetings.

When pressed further, he admitted that by 'hours' he meant no more than two hours. Atwood conducted two home visits in which he interviewed the foster carers and made some casual observations of how the foster children acted in their company. He made a report that the carers were 'of the highest calibre seen' among the candidates applying to Young Hope. At news of this means of assessment, Natalie Collins visibly blanched.

*

I wondered how Anna and Nathan would cope with having to relive the nightmare of losing William before a packed courtroom. On the inquest's first day, they had entered to stares, nods and whispers – Anna in her pale pashmina wrap exuded a quintessentially North Shore vibe. She wore the evidence of her expensive tastes with confident ease, but looked like a frail bird, thin-framed and delicate. With her porcelain skin and high cheekbones, Anna could convincingly play the role of an heiress in *Downton Abbey*. Her intelligent brown eyes didn't miss a thing. She was frequently fingering a tri-coloured trinity ring worn on her left hand.

Nathan appeared in a crisply ironed business shirt and skinny jeans. He's about six feet tall with a medium athletic build. He comes across as confident, if not slightly salesmanlike. Nathan's salt and pepper hair was cut stylishly and he sported silver cufflinks and a very impressive watch. I considered offering him my Peugeot 308 for it.

Escorting the foster mother like an awkward bridesmaid was Captain Michelle White of Young Hope. She had thick strawberry blonde hair that looked to be double the volume of Anna's. I could imagine her in her Salvation Army officer's blazer. Michelle's floral print blouse interrupted Anna's sartorial eloquence, as did her habit of passing crumpled tissues to her companion every five minutes.

When I first heard Anna Wyndham speak, there was a note of affectation in her voice. For me, her self-assuredness didn't engender empathy. It irritated. As for Nathan Thomas, he seemed too casually dismissive, an attitude at odds with rumours of his emotional breakdown at the scene. They were well-mannered, composed and smartly dressed, their attire revealing their comfortable, upper-class North Shore status. Their situation couldn't have contrasted more sharply with that of the birth family. The expensive cologne of success clung to one pair, while the whiff of booze and cigarettes followed the other. But Australia is a land that champions the underdog.

Anna and Nathan's house is in a leafy, quiet suburb on Sydney's North Shore. These folk have in-ground swimming pools, not inflatables. They drive BMWs, not Kias. They can access the best childcare. They go to Bali, like their compatriots do, but they stay in the hinterland. There's extra money for toys and clothes, and you don't have to wait until Thursday. The future holds promise: a private school education, university and satisfying employment. Privilege is the currency that buys them acceptance in the community.

William and Lindsay's foster parents were eminently suitable carers from FACS' point of view. The Department enthusiastically supported the placement of the children into their home. These were people with the means to provide, financially and emotionally. In a police statement, Anna described her motives as altruistic.

'I've always wanted to open my house to children who needed care. I've always known that when I was in the position to be able to do so, I'd want to care for children who needed love and security.' But the keyboard warriors saw things differently. Their online attacks on Anna and Nathan's motives for fostering the Tyrrell children were unrelenting. It was characterised as a case of rich people buying themselves an instant family. I asked one of them about this in a chatroom exchange.

'Do you think it's possible they are kind-hearted people who just want to give disadvantaged children better lives?'

'No – that only happens in the movies.'

'But what about the significant cost to the couple?'

'Cost? They get tons of money for each kid they take on. They're vampires.'

'But these people are pretty well off already.'

'Rich bastards. There's always some other motive with them.'

'What about the other costs? Foster care can be very hard, physically and emotionally.'

'Those people have no feelings. Just look at her. Could she get her nose any higher in the air?'

Mainstream media majors in the spectre of a class war in Australia, but unlike the race wars that fill the news, it's subtle. There persists a lamentable, ignorant view that wealthy people are inauthentic; that they're disconnected from working-class Australians. Lots of people see wealth as a matter of sheer good luck, not hard work. I could see that the foster family were often targeted out of the basest of motives – envy.

People claiming to represent working-class Aussies inflamed the situation, digging dirt on the foster family that might bring them down a peg or two. There's something peculiarly Australian about disliking successful people. We don't merely cut down tall poppies; we crush them. Then, for good measure, we press out the juice and get high on it. We are among those rare people of the world that wear the underdog tag as a badge of honour. Even when we're underdogs because of our own bad behaviour.

Moreover, the notion that impoverished people are hard-wired for disaster is not always borne out in reality. Plenty of Australians work hard to overcome disadvantage and enjoy success. Socio-economic hardship and lack of education are certainly factors that can throw families into turmoil. But they're not the only factors that put kids like the Tyrrells at risk of family violence and substance abuse.

At the first adjournment for the day, I happened to meet Natalie, Brendan and Allana Smith in the elevator. I introduced myself, explaining that I was an author from the Kendall area. They invited me to join them at their table in the café. I thought it was disgraceful that they hadn't any legal representative at the proceedings and told them so. Brendan seemed unaware that he could have had a rep at the bar table. By the inquest's next sitting, with Allana Smith's encouragement, they would obtain a barrister through Legal Aid to represent their interests.

With her straight, dyed-blonde hair and tanned, toned body, Natalie Collins doesn't look like anyone's grandma. She exudes a convincing rock chick vibe, an impressive feat for a woman about to turn sixty. The first time I saw her in court she was fiddling nervously with the twin gold and silver crosses on chains around her neck, slipping them on and off her chin as she listened.

One of the first things William's family discussed at the court's coffee shop was their negative view of FACS. They were irritated by Katherine Alexander's description of William's foster status, namely her statement that, 'When he disappeared, William was under the parental responsibility of the Department of Family and Community Services (FACS).' It did seem a distasteful choice of words to characterise children as being 'parented' by a government department.

Natalie confirmed for me that William Tyrrell was on FACS' radar before he was even born. She eyed me across the table, giving me the impression that she had quite a bit to say, but was holding back while she was in the company of the others. I would find out more about the family as we drank our way through a bladder-wrenching volume of coffee to fill the time eaten up by the interminable adjournments.

I learned that when Karlie Tyrrell became pregnant to her then boyfriend, Brendan Collins, her family situation had been marked as one to watch. Domestic violence and substance abuse are twin red flags that draw departmental attention to a pregnant mother; FACS had temporarily removed Karlie and Brendan's first child, Lindsay, for these reasons.

By the time the inquest had rolled around, Allana Smith was convinced that William's foster parents were hiding something. And she had a lot of support. She attended the inquest in the capacity of a children's welfare advocate, seeking to bring attention to the plight of children in unsuitable foster care placements. She admitted that – regardless of the evidence – an outcome clearing the foster parents' names would be unsatisfactory. She had a lot invested in this case and she wanted her pound of flesh.

Allana is a victim of the worst extremes of the FACS system herself and lays the blame for her truly awful childhood in foster homes at their revolving door. I feel deeply for her. On the inquest's first day, she couldn't get past the revelation that FACS weren't asked to conduct a review of Anna and Nathan's suitability as carers after William went missing. And that they still had Lindsay.

One afternoon during the inquest, Allana declared to a contact in the press that William had been 'hand-picked', earmarked for adoption well before long-term orders were in place. She suggested FACS purposely kept William's foster status secret to avoid scrutiny over the circumstances of his placement. Put simply, she didn't believe they enacted due process. Allana theorised that Anna and Nathan procured the children via a preferential, fast-track method. She posed awkward questions.

During our conversations in the coffee shop, I could see that Allana's personal take on this case and Natalie's understandable bitterness over the loss of her grandson was a match made in conspiracy heaven. Allana's persuasive powers cemented Natalie Collins' opposition to the foster family and to the system, although admittedly, Natalie didn't need much persuading. Brendan Collins, however, was wisely reserving his judgement.

*

A few days into the inquest, Deputy State Coroner Harriet Grahame asserted that there was no evidence that William's foster care status had anything to do with his disappearance. As she explained this, the Coroner fixed a steady gaze on William's biological grandmother. I watched as Natalie raised her eyebrows in silent response to the Coroner's intimidating glare. We were being repeatedly assured that William's FACS status played no role in this tragedy. Given this, I struggled to understand why FACS went all the way to the Supreme Court to prevent Allana Smith from revealing William's foster status to the public.

Allana's David versus Goliath victory seemed to invest her views with credibility. But, in the years since her win, she's become increasingly prone to throwing inexplicably angry accusations at William's foster parents that simply can't be supported by facts. In one Facebook rant, Allana declared:

I'm getting JACK of lies. Mummy Monster and Daddy Monster were against most contact visits because that would mean the children could maintain a relationship with their REAL mummy and daddy. Well, they had to KNOCK that RIGHT outta the kids. And the cops want to sell us the 'old man paedophile' story. Look past the smoke and around the mirrors people, because you are all still being hoodwinked.

It wouldn't be until the second sitting of the inquest that Brendan's barrister would make her first appearance. Michelle Swift reminded me of a blonde-haired version of Enid Blyton's troublesome doll, Naughty Amelia Jane. Slightly dishevelled in her navy pin-striped suit – her uniform throughout the entire inquest – Swift looked as rushed as her name implies. As she rose to address the Coroner, she'd self-consciously run a hand through her long mane, as if to tidy it up. She could've done with a scrunchie borrowed from the School Prefect.

Swift was provided with the brief of evidence just a week ahead of the inquest's second session. But due to the dossier's astronomical size, the court would only fund a single printed copy. The family needed more for the members of their legal team. This, combined with the fact that Brendan and Natalie were unable to channel their queries through a representative at the first sitting, didn't do much to reassure the public gallery of open justice in action.

3

STACKING THE DECK

I may be able to navigate the world of words like a boss, but my orienteering skills in the average city are another matter entirely. In March 2019, life had become a blur of train and cab rides, days in court taking notes but, most often, waiting. I detest Sydney, and I don't like being away from home. I got pretty cranky. Needless adjournments, court closures and repeated delays didn't improve my mood.

After each adjournment, media platforms were heaving with activity. I saw a well-known journo feverishly banging out an article for news.com.au on her laptop. Although it must've been hard to run in those thongs, she led the race to file a story, if only by a nose. Radio reps had no need to pap the key witnesses, but they still tried to elbow the photographers into the rails. News – real, fake and sloppy – whisked up suspicion like the egg whites in a news anchor's omelette. By the first morning, we'd already hit fever pitch and things remained that way throughout the proceedings.

By the time I'd missed the elevator and walked down the winding staircase to the café, one Network Ten podcaster had already tweeted her battery flat. I wondered who else had been in the media room that morning. It must have been full because every nanosecond a new story appeared online. Photos too. I even saw myself in the background of one picture. After some fortification with coffee and banana bread that I feel sure is served in Heaven, I returned to court. Noting a stain on my jacket's lapel, I resolved to wear courtroom black the next day. I wrote a reminder in my notebook.

Natalie, Allana and two of their supporters decided it would be a good idea to meet up with me for dinner the next evening. They wanted to give me their take on the birth family's relationship with FACS. Details provided by Natalie at that dinner powerfully illustrated for me the dilemma case workers face as they try to keep children safe. We met up at my hotel in Lidcombe and ordered pizza. I wrote notes as Natalie began to talk.

Shortly after FACS took custody of Lindsay – while Karlie was pregnant with William – his parents had ostensibly broken up. Natalie said FACS told Karlie the break-up was a good thing, because they believed that home to be a disastrous setting in which to raise children. But in reality, the couple had reconciled in time for William's birth, lying to FACS about the split. Karlie told her family that FACS was satisfied she could care for William on her own. They wanted her to cut Brendan loose. Certainly, when FACS discovered Brendan would be living in the home too, things went pear-shaped.

But according to his mother, it seems it wasn't Brendan who worried FACS; it was the beast that was conjured when the two parents lived together. In order for Karlie to keep her son, FACS needed assurances that the home environment was stable and safe. She needed to prove she had family support. But neither her mother or father were in a position to help. FACS took things a step further, officially ruling that the couple couldn't be in a live-in relationship, saying it created an unsafe environment for their children. It would only be a matter of time before both children were removed from these struggling parents.

With baby William on the way, the family needed support in various forms. Natalie told me she believed the children's removal could have been temporary if Karlie and Brendan had responded appropriately to FACS' intervention. But instead, they continued to lie to authorities. In his inquest testimony, Brendan Collins admitted he and Karlie had deceived FACS into believing they had permanently separated in 2011. They did this hoping to keep custody of William. But the couple were soon spotted together at a video store. In a process that seemed to Natalie too rapid to be fair, the Family Court issued an order: surrender William to FACS.

Baby William had a little more time at home than his sister, leaving when he was eight months old. He was officially placed with Anna and Nathan on 8 February 2012, but wouldn't join them until five weeks later. While the foster family waited for compliance with the court order, the birth family had hatched a different plan. The event some have described as 'William's first abduction' was unpacked at the inquest in 2019.

When case workers went to collect William on the agreed day, they encountered an empty house. The couple had absconded, hiding the child from authorities. They went on the run – quite a commitment. The response to this misguided course of action was swift. Police assembled Strike Force Duncraig and scoured the Ryde Police District, wholly dedicated to locating William and his parents – the villains who'd dared to kidnap their own son.

The couple had some help. Natalie told me she organised for Darryl Clifford, her estranged husband, to shelter them. Clifford told police the couple had lied to him to get his help; he'd called authorities when he'd learned they'd deceived him. Natalie was bitterly disappointed that Brendan's father was not prepared to help them when the heat was on. Neither she nor her son have much contact with Clifford anymore.

After a few weeks, the couple left Brendan's father's place, hiding out at a small flat in Gordon, on the North Shore. Natalie paid their rental bond. Karlie wasn't able to see Lindsay for five weeks, staying in hiding with baby William until the Strike Force caught up with them on 15 March. William spent a night in hospital under observation then arrived at his new home with Anna and Nathan under a shiny new set of court orders. His parents' decision to cut and run had sealed William's fate, it seemed.

Natalie told me with some pride that the abduction was all her idea. But when he took the witness stand, her son would heroically step up to assume full responsibility, saying his mother was unaware of their plans. Apparently everyone wanted credit for the manoeuvre because Karlie Tyrrell also contradicted this. From my talks with Natalie and Brendan, it seemed clear the plot had involved the cooperation of all three.

*

Karlie's court appearance was somewhat dramatic. She arrived on day five of the proceedings, amid an urgent media scrum. Photographers descended like mutton birds. Like the rest of William's natural family, Karlie used the public entry into the court complex. She took a seat on the opposite side of the room from me. I'd landed in the foster family's camp that day due to a seating crisis in Switzerland. I could see William had his mother's eyes and smile. Hers are dark brown; his, hazel, but it's easy to spot the resemblance. From photos, I knew Karlie had long brown hair until her second child was born. At the inquest she wore it shorter, which suited her face. Karlie Tyrrell is petite and pretty, when she smiles.

With Brendan's family and friends by her side, it appeared that Karlie Tyrrell was enfolded in a warm network of support. They hugged her; she seemed to reciprocate. She looked comfortable in their presence. I was puzzled – was she enjoying this display of coddling? Then, I realised: the family were working hard to ensure she didn't have a 'moment'. Despite the outward display of solidarity, there was a deep rift that has only widened since the inquest.

A solemn silence signalled a heightened state of alert in the courtroom. The court officer called Karlie Tyrrell to the witness stand and she took the oath. Mr Craddock began his questions, sympathetically leading the young mother through the events of 2012. He began with the time when FACS obtained the order to surrender baby William to their care. Mr Craddock asked Karlie to articulate her reasons for disobeying the court's ruling.

'I just couldn't imagine handing over my son,' she replied, looking not at Mr Craddock but at the Coroner. Karlie shook her head with genuine sadness. It was a heartfelt appeal to a fellow mother. She re-told the story of William's abduction from her point of view, up to where the couple were discovered and had to hand their son over. Karlie talked about her relationship with Brendan and their efforts to keep custody of their children.

At one point, Karlie slipped up. She mentioned Brendan's name, instead of calling him 'the father'. Tracey Stevens was questioning her at the time. It was incredible how quickly Karlie became irate.

'They all know our names,' she snapped. 'What does it matter anyway?' Someone patiently explained the protocol was there to protect everyone's privacy, including hers. Turning to the Coroner, Karlie boiled over, saying, 'But you made my name public.' Stevens continued her questioning, asked Karlie if she would please listen to what she was saying.

'Yeah, I'm listening,' she retorted. I could see Karlie was close to blowing her top. She wasn't listening anymore. She was seething. The formalities of court procedure were preventing her from expressing herself freely. Ms Stevens patiently continued, asking questions designed to tightly focus the witness's responses.

'I'll lose it!' she growled at one point, eyeballing Ms Stevens menacingly. Natalie Collins caught my eye, eyebrows raised as if to say, 'See? I told you she was volatile.'

It was clear at the inquest that Karlie couldn't hold her anger in long enough to make it through a short period of questioning. This was an occasion to be on her best behaviour – and sadly, it seemed that was her best behaviour. When Karlie had finished giving evidence, Natalie Collins hugged her in a motherly gesture that Karlie really seemed to need at that moment.

*

The night after Anna gave evidence at the inquest, I re-read my notes. In a police statement, she recalled the hopes she and Nathan had held for their future. 'We'd always spoken about what we wanted to do, the type of children we wanted to have. Not just one – preferably siblings, so we could help a family. Help two children. And just as we were completing those classes, a scenario came up. The Department even told us we'd be perfect for these kids. They'd be perfect for us. And so, it all fitted into place. I mean, the ink wasn't even dry on the paper and the children were already being transitioned over to us. So it was pretty quick.' I took off my reading glasses and rubbed my eyes, trying to erase that phrase 'a scenario came up'.

Anna's testimony indicates that FACS must have told the couple when they took in Lindsay that William would be surrendered very soon and that they'd be awarded permanent custody of both siblings. If FACS had a court order to remove William when this conversation occurred, their twelve-month timer must have begun ticking while he was still in utero (FACS must have a child on their books for twelve months before that child is eligible for long-term care orders or adoption). That sounds Orwellian, but there's no denying that children are most vulnerable when they're infants. It can be a matter of life and death.

Natalie Collins told me that when William was first placed into foster care, his parents had high hopes of having their boy returned home. They felt Karlie might be able to regain custody of William if FACS believed Brendan was no longer in her life. During this time, he didn't see his daughter for over a year. This was necessary, they felt, to keep up the pretence they were no longer together. It was hard, Brendan said, but he felt it'd be worth it when William was returned. Sadly, it was already too late to get Lindsay back.

Brendan and Karlie went to counselling, anger management sessions, substance abuse courses and parenting groups. They moved to a bigger home, a place more suitable for children. Brendan told police that FACS wouldn't even do an inspection of the place, giving him the impression they had no chance. I wondered as I read that report whether Brendan realised the gravity of his children's situation. FACS had rightly determined they were unsafe at home until things changed. And the house had nothing to do with it.

By late 2012, both children's futures were inked into finality. Karlie and Brendan would never be able to regain custody of their children. William and Lindsay would be in foster care until they aged out of the system at eighteen. But all was not lost, the young couple was assured. Young Hope encouraged the birth parents to continue 'safe relationships' with their children. Case workers supervised short visits, first weekly, then monthly, then by 2014, every two months for just an hour – plenty of time for kids to form those valuable family connections, apparently. I wondered why Karlie and Brendan didn't fight this strict schedule harder.

Then, I found the answer and it unsettled me. I found myself naming it 'the FACS Trap'. In these parents' minds loomed the spectre of losing their other two children. Did the couple realise their family's future was in their own hands? They must have had some inkling, because – for a time – they were able to keep Francis and Connor.

Luck was temporarily on their side. The Tyrrells had been transitioned from an old DOCS department to a new FACS department, across different zones in Sydney. They moved from

Ryde to Granville, where they became part of Young Hope's caseload. There were new processes and different assessors who, for a short time, gave them the benefit of the doubt. They could keep Francis and Connor for the time being. But for Lindsay, then already under long-term orders, there was no going back. For William, his progression from short- to long-term care orders would be a matter for Young Hope to determine.

Now I'm no mind reader, but I'm thinking at this point you might have just asked yourself a bit of a knotty question. Perhaps you even asked it out loud. The police certainly did. In fact, in September 2014, they interviewed Brendan Collins and asked him straight out, 'Did you take William?'

Brendan was adamant in his denial. 'No. I knew it wasn't the right thing to do. I learned from last time that I needed to change and earn FACS's trust. I knew I needed to be a better person,' he added meekly.

*

From the outset, Karlie and Brendan were informed that the foster carers were not comfortable meeting them. They were told they needed to respect the carers' privacy, cutting off access to information about how their kids were faring. They'd have to rely on written reports instead. All communication was to go through Young Hope case workers.

Access visits usually involved Ben Atwood coming to collect the children from home. He would take them to the pre-arranged meeting place. But by August 2014, Anna had started taking the children to visits herself, slipping away before the birth parents arrived. She hoped this might minimise the children's anxiety.

On Thursday 21 August, Anna took the children to an access visit. The June one had been cancelled. Brendan had needed to work that day and Karlie was sick. The last parental access visit had been at a park, back in April. The goal of these meetings is to help foster children make sense of their identities. Like little saplings, they had roots embedded in the soil of their old lives. No doubt it was Anna's hope that in their new lives they'd sprout verdant leaves and good fruit. She was taking the children to what would be William's last visit with his birth family. Karlie and Brendan would never see their son again.

Case workers' reports are quite detailed, allowing me to reconstruct the scene for you here. That Thursday, Anna parked at the Macquarie Centre and walked the kids up to Chipmunks Playland to meet Ben Atwood from Young Hope. He was waiting outside the entrance, his shiny, bald head unmissable even from a distance. Ben looks like a stick figure, he's so thin-framed. If you were to assess him by his fashion sense, he could be a bank teller. Always just a touch too formal, as though he wears the powers granted to him by FACS as a badge of pride.

'They've been up to here this morning,' Anna whispered, indicating her neck. 'Hyper. Especially Lindsay. She's been engaging in lots of dialogue about Brendan and Karlie all the way here. Oh. And here's a spare pair of undies for William.' As everyone sat down Lindsay proceeded to climb all over Ben, trying to hug him around the neck. He politely disentangled himself.

'Mummy, why are you leaving us?' William and Lindsay asked when Anna went to leave. Ben Atwood's report shows there was an imperative from FACS to hurry things along so that the birth parents and the foster parents wouldn't cross paths. I found this fairly compelling evidence that FACS were aware of animosity existing between the parties, despite official denials.

'It's just for a little while. Mummy will be close by doing some shopping, okay?'

The case worker had called Karlie to confirm the visit beforehand. He'd explained that William had given himself a black eye. He'd fallen while climbing on his foster mother. Another report I read said it was his foster father, and noted William had spent a night in hospital, just for observation. The bruise was the only injury reported, and Ben did write excellent reports, so when I sat comparing both documents, I went with his version.

Brendan and Karlie arrived with their son Francis in a stroller. It must have been hard for William and Lindsay to grasp where this baby fitted into their lives. The couple greeted the children with huge smiles. Both crouched down and gave them hugs, awkward for Karlie. Ben had helpfully documented everything at this visit, even capturing the sense of what was said.

'Are you pregnant?' Lindsay asked Karlie.

'Yes, I am. You're going to have another little brother or sister.'

'You have crazy hair,' Lindsay told Brendan.

'Yeah, I do, don't I?' he laughed. 'Do I get a hug?'

'No.' The little girl leaned into the stroller to look at Francis and smiled at him. Karlie looked at William, taking everything in – his 'geeky' haircut, as she would describe it later, a superhero onesie of a type she didn't recognise. She noted the bruise, faded but still visible near his eye. She wondered if the kids were too skinny.

Brendan paid the admission fees and they went into the play centre. There were other people with them this time. A psychologist from the Child Protection Service sat at a nearby table, trying to remain unobtrusive. A second case worker was there with Ben, as policy dictated because of the number of children present. Apparently three adults are no match for three children under four – and two disempowered non-custodial parents.

After trying unsuccessfully to get William and Lindsay to play with them, Karlie and Brendan changed tack. They bought sliced fruit and juice boxes for morning tea. Karlie encouraged the kids to sit at a table. Lindsay obliged, but William wouldn't stay put long enough to eat something. Karlie and Ben took turns chasing him down when he ran off, heading for the big slide.

'Logan from day care is here,' Lindsay announced. She pointed to a boy of about four. 'Logan's not my brother,' she added.

'You have two brothers, Lindsay,' Karlie replied.

'I only have one brother.'

'You're only saying that because Francis doesn't live with you.' Lindsay ignored her and wandered off to play with Logan. 'Come on, Lindsay. Don't you want to play with me?' Karlie called after her daughter. Lindsay shook her head. 'Mummy Karlie's here. Daddy Brendan's here. We'd like to play with you.' No response.

Ben suggested they try some 'cooperative play' so Lindsay didn't feel she was being taken away from her friend. Karlie went over to Logan's mother and introduced herself, asking if her daughter could play with Logan. She must've known what cooperative play was, because in no time all three children were taking turns on the big slide.

Karlie and Brendan waited at the bottom.

'Wow Lindsay, you're going so quick!'

'Me too!'

'Ooh! Well done, William!'

After a lunch of chips and nuggets, Karlie produced a birthday present. William had turned three on 26 June, which went uncelebrated by the Tyrrells because of the cancelled visit. He opened the belated card. *Happy Birthday, love Mum, Dad and Francis xxxx.* William was delighted with the *Planes*-branded light-up sneakers and a summer outfit: *Giggle and Hoot* t-shirt and shorts.

'I like them!' the little boy exclaimed, holding up one shoe in each hand.

'Wanna put 'em on?' Brendan asked.

'Yes please.' Brendan put the new shoes on William's feet and laughed as William stomped around, making the lights flash red.

'Come on. Come over here and see what else we've brought you!' Karlie said, pulling another package out of the bag. Lindsay tore the parcel open and stroked her new pink light-up shoes, delighted she'd been given a present too.

The children climbed the cargo net, shot the cannon and romped in the ball pit. But each time one of their parents joined them, they'd sidle away to do something else. The psychologist observed, scribbling. Ben observed, scribbling. The other case worker observed without any scribbling. She was just there to make up the numbers.

When Ben submitted his report, he noted that Karlie took Lindsay to the ball pit where they played together for a short time. Karlie said something Ben couldn't make out from where he was sitting. Lindsay would later tell Anna about it.

'One day you might come and live with us again, at your real home,' Karlie had whispered. This prompted an angry reaction from the little girl.

'You're not my mum! Anna is my mum!' Lindsay shouted in her mother's face. Ben wrote that he could see the pain in Karlie's face. But in his report, he called it 'tension'. When she regained her voice, it sounded tight. She coaxed her daughter to come back and play. Ben looked at his watch.

'It's right on twelve o'clock, guys. Time to go. Two hours are up.' Ben started packing things away.

'Can I have an ice-cream?' Lindsay asked her mother.

'Hey, William, want an ice-cream?' Karlie asked. 'Tell you what. Let's go to the loo, then we'll get an ice-cream.' Lindsay was still stand-offish, but William was jumping with excitement. Lindsay took herself to the toilet without any help, then washed and dried her hands. She peeked at Karlie under the stall door and gave her a little wave. William went to the men's bathroom with Brendan then met the others at the ice-cream counter.

'Smarties ice-creams, okay?' Two little heads nodded. Ben's meticulous notes tell us Brendan hissed something in Karlie's ear. After the ice-creams, there was another bathroom visit to clean up their faces. Anything to stretch out those precious minutes. They were just beginning to warm up again. William had even let Karlie give him a cuddle as he sat on her lap.

'It really is time to go. I'm sorry,' Ben said, glancing over Karlie's shoulder, motioning for the newly arrived Anna to stay out of sight, while maintaining a smile for the children. A series of half-forced hugs and kisses signalled the finale, then Ben breathed out a sigh as Karlie and Brendan left. Anna appeared the second they were out of sight.

'Ben, it's ten past. It's not right that they spin things out like this.'

'We had ice-creams,' William said excitedly.

'Wow! aren't you lucky? Ice-creams!'

'Mummy,' Lindsay asked, curling her arm around Anna's leg, 'Why does Karlie say she's my mummy?'

4

BLINDSIDE

It strikes me that William Tyrrell's story is replete with names. Secret names, redacted names, street names, nicknames, namesakes. They are a recurring motif in the story. From the outset, we see William and Lindsay rebelling against their birth names. Their sense of self is wrapped up in their wish to use their foster father's surname. Ironically, that very name is fiercely protected, kept secret from the public.

When he vanishes, Australia recognises William Tyrrell more by a visual image than by his name.

'You know. The little boy in the Spiderman suit.' Searchers looking for William call his name until they are hoarse. A media campaign bears his name. 'Where's William?' it asks Australia. Irony can be amazing and it can be amusing. But it can also be cruel. FACS order William's birth parents to give themselves different names when they are in contact with the kids – not Mummy and Daddy. I can imagine as a parent that accepting a different name for yourself forces a gutting acceptance of a diminished role in your children's lives.

The staff at William and Lindsay's Sydney childcare centre knew the Tyrrell kids were in foster care. They'd been going to day care three days a week since 2012 and their names were causing confusion. William had managed to con someone into writing his preferred moniker on his story portfolio. He wanted to be William Thomas, not William Tyrrell.

William's confusion showed up in his behaviour. He was a demanding child, always on the go. Anna described him in her police statement:

'William was a special little boy who drew attention from everybody, even when walking down the street. Something about him drew people.' But Anna also journalled her less glowing observations of the children for FACS, writing of anxious and aggressive behaviours, including hitting and biting their carers and each other. The children would punch and slap each other a lot, and anyone else who happened to be in the way. All this activity left them unnaturally fatigued. They had poor concentration and would flatly refuse to do simple tasks requiring focused attention. They whined, cried, screamed, bit their nails. Anna wrote of night terrors and diarrhoea. This unpleasant combination seemed to affect William before and after access visits.

As I pieced together a profile of this foster family, discrepancies emerged. There's a good deal of variance between the pictures Anna and Nathan painted of their relationships with the children. Nathan acknowledged things were tough at first, but said their struggles were nothing out of the ordinary. In his police interviews, he downplayed the troubles at home, focusing on the emotional positives. He told police of his affection for Lindsay when they first met.

'She's such a gorgeous little girl. Fun and giggly and adventurous. Just a good, decent, beautiful little girl.' As for William, he spoke of him as if he was a different child to the one his wife described in her journal.

'He's a flamboyant little boy. He's full of beans. Huge smile.' Nathan's tone changed when he reflected on the first time he saw his foster son. 'When I met William, you know, it was like – he was mine. There was an instant connection. Like he was my own boy. I was his world and he was mine.'

Anna told police of watching this close relationship form between her husband and foster son. 'Nathan and William bonded from the second they met. They were like two souls that had found each other. This was not a relationship that needed to develop. It was there immediately. Nathan and William would play together, laugh together, just do normal father and son things. They just understood each other. Always together.'

In contrast, William's relationship with his foster mother stalled for a time. He resisted receiving her affection. Recalling her own childhood spent around horses, Anna described William as 'head shy'. He'd flinch away from her if she got too close. Despite this, William was not scared of the dark. According to his foster mother, he would sleep with the door shut.

I watched a videoed police interview in which detectives asked Nathan whether he noticed any difficulties faced by William due to his rough start in life. Nathan's body language and tone softened whenever he spoke of the little boy. He shook his head and stared at his hands as they toyed with a pen on the desk. When he answered, he used the present tense in a gesture of weak optimism.

'No. He's a tough little kid.'

But in reality, the toddler's behaviour must have given his foster parents cause for concern. It ranged from noisy and boisterous to downright obnoxious. A troubled sleeper, William would actively fight going to bed most nights. He'd lie there, waving his arm in an arc above his head for hours, determined to keep himself awake. In and out of bed all evening, he'd keep Anna and Nathan on patrol. This must have been a rough introduction to parenting. But at the inquest, Nathan only seemed to remember the good times.

I can't write about William's medical history here. Non-publication orders remain in place where matters of health are concerned. The law is finely nuanced when it comes to privacy, and that's fair enough. I can tell you William suffered from asthma every so often, a fact revealed in the emergency call his foster mother made when he vanished from Kendall. I also discovered that when William was ill, he'd always ask for Nathan.

Anna worked with professionals to help William develop coping strategies, including deep breathing, to improve his behaviour. She saw little habits she wished to modify in Lindsay too. The little girl would try to physically mother other children, particularly William. Childcare workers called it 'parentified behaviour'. Such habits are often seen in children who've had unsettled home lives in their early years.

The children's problems didn't end there. Both would go toe-to-toe with Anna, leaving her frustrated and exhausted. She described her foster daughter screaming at the top of her lungs, defiant and refusing to listen to instructions. Anna confessed to the case worker she was second-guessing her own parenting strategies. It seemed no progress was being made.

Ben couldn't offer much help. After all, he wasn't a parent. He confined himself to writing very detailed reports. In them, he observed William to be oppositional and unsettled, snatching things off his sister, pushing her over, punching her and other children. Sometimes, little William would arm himself with objects likely to leave a mark. During one visit, he hit Lindsay over the head with a plate. A day earlier, he'd bitten her on the head. Both children engaged in constant nervous chatter, screaming and fighting like cats.

Abruptly, they'd switch to infantile behaviour, going completely limp. They'd suddenly refuse to walk, demanding to be carried. This would persist for a while, then there'd be another shift, this time toward clingy behaviour. They'd seek out incessant snuggling, hand-holding, following Anna everywhere, thumb-sucking and crying and demanding to know where she was even if she momentarily left a room. The children needed constant reassurance, prolonged attention and soothing. Ben wrote it all down meticulously.

Anna vented her feelings to Ben, saying she believed three things precipitated these behaviours: access visits, talking about access visits and being around gifts received on access visits. In Anna's view, this was the outworking of trauma. But, against her repeated requests to vary it, the contact schedule remained in place. She was blithely reassured by the case worker that these troubles would pass. The lines between everyone's best interests began to blur.

Reports reveal William and Lindsay also wrestled with self-confidence because they were confused about their parents. Sometimes, the children called Karlie 'Other Mummy'. At other times it was 'Mummy Karlie'. Ben commended Karlie on her compliance with Young Hope's directives in using this name during access visits. He understood it was hard. But increasingly, and heartbreakingly for Karlie and Brendan, the kids would simply call them by their first names.

In fact, Lindsay's birth surname would elicit such a negative reaction from her brother that she'd wield it as a weapon. In an email to Ben Atwood, Anna wrote that one day, her foster daughter told her she'd said a naughty word. When Anna pressed for a confession, she discovered the word was 'Tyrrell'. Anna explained that her surname is not a naughty word at all, but Lindsay wasn't convinced.

Despite these difficulties, the childcare centre's staff saw consistency in Anna and Nathan's parenting. Staff described them to detectives as caring, confident and fair. Anna told police that by William's second birthday, he was much more positive toward her. Anna told police about it in her first interview.

'Things changed for William when he reached the two-year plus age. It was like all of a sudden he settled down. He seemed to feel much more secure in his environment. His relationship with me turned around completely and we'd been sharing an extremely good, loving relationship since then. In fact William began shifting his focus towards me over Nathan.' The family became close, and William was getting on better with his sister, she said, noting that previously fragile relationships were steadily strengthening into loving family bonds.

*

By all accounts, William was a lively and active participant at the childcare centre they attended. Lindsay spent her time in the Preschool Room, but she loved visiting the Toddler Room to see what her brother was doing, which often involved causing more than his fair share of mischief. Once, William took a pair of scissors and tested his hair-cutting skills on some unfortunate playmate. He was 'experimenting'. Staff told investigators that prior to William's disappearance, both children had seemed content. They told police Anna was 'a very confident and fair woman'. She'd get down to eye-level when 'engaging in dialogue' with the kids. They noted she always spoke to them in adult language. One staffer described Anna as 'the perfect parent'. As for Nathan, he was viewed as 'consistent in a good way when it came to disciplining the kids'. But staff must have seen the fallout from access visits that continued to plague the family.

As well as dealing with the tyranny of two challenging children, Anna had paperwork to do. Foster families need advance permission to travel. Anna applied for pre-approval to travel on a bulk basis, which can be granted for three months at a stretch. It was under this arrangement that the family would make their fateful trip to Kendall.

For overseas travel, there was additional paperwork, as if the process wasn't tedious enough already. The children had passports issued in their birth names. They had been to a Balinese holiday resort in July 2014. On this trip Anna bought the children two new dress-up costumes. Lindsay chose a blue Elsa dress made popular by the Disney film *Frozen*. She proudly showed it to Ben on his next home visit. He put it in his newest report. The costume they bought for William would be shown to the whole nation. His red and blue superhero outfit would become a powerful emblem of loss, seared on our collective memory.

Anna's parents, Phillip and Nancy Wyndham, retired to Kendall on the Mid North Coast of New South Wales after their four children left home. Anna has a sister and two brothers. Their father had passed away in February 2014, having lived in the house the couple had built at 48 Benaroon Drive twenty-two years earlier. It's a single-level building, but one side is at second-storey height because the block slopes down dramatically.

I hadn't known Nancy Wyndham before her foster grandson went missing. Early in 2015, my Kendall friend Jen pointed her out to me at the community hall. The image that comes to mind as I try to describe her is of a delicate wading bird. She's petite and wire-thin, and her long-fingered hands move mesmerisingly when she talks. Her hair is white and fine as fairy-floss, but although she looks her age, her speech and body language give her a more commanding presence than that of your average granny. Her slight frame gives the impression that she'd blow away in a strong wind.

But I had been told by locals who've worked with her on various projects that her frail looks belie her toughness. She walks around town with purpose, works tirelessly in her impressive gardens and is a great letter writer, making comments on all manner of local issues in the *Camden Haven Courier*.

In 2014, Nancy was an active woman who liked to involve herself in a good cause. One was the community dream of building a sparkling swimming pool. Phillip and Nancy got the pool project off the ground, or more precisely, in the ground. Their small team started the Kendall Op Shop and all proceeds went to the pool fund-raising effort. The venture raised more than $300,000. But this herculean achievement was soured by allegations of misconduct. The new pool hadn't been open a week before accusations of financial misdealings were publicly levelled against the Wyndhams.

As I gathered material for the book, locals who know her well told me Nancy wasn't one to suffer fools gladly. She would confidently speak her mind, a fact that Anna confirmed in a police statement about her mother: 'She's very vocal, very opinionated.' When they were working on a community project she got people offside. 'Mum's had run-ins. She held people accountable for commitments they'd made. People tried to discredit their reputation and really do some damage. One of them ended up taking all the credit for the pool.'

Because my friends in Kendall knew I was writing about the case, they'd sometimes get people I didn't know to contact me. Some wanted to give me information – others to install themselves into the narrative. They took me into their confidence, relating all manner of intriguing stories they hoped would find their way into print. One of Nancy's neighbours mirrored Anna in describing Nancy as 'very opinionated' and another described her as 'a tough woman'.

She rose to leadership positions, including secretary of the Kendall Community Centre Reserve Trust. But her self-assuredness put more reserved people offside. When the mud-slinging began, some of it sullied the pool project, at least for Nancy. After facing allegations of embezzlement, and even worse, the cardinal sin of making decisions without involving the committee, she pointedly withdrew from the Op Shop. She also quit the pool committee and other volunteer roles after that episode, declaring she'd prefer to focus on growing her begonias. Perhaps it's because she knew flowers don't talk back.

In 2014 during initial police interviews, Nancy told police her daughter was 'a city girl' who hadn't approved of Nancy's decision to stay in Kendall after Phillip passed away. There were gardens and an acre of lawn to maintain, and it was such a long drive from Sydney. She understood it wasn't easy for Anna and Nathan to get away from work and commitments involving the foster children. They hadn't been up to Kendall since Phillip's funeral. So when Nancy heard that they were coming up, she was quite pleased to be hosting a visit. She was expecting them to arrive on Friday morning, 12 September.

According to both Anna's and Nathan's earliest police statements, certain stars had aligned so they could leave on Thursday afternoon. Nathan had his afternoon meeting cancelled. His diary had only one entry for Friday, a sales demo to be done by teleconference. Nathan later told police that he'd imagined he'd do it in the car while Anna drove them north to Kendall. But he'd rethought. Two excited kids in the Land Rover would surely derail his sales pitch. Better to land at Nana's Thursday night and do the demo Friday morning instead. He'd drive to a parking spot with better internet.

Then there was the problem of Katy and Ned – Anna's cats. Anna told police the couple relied on two regular house-sitters, but when she called them, both were unavailable. The two cats would need to be booked into boarding care for the weekend. In their separate interviews, the couple sketched out their next movements for police. When Nathan got home, Anna was packing the children's gear. The cat carrier appeared and the skittish Katy went into hiding, sparking a merry chase. They eventually reached the cattery with Katy and Ned. The payment receipt was time-stamped 3.15 pm. The final order of business was to collect the children from the childcare centre.

The kids were beside themselves with excitement. Both Mummy and Daddy had come to pick them up. They were going to Nana's a day early. And they'd get to stop at McDonald's, a rare treat reserved for long trips up the highway. Anna said at the inquest, 'I think I told the staff that we were travelling up to Mum and Dad's that afternoon. I may have mentioned it was at Port Macquarie. I don't say it's at Kendall because no one knows where Kendall is.'

Port Macquarie is thirty minutes north of Kendall. It's a blue-water paradise that attracts boating, fishing and surfing enthusiasts, motorhome adventurers and whale watchers. The place also offers more sedate attractions including winery tours, farmers' markets and a thriving arts scene. Usually serene, it heaves with activity in the tourist season – summer holidays. But increasingly, the tourists end up staying, embracing a sea change. It was recently named one of the fastest-growing towns in New South Wales. 'Port', as the locals call it, has everything sea-changers could ever want – schools and universities, hospitals, good shopping, an airport and a zoo thrown into the bargain.

While young families opt to live in Port, retirees prefer the little towns of the Camden Haven. All the mod cons are just a short drive up the highway. If you've retired to go fishing and boating, Laurieton and North Haven are the places to be. For country folk who raise gardens and animals, Kendall is the obvious choice.

Between Kendall's highway exits to Kew and Wauchope are two villages that would come to prominence in the William Tyrrell investigation. Just west of the highway, you'll find Herons Creek. It is home to a small cluster of dwellings and a heritage-listed chapel lovingly restored by the community. A little further west of Herons Creek is a heavily forested area called Logans Crossing. Both sites are close to the Pacific Highway and were once key to the timber milling industry on the Mid North Coast.

Kendall was named for its most famous resident, the poet Henry Kendall. He worked in forestry before deciding to find out if the pen was mightier than the axe. Turns out it was, but it couldn't conquer the bottle. Kendall drank himself to death at forty-three. Still, he left us a legacy of stirring poetry. His lyrical images of tinkling waterfalls and bellbirds ringing their calls through misty rainforests continue to resonate in 'The Poet's Village'. That's how the town is affectionately and proudly signposted.

Driving west, you encounter the verdant fields of the Lorne Valley, bisected by the modest Camden Haven River. The place is alive with birds: rosellas, cockatoos, graceful grey herons and white egrets. The forested foothills dotted with dairies and hobby farms are watered by heavy dews that turn everything green. Sage, myrtle and mossy bushrock form clusters at the edges of grassy fields. Pale riverside willows contrast with olive-crowned eucalypts and luxuriant bottle-green bushland. In summer, purple jacaranda carpets adorn the greenscape, but that September, the bright red flame trees were blooming early.

*

After two decades of visiting Benaroon Drive, Anna was familiar with some of the neighbours. She knew Nancy was friendly with the Millers, adjacent to her mother's. She'd met Paul and Heather Savage, diagonally opposite, and the Crabbs just up the hill.

William's first visit was in the winter of 2012. The following year, they'd gone to a Christmas street party. Certain neighbours knew Nancy's daughter had foster children. Some had seen William and Lindsay riding their bikes at number 48. But Nathan preferred his bikes supercharged. He'd enjoyed some good times over the eight years or so that he'd been visiting the in-laws, trail biking and four-wheel driving on the fire trails through the bushland. He knew those trails reasonably well and frequently forayed right into the state forest, sometimes with the kids.

Anna's mother was planning to sell her home. She had already lined up a prospective buyer. After Phillip died, Nancy had talked about throwing out some of his things; items that Anna didn't want discarded. It seems they differed over what constituted 'rubbish'. On this visit, Anna would help her mother sort things out. Perhaps they might squeeze in some house hunting. They also planned to visit the grave of Opa, as the children called their Dutch foster grandfather. They hadn't yet seen the headstone that had been installed after his funeral.

Police statements tell us that before departing the day care centre for Kendall, Nathan and Anna geared up for a hassle-free journey. He set up the car DVD player. She gave William and Lindsay a snack. With the kids buzzing animatedly in their seats, they were off. They fuelled up at the Shell service station on Mona Vale Road and stopped again at the 7-Eleven servo on Wahroonga's outskirts, the last amenity before the Pacific Highway becomes the M1. Nathan grabbed some food and drinks to keep the kids occupied.

As the family drove north, they talked about the surprise their early arrival would give Nana. Then Nathan began to second-guess this plan.

'You know, we should call her and give her a heads up. Probably shouldn't just lob in,' he said to Anna as they were driving towards Kendall. His wife agreed. She contacted her mother en route. Anna called at 3.50 pm and left a voicemail message. At 4.00 pm, her mother called back.

'We're on our way up now. I hope you don't mind. We thought we'd come a day early,' Anna said. Nancy received the news with consternation. She wasn't feeling well. Now she had to prepare for visitors sooner than she'd planned.

Anna told her not to fuss. 'I'll make up the spare beds myself when we get there, Mum.'

They reached the Central Coast and made a quick toilet stop at the Caltex Service Centre that straddles the highway at Tuggerah, just west of Wyong. Police would later ask Anna whether she thought they could've been tailed. She didn't know, but doubted it.

'We parked the car just outside the complex and used the toilets.' They were there for just a few minutes. They didn't buy anything or speak to anyone. Further north, they'd almost reached the McDonald's restaurant at Heatherbrae, on the outskirts of Newcastle. It's a popular rest stop for Pacific Highway travellers. While they idled at the traffic lights, Anna sat, smiling across at Nathan at the antics of the kids. They were bouncing around in excitement at the prospect of a Happy Meal for dinner.

'Why aren't you going, Daddy?' little William asked from the back seat.

'It's a red light, mate. If it's red, you have to stop.' The light changed. 'See? Now it's green. That means it's safe for us to go.'

Four years after William vanished, I watched CCTV footage of that visit to McDonald's, Heatherbrae. The vision is time-stamped 6.25 pm and it's dark outside. Nathan walks into the store with William riding on his shoulders. Anna folds her arms as she studies the overhead menu at the counter. Lindsay waddles sleepily at her feet.

They order meals and spend around fifteen minutes eating. They sit on barstools at a high bench by the front window. There's an enticing view out to the children's playground from their seats, but there's no time for play now. It seems Anna is conscious of the time. At the inquest she said she didn't want to arrive late and keep her mother from getting to bed.

The foursome exit the restaurant at 6.40 pm, a time consistent with Anna's estimate. This is the last video footage taken of William Tyrrell. I was chilled watching it. The faces are indistinct, then suddenly, the lens catches William at a particular angle and his features are sharply defined. His position high on Nathan's shoulders puts him closest to the camera. He looks different in this image, older somehow. Perhaps it's the interior lighting.

The automatic doors open for them.

*

They'd just driven through the Heatherbrae roundabout when Anna realised the children weren't wearing night-pants. They were still supercharged from their Happy Meals, but with full tummies, they might soon be asleep. Nathan pulled up beside the highway. They changed the kids into nappy-style pants. It was just a few minutes. The area was unlit. It was pitch black. They saw no one, no cars, nothing unusual, and nothing to indicate they were being followed on their journey north.

Travellers to Kendall exit the Pacific Highway at Kew, a scattering of shops and service stations. Before the bypass was built in 2011, it was a pit stop for holiday-makers running low on fuel. Kew's Royal Hotel was once a popular watering hole, and travellers have long been attracted by its legendary reputation as a bikie haunt. Trouble might brew at the Royal if you wear the wrong patch, or if someone reads your iconic 'Far-Kew' t-shirt and takes it personally. This is Bandidos territory.

But for your average suburban dad, it's a cool place to grab a Chiko Roll, rub shoulders with some leathery guys and contemplate growing a beard. The stop fortifies them as they head north to do battle with the in-laws. Revving up the family station wagon, they take off in a cloud of what they'd like to think is a heady mix of exhaust fumes and burning rubber. But it's actually just the dust from the hotel's dirt carpark.

Turning left at Kew takes you to Kendall, just five minutes away. Turning right takes you to Laurieton. Kew is home to a monstrous piece of only-in-Australia kitsch: the Big Axe. Poised menacingly over the carpark of the tourist information centre, it's sufficiently arresting to divert a driver's attention, but not really Instagrammable. Not in comparison to snapping a selfie with a bikie outside the Royal.

Nathan, Anna and the children arrived in Kendall at 8.50 in the evening. Nancy was watching television. After the usual flurry of welcomes, Nathan unloaded the car. Anna and Lindsay would share one double bed and Nathan and William would take the other. They habitually separated the children so they didn't wind each other up. Anna and Nathan sorted out sheets and doonas, put the children into their pyjamas and bundled them into bed.

'You can't do any washing, I'm afraid. The machine is in pieces,' Nancy announced as soon as they arrived. 'I had the repairman order the part two weeks ago.'

'Two weeks? That's ridiculous. He can't expect you to go all that time without a washing machine. When does he say the part will arrive?' Anna replied.

'Well, I don't know ...'

'We need to find out what's going on.'

'He'll just turn up when he has the parts, I assume. It's how we do things up here,' Nancy countered.

'I'll call him first thing in the morning,' Anna sighed, exasperated.

From this point in the evening, facts become tangled, setting tongues wagging among the foster family's critics. The first point of contradiction centres on bedtimes. During separate police interviews conducted the week William vanished, both parents said they were the last to bed. Nathan said everyone went to bed soon after they arrived, while he stayed up working. He was on his laptop preparing for the meeting next morning. He claimed to distinctly remember being last off to bed – at around ten.

'Anna was tired. Anna's mother was tired,' he told police. 'I still had a bit of work to do on my computer and I sat there probably, I don't know, half an hour. I had two glasses of wine. I had to get some emails off. Then I shut it down and went to bed.' Then he added, 'And I didn't get up until the next morning.' I wondered if this odd statement simply meant he rarely slept through the night uninterrupted, given William's sleeping difficulties.

But Anna contradicted her husband's statement, saying Nathan was tired from the drive and went to bed before her, at 9.30, just after the children. 'He got changed and went to bed pretty much at the same time as William.' Meanwhile, Anna said she sat talking with her mother about how they'd been coping after Phillip's death in February. 'Shortly after that, I went to bed and left Mum watching television.'

Because of discrepancies like this in the foster parents' recall, speculation has made some mighty leaps. For example, some have questioned whether William Tyrrell was ever actually at his foster grandmother's house at all. Did anyone even see him there? Did those foster parents stage William's disappearance? Would it be easier to fake an abduction in quiet Kendall or busy Sydney? Theories grew like noxious weeds. The police repeatedly addressed them, but not to everyone's satisfaction.

Detective Chief Inspector Gary Jubelin would steer Strike Force Rosann for four years. At its peak, the Strike Force had twenty-six full-time detectives. Early on, Jubelin dismissed suspicions about the foster family as nothing more than vindictiveness. He went on the record with the emphatic comment that he'd personally interviewed them and was satisfied they were telling the truth about what happened that day. 'I'm saying they've had nothing to do with it,' he said.

Certainly, evidence exists that appears to support aspects of the foster parents' testimony. Security footage and data from point-to-point cameras on the Pacific Highway confirm the timing of the journey, but, aside from the McDonald's CCTV footage, it's not possible to confirm the number or identities of the car's occupants. Statements from Nancy, Nathan and Anna mirror each other on the claim that they arrived in Kendall between 8.30 and 9.00 pm that Thursday. And it seems they have an independent witness.

Heather Savage, the neighbour diagonally opposite Nancy's house, was making up the spare bed for her own visitors, expected on Friday. She said she saw the tail-lights of the foster family's car as it pulled up sometime after 8.30 pm. She didn't see the occupants.

In public discourse around this mystery, most onlookers didn't initially know about the foster care situation. Then the key disclosure came – the people William lived with were his foster carers, not his birth parents. This intrigued viewers watching a *60 Minutes* interview aired in 2015.[5] The exclusive promised to give us our first look at them. A vision emerged of two silhouettes, sitting in silence as the interviewing journalist Michael Usher wept. Afterwards, Anna and Nathan remained in the shadows, occasionally issuing careful statements via a public relations firm. They remained anonymous.

By the time William's grief-stricken biological mother appeared on the *Sunday Night* television program in 2018,[6] sympathy for the faceless foster family had lost traction. They began to seem detached, irrelevant. And they weren't giving anyone access.

Before this book was published, I made a point of contacting William's family members personally (or attempting to). His birth father, uncle and grandmother and their friends all gave me their support in March 2019. But in 2020, when she saw me publicise my author's note, Natalie Collins publicly sounded off about being sick of people writing books about her grandson. I found it entirely understandable.

I also let William's foster mother know of my intentions in person but when I spoke to her at the second sitting of the inquest in Taree in August 2019, I couldn't get a read on her response.

'Could I talk to you for a moment?' I asked Anna as she was preparing to leave for lunch. She had paused to fold up a shawl she'd hung over the back of her seat.

'No.' The reply was swift and matter-of-fact. Her raised eyebrows seemed to be inviting me to mount a challenge, so I persisted.

'I'm not after information. I just wanted to let you know what I've been doing here at the inquest.' No reply, but she shifted her position to face me, signalling that I had her attention.

'I'm a local author writing a book about the case,' I told her. 'Just in case you were wondering why I've been here.'

'Yes, I had wondered,' she replied. She thanked me for making myself known to her and left. I thought, under the circumstances, that she was gracious to even listen.

Far from being 'just the carers' – as Anna bitterly complained to Young Hope and to police – they saw themselves as William's parents in every respect except biology. But social media influencers declared they had no right to feel bereaved. *Who do those people think they are? What about his real family?* Now he's been taken from them twice.

The sequence of events that Thursday night in Kendall varies in Anna's and Nathan's separate statements, but experienced investigators know this is unremarkable. In fact, statements that are too similar can make detectives suspect collusion. Still, to armchair detectives, it appeared downright shady. First, these people from somewhere in Sydney won't even identify themselves. Who knows who they are and what they're mixed up in? And later, at the inquest, the couple couldn't agree on details about what happened on the worst day of their lives.

63

5

A ROLL OF THE DICE

The year 2014 was one of tragedies, not least for Malaysian Airlines. In March, flight MH370 vanished and just four months later, MH17 was shot down. In Sydney, a lone terrorist raised a siege at the Lindt Café in the Sydney CBD, causing the deaths of two people just going quietly about their business. Australia lost Phillip Hughes to a freak cricketing accident.

Globally, the tragedies kept coming. In Africa, it was the Ebola epidemic and the Nigerian schoolgirl kidnapping; in Eastern Europe, there was fighting in the Ukraine and Crimea. In the Middle East, another deadly conflict between Israel and Hamas took more lives.

But some positives for world progress also came in 2014. Pro-democracy protests in Hong Kong commemorated the Tiananmen Square massacre. Russia hosted the Winter Olympics in Sochi and Germany surprised Brazil with a thrilling World Cup win. Social media gave us Grumpy Cat and the Ice Bucket Challenge. Commuters in Sydney and Melbourne stood against racism and bigotry one person at a time in the 'I'll Ride with You' campaign and for good measure, 'dabbing' became a thing.

Off-world, the European Space Agency managed to land the Rosetta spacecraft on a comet speeding between Jupiter and Mars. But, despite being able to pinpoint a tiny heavenly body hurtling through the vast backyard of our solar system, we couldn't locate a toddler in a tiny regional town.

Since 2014, I've been curious whether the rest of the world knows about the case. Various social media forums have enlightened me. Threads have featured participants from across the globe, predominantly the United States, Canada and the United Kingdom. These were the same people interested in other mysteries involving children; JonBenét Ramsey, Madeleine McCann and Australia's Daniel Morcombe. Many followed William Tyrrell's story from the time he first went missing. The adorable face of this little boy touched the hearts of parents everywhere. Roaring at the camera in his Spiderman suit, he looks happy, energetic, invincible.

William had faced struggles since infancy but his foster mother told police that he was really settling down by 2014. Perhaps, like so many other kids, he was attracted to Spiderman because he's brave and strong and has a cool costume. But if he'd had the chance to grow up, I wonder if William would've seen an even worthier quality in that particular superhero. Like many fans, I love Spidey because of his vulnerability. He's an orphan, so, like a foster child, he's struggled to find his place within a family, and by extension, in the world. He's known great sadness, weakness, fear. Adults know that behind the mask is just a vulnerable kid – very brave, and very human.

Anna mentioned to police that William's Spidey suit had a hood that went with it. They'd left it at home that weekend, a fact that I found beautifully poetic. Because it meant that little Spiderman was perhaps one of the few figures in this case that we see without a mask.

*

When it was Nathan's turn to speak at the inquest, details emerged that highlighted subtle differences between his and Anna's account of the fateful morning. At the inquest, he recalled how that day began. High-pitched giggles let Nathan know that William was already up. He changed the toddler out of his night-pants.

Anna sent Lindsay out of the bedroom, hoping to get some more sleep. Meanwhile, Nathan tried to keep the children occupied. 'He woke up and then, you know, he's giggling. He's all over me, wanting to play. And then we watched some shows on my phone.' Nathan had already downloaded *Fireman Sam* to the device. He held it for the kids as they lay on either side of him. This amused them until Anna rose. But she didn't get much of a sleep-in.

Anna told the court she woke early on Friday 12 September 2014. I watched her expressive eyebrows raise and lower as she took us back to the events of that morning. Anna said she opened the verandah doors at about 6.30. Letting in fresh air each morning was a practice she'd inherited from her mother.

Her next recollection would become a critical factor in the investigation. Anna allegedly saw two cars from the vantage point of her verandah, though she wouldn't mention this to anyone for two days. She told the court she remembered them on Sunday 14 September, while driving back from Port Macquarie airport after fetching her sister. She said there was a sudden, blinding flash of recognition, the force of which caused her to gasp, 'Oh my God! There were cars! I've forgotten the cars.' Anna described as 'burned into her memory' the image of two cars parked on the edge of the street that morning. They were older models, 'scungy', Anna called them. The first was a grey sedan.

'I don't know what model it was – very straight at the front and back. It was shorter in length than a Commodore,' Anna recalled. Parked behind the grey car, less than a metre away, was an off-white station wagon. 'I thought to myself, *that's odd.*' She found it strange that they were parked between two house frontages with both driver-side windows down. She remembered thinking that would never happen in Sydney. They were parked as if visiting the house across the road, but very close together.

The station wagon had a boxy back-end and a short front. Both cars had tinted windows. The vehicles were dirty and the wagon had damaged paintwork. Neither had any hubcaps. In a different police statement, Anna said the off-white car was in front of the grey one. Nevertheless, she was confident in her recall of the other details.

Anna was adamant when she spoke about the cars at the inquest. 'I had a very clear, unobstructed view of them. I would give a rough estimate of about 6.40 am, very shortly after getting up. I still look for these cars to this day when I am driving around. Some time ago, I saw a vehicle that looked so similar to this white station wagon. The vehicle that I saw was a Camry station wagon.'

On Sunday the 14th, Anna returned to Kendall at 6.15 pm and went to the command post. Police took a description of the cars she'd sighted. They brought up some images of older model cars and, scrolling through, she considered their style, vintage and features. She decided the gunmetal grey vehicle could be a BA Falcon or a VN Commodore. (I remember a lively discussion unfolding at the Kendall Club that centred on this piece of testimony. One fellow shook his head, saying, 'When an Australian can't tell a Ford from a Holden, it makes you wonder what the hell they were doing in the 1980s. I mean, weren't they watching Brocky and Johnson like the rest of us?')

The police wouldn't mention the cars publicly until 2015, but at the coronial inquiry their presence was treated as a certainty. Intriguingly, Nathan told police he hadn't seen any cars there when he'd left the house that morning. He was never asked to repeat that assertion at the inquest. But in an interview with police in 2016, he was emphatic – if Anna said she saw the cars, then she saw the cars.

We know William and Lindsay were keen to see Nana that morning from statements all three adults made to police. The children went to open her bedroom door and wake her, but Anna told them to leave her in peace and go play. Nancy kept toys in the house for when they visited. According to Nathan, they included a stuffed fabric Spiderman toy bought at the Kendall Op Shop on a previous visit. But in another small contradiction, Anna told police they'd brought this toy from home. She said she remembered packing it with William's clothes.

'For William I packed some clothes, pyjamas, Pull-Ups, toothbrush, pillow, blue *Monsters, Inc.* slippers and some toys including a truck, motorbike, soft Spiderman toy, a red outfit and a fireman's hat. Oh, and a Spiderman bag with some little cars.' Reading this, I remarked to myself that Anna's reports were almost as detailed as Ben's.

The Spidey toy can be seen in the photos Anna took of the children that morning. The kids also played with a flushing-toilet toy, a steering wheel and a doll in a pram.

'William and Lindsay sat alongside the three sliding doors that I'd opened earlier that morning – the same doors I exited when I saw the vehicles.' Reading through these statements, a couple of thoughts occurred to me. First, I doubted if I'd remember with such exactitude which items I'd hurriedly packed for my children. And second, if Anna was mistaken about packing the Spidey toy, could she also be mistaken about seeing those cars?

Anna gave the kids some liquid probiotic yoghurt to take the edge off until breakfast. William wanted to put on his two-piece Spiderman suit. There was some disagreement about wearing a singlet, but they reached a compromise. He put on a Spidey t-shirt underneath the thin polyester costume. If he became too hot, he'd still have a top to match his pants. This made the little guy happy.

The children were playing on the high verandah that morning. The railing made it safe, and Anna could watch them from inside the house. She said anyone on the quiet street would have been able to hear William's and Lindsay's voices as they played. Six days later,

Anna Wyndham would feature in a walk-through video describing the events of the morning to detectives. (Walk-through videos are routinely filmed in missing persons cases to reconstruct the events of the day.)

In Anna's walk-through video, she couldn't recall whether she was the one who let the kids onto the verandah. But earlier, she did recall opening the door to let in the fresh air. In other reports, she'd said she was looking for a kookaburra her mother had tamed to hand-feed on the verandah. Taken collectively, the different versions form a tangle. Often it's hard to follow the threads to arrive at the facts.

Meanwhile, Nathan prepared for his morning meeting. The children were making a bit of noise, and according to Anna's testimony, Nathan grew frustrated.

'You do you; I'll do the kids,' she said. She distracted William and Lindsay with an activity – making cards for Opa's grave. They intended to visit it later that morning.

Anna's mother couldn't accurately recall her son-in-law's movements that morning. At first, she said she'd had breakfast with her daughter and the children; Nathan had left the house before she got out of bed, around 8.00 am. 'We all got up and did the routine of breakfast, you know, milk and all those sorts of things,' said Nancy. But Nathan's statement puts him with his wife at breakfast. These details are complicated by a later addition in Nathan's statement. He said he had coffee and toast while William and Lindsay were fighting over a toy, an electronic gadget shaped like a car's dashboard. It had a steering wheel that turned, a horn and an ignition key and made sounds. Nathan couldn't recall whether these fights occurred before or after breakfast.

Later, Nathan added a detail about William: 'I think that he was having breakfast after I left.' In his statement, Nathan is clear both women were out of bed before he left. They were getting eggs, toast and Weet-Bix organised when Nathan asked when the pharmacy opened. He had to fill a script. Reports vary as to the exact time Nathan left the house. Early media reports said 9.15 am, whereas testimony from both foster parents at the inquest estimated it was no later than 9.00 am. A security camera captured footage of his car passing the Kendall tennis courts at 8.49 that morning.

Among the online sleuths, a key question has been why Nathan felt it necessary to go out for that meeting. Detectives asked him for us.

'Because the internet access up there is absolutely abysmal,' he replied. As a local, I can attest that many areas up our way struggled with internet service before the National Broadband Network (NBN) came through. Even now, we have other names for the NBN up here, No Bloody Network being my favourite. Nathan intended to use a software tool called 'Go To Meeting'. Users can host online meetings with it, provided there's a decent amount of bandwidth to handle the data. He conducted the meeting out of his car while parked at Lakewood. Anna's statement aligned with Nathan's on this issue.

'The work demo Nathan had to do was always booked in for that morning. Often when we visit, Nathan will go where reception is best, as reception in Kendall is not the best and his work calls drop out. He often takes his laptop and does work in his car.' Nathan drove the most direct route through Kendall to Kew, then onto Lakewood. Nathan said he arrived at Lakewood at about 9.15.

His meeting with a client in Queensland accounted for thirty-nine minutes. Nathan missed a call from a recruiter during the meeting. He retrieved her voicemail message and at 9.45, returned her call. Then he went to the pharmacy.

The shopping precinct of Lakewood has a Woolworths supermarket and a sprinkling of shops that service the housing estates between Laurieton and Kew. It's a ten-minute drive from

Kendall. In a police video, Nathan reconstructed his movements that morning. He recalled with undisguised pride that as he pulled his brand-new Land Rover Discovery into a car space, two tradies walked past him exchanging envious glances, as if to say, 'Nice car!'

Nathan's enthusiasm for his new toy had certainly rubbed off on the kids. They'd delighted in showing it to Nana that morning. They'd sat in the car and Nathan had started it up and run through its features, much to William's delight. Shortly afterwards, he unloaded the kids' bikes then left the house.

Anna had no memory of her husband showing her mother the new car. She theorised about whether Nathan might have supervised the kids riding their bikes for a while as she showered and got dressed, around 7.50 am. Anna said that after he left, she and Nancy supervised. The kids put on their helmets and rode their bikes on the driveway.

'He'd already left. They were riding their bikes where his car had been parked. Mum and I were sort of walking them up and down the driveway as they rode.' The children alternated between doing circuits on the driveway and racing each other with Nana giving the 'Ready, Set, Go!' Then they tackled the sloping footpath.

'Lindsay ended up riding down the footpath towards the front stairs. As she rode down there, she lost her balance and fell off into the garden. She hadn't hurt herself and got straight back up. Just then, William rode down that same footpath and deliberately crashed his bike into the garden.' It was then that Anna noticed yet another car.

'I saw a dark green/grey sedan drive past Mum's house, up Benaroon Drive. The car just nosed into the Millers' driveway and then backed back.'

'Whose is that car, Mummy?' Lindsay asked. Anna assumed it belonged to the Millers. In her initial police statement, she said she saw the car for less than ten seconds. In that time, though, she noticed it had black plastic louvres, bronze-centred wheels and tinted windows. Anna said it was green, grey and teal in different interviews. At first, she described it as a Ford LTD. Then later, that changed.

'I believe it was a Holden Commodore. Very dark teal green, almost grey. It had a slight metallic look.' More details were added in different statements as time went on. 'I can't remember whether the windows were down. I could not see any of the occupants.' But by the time of the inquest, she had clearly recalled the driver, previously unmentioned. Anna presented the experience in minute detail to an enthralled courtroom, stating, 'I can see him today.'

We heard he was a very large man, thick-necked, with his body at quite a distance from the steering wheel, too bulky to fit behind it comfortably. He had a beer belly. She said the image of the man's face was 'burned into her brain'. She distinctly remembered his round eyes, and his clean-shaven but weather-beaten skin.

'The driver was in his late fifties. His hair looked like it had been red, but had faded with age. But he wasn't balding. I could clearly see the top of his head.' Then she remembered another key fact, a rather unforgettable one. The man had given her a challenging look. She added some imaginary dialogue to illustrate the unspoken exchange.

'He looked at me as if to say, "I know you're watching me. Well, I'm watching *you*."' Strong visual memories initially absent, then recovered, overshadowed her testimony with doubt.

In a 2016 interview with Detective Chief Inspector Gary Jubelin, we heard a very different version of this sighting.

'I remember seeing an older gentleman in it, grey hair and you could see that he was a slightly larger man driving.' Jubelin wanted to know if there was anything else that drew her attention to the car.

'If I think about it, he didn't look over. He just kept driving straight ahead.'

'He didn't look towards you?'

'No. He didn't look towards us.'

Oddly, Nancy made no mention of seeing or hearing this teal-coloured car, nor its driver. Anna never mentioned it to her until after she'd reported it to police. On social media, onlookers seized upon this sighting, questioning its authenticity.

Well, it turns out a car was indeed heard (but not seen) around this time of that morning by Mr and Mrs Crabb. By the time of day, the fact that no doors were heard to open, the turn it made and the sound of the engine, they took it to be the postal worker's vehicle. (In these parts, due to long distances, the postie drives a car, not a motorbike.) Mrs Crabb said it was going quite fast. The public would never hear whether the police had ruled out the postie. Presumably, it would be simple enough to check with the post office which driver (in which vehicle) was on duty that day. Actually, I did some digging and discovered that the postal worker – a woman – had been in Benaroon Drive about ten that morning. We can't rule out the possibility that it was the postal worker the Crabbs heard.

The Crabbs heard that car but none of the other neighbours did. It seems possible then that vehicles can sometimes enter and leave Benaroon Drive without being seen or heard. This lends weight to Anna's testimony regarding the two initial cars, those parked across the road at around 6.40 am. She could have been the only person in the street to have seen them.

In her police statement, Nancy was adamant that you can't hear cars coming up the road from her back patio. One fine day, I decided to test this theory out for myself. Shamelessly trespassing in the vicinity of the patio, on the fringe of the property – all in the interests of good research – I had a friend drive up the road, following the trajectory of that vehicle as Anna described it and I found it to be quite true that I could not hear the car from that position until well after it had turned the corner.

We are left with two clear possibilities. If Anna is telling lies, they have been poorly conceived. She must have known that no one else would corroborate her story. The other possibility is that she did, in fact, see those cars. No one connected with those vehicles has ever come forward. This could be how William was taken from Benaroon Drive. If he was snatched from Batar Creek Road, it would've been even easier. There's no one around. Few houses fronting the road. Easy to stop, scoop him up and drive on.

William was growing bored with bike riding, even with the added interest of repeatedly crashing into the garden. Anna took him past a bed of scarlet begonias to a celery wood tree in the front garden. There they played chasey, Anna as 'Mummy Monster' and William the hapless victim. Their shrieks and laughs startled the birds.

'When William was running away from me, he was squealing. I caught him and he was screaming and laughing as I tickled him. Neighbours or people on the street would have been able to hear him.' At one point, William slipped and fell, but it was just a small tumble and it didn't make him cry.

Anna told the court that when William tired of this game, she was relieved because, frankly, she was over it too. This urbane admission drew gasps of shock – perhaps feigned – from the couple's more vocal critics. One later remarked that a foster carer who'd admit to being bored with a child's game is not fit to be a parent at all. A pretty harsh judgement, but harsh judgements in this case have been the order of the day.

Nancy's garden featured some native trees, planted to attract the birds. Green-suited lorikeets and red-hatted rosellas fed on nectar. Pink-and-grey galahs squabbled over seeds on the ground. During their walk around the garden, William attempted some tree climbing. Anna lifted him into a good climbing tree, but, she said, he wasn't keen. She told the court that William became spooked when he tried to move from one branch to another.

'No Mummy, too high. Too high. Get me down.' To encourage the little boy to push his boundaries, Anna reassured him that he was secure.

'See? You're safe. I'm holding you.' But he insisted, so she lifted him down. At this testimony, more gasps were elicited from the foster family's critics.

'Fancy forcing a frightened child to climb a tree!'

On her way back to the house via an acute slope of yard, Anna slipped and hurt her hand on a sharp stick. She would show her mother a small injury, a red patch on her palm. William found the ground there too steep. He didn't want to climb up that way, so Anna showed him how to skirt the base of the hill where the ground was more level. She was pleased that his natural caution made him reluctant to run up or down that slope. He'd be unlikely to try it if he happened to be on his own, Anna thought.

Anna said she noticed the two strange cars for a second time. It's a wonder Nathan didn't see them when he left the house at around 8.35. Perhaps they left and then returned later that morning. The closest resident – Anne-Maree Sharpley – didn't see the cars either. She checked the road as she reversed her car out of the driveway into Benaroon Drive at 8.40 am.

Neighbour Peter Crabb said he didn't see any cars parked on the street either, not when he and his wife left and not when they returned home at about 9.30 am. A heart scare had prompted Peter to add more exercise into his daily routine. So every morning, rain or shine, he and his wife, Sharelle, drove to North Haven for a brisk walk along the riverside bike path. Their walk took at least an hour, putting their departure from home at around 8.00 to 8.30.

According to Anna, no sooner had she and William returned to the house than Lindsay piped up, wanting to play the chasing game as well. Anna took both children back down to the front yard where they played some more. She noticed the cars were gone.

As they walked back to the house, Anna told the kids about going to see Opa's grave and drawing some pictures for him. They began collecting leaves and twigs to stick onto their cards – a craft activity they'd done at day care. They made their drawings on the patio while Anna and Nancy sat watching them. Next, the children played a dice game, rolling them on the verandah and counting up the dots. Lindsay counted the dots with Anna, then did the same number of little jumps.

But William was boisterous, throwing the dice roughly. Anna showed him how to roll them gently, just letting them tumble out of his hand. Nancy took up the theme and asked William to play nicely, but he didn't readily quit. He liked the sound the dice made on the wooden slats when he threw them hard. It's a bitter irony that the children played with dice that morning, because it seems that chance was the single force that would soon determine William's fate.

Lindsay wanted Anna to help her attach some leaves to her drawing. Anna wrote Lindsay's message to Opa and helped her stick the leaves on her picture. She stuck some things onto William's picture as well, but he'd lost interest by this time. The children played on and off the patio while Anna and her mother sat talking. Anna went inside to get her Sony digital camera and take some shots for a life story photo book she was making.

Anna took five shots of the children playing on the deck. As the pictures of the children innocently amusing themselves on their grandmother's patio were shown onscreen, I felt my own eyes welling up. I looked over to see Natalie Collins weeping at the sight of the last photo ever taken of her little grandson. As I watched her, I recalled a comment she'd made to a national newspaper before the inquest began.

'They're never going to find William — I just know in my heart he's dead.'[7]

*

Anna's testimony continued to take us through the events of that morning. Just before ten o'clock, Anna and her mother decided it was time for morning tea. Mr Craddock described Anna's finicky tea preferences with maddening precision. Early news stories said Anna was inside making tea when William vanished. In a subsequent report, we heard it was Nancy who'd made morning tea that day. But neither woman was inside making tea when William disappeared.

One newspaper has the tea-making occur before any photographs were taken: 'William's foster mother made cups of tea before snapping the iconic photo of the three-year-old boy sitting on the deck dressed as Spiderman at 9.37 am.' But this error was easily corrected when a small but significant detail was noted in court. No teacups were visible on the little table between the chairs. Clearly they hadn't yet had morning tea.

In the photograph, we see Nancy dressed in a pink blouse, fawn jacket and trousers. She's wearing socks and blue slippers, and is reading what looks to be a local newspaper called *The Independent*. Now defunct, it had a distinctive sky-blue masthead and was issued every Wednesday. This must have been last week's paper, since Nathan was yet to bring the latest one home.

In the last pictures Anna took of the children together, they are sitting on the deck. Lindsay is bent over, working on her drawing; William's drawing is in front of him. He's playing with crayons from a yellow ice-cream tub. Lindsay is wearing a blue dressing gown, with her play clothes underneath, and sandals. William is barefoot. His open-toed, velcro strap sandals are visible near the back door. Anna confirmed William wasn't wearing his shoes until a little later. He put them on just before he vanished.

'I can see that he has no shoes on in this picture. I have seen that in the previous photos; William's shoes are by the back door.

I cannot remember it happening, but William would have taken his shoes off when going inside after the walks we did.' Anna had wanted William to put his shoes on when he was getting his feet dirty from the muddy area under the clothesline. Prickly bindies lurk in the grass of most Aussie backyards, so shoes are necessary.

There's a pot plant and a sunhat on the table. Near the two steps down to ground level is a planter box on legs, containing colourful petunias. Another small table supports a plant in a pink plastic pot. A white timber seat with a padded cushion is under the window-sill. A pink play stroller, a couple of toys and two drink bottles – lime green for William and pink for Lindsay – complete the picture of this ordinary morning in Kendall.

The other notable feature of the photo is the one everyone immediately recognises: the little boy's Spiderman suit. It's of a design only manufactured in Indonesia: 100 per cent polyester, red on the front and mostly royal blue on the back and under the sleeves.

The image of William – open-mouthed in mid-roar – that made the little boy's face recognisable throughout Australia is highly significant because police used it as a 'proof of life' exhibit to piece together a timeline of events that morning.

Suspicions were raised when it was discovered the Exchangeable Image File Format (EXIF) metadata timestamp had been altered. It shows a 'Created' time of 07:39:54 and a 'Corrected' time of 09:37:44. Pressure for an explanation intensified, not least because in Mr Craddock's opening address to the inquest he'd explicitly set up that shot as the anchor for the morning's timeline.

'William was on that deck at 9.37 am. Of that we can be sure,' Mr Craddock told the court. But could we? Between the inquest's final two sittings, media disseminated the official explanation: Anna hadn't correctly set the time on her camera when she'd first bought it. But this didn't satisfy everyone and gave rise to wild speculation about what happened in those 'unexplained 118 minutes', as the *Daily Mail* put it.[8]

The timeline is absolutely vital to any missing persons investigation. And unusually, we had a photo that quickly became the unassailable reference point. But counsel assisting the Coroner made his position clear – questioning the foster mother and grandmother's timeline, as sketched out for detectives, was off-limits. Critics slammed Mr Craddock for refusing to question the veracity of the timeline ... until the reason was revealed in 2020.

Anna's $200 camera wasn't a particularly complicated device and she'd had no manual for it. By pure chance, one image taken on 1 September – eleven days before William vanished – had captured a television on which Channel 7's *Sunrise* program can be seen going to air. The news segment is shown with an onscreen clock displaying the time of the live broadcast: 118 minutes earlier than the timestamp attributed by the camera. And thus, the truth about the altered timestamp was revealed. Anna had simply never set the camera's timer when she bought it. End of mystery.

*

Anna was hoping Nathan would be home soon, so they could get on with their day. The couple cited different plans for the afternoon, again creating suspicion about events that occurred that morning. Nathan mentioned house-hunting with Nancy as a priority. But Anna said they had no plans beyond visiting Opa's grave.

Detectives interviewed Lindsay about the moments leading up to her brother's disappearance, but she couldn't shed any further light on what had happened to him.

'William was playing on the balcony and then he went off and he was finding Daddy's car.'

'Was anyone else here?'

'My Mummy and Nana.'

'What were you doing on the verandah?'

'Playing. Um, drawing.'

'And you said William was playing like a ...'

'Tiger. Um, he kneeled on the ground and then he said, "Raaargh!"'

We learned from Mr Craddock that Nancy prefers her tea weak, with a dash of milk. He encouraged Anna to describe how she likes to let her tea steep until it reaches a colour to her liking. Then she lets it sit until it's a drinkable temperature. Anna told Mr Craddock she remembered sitting down, sipping her tea, watching William running around.

The timing isn't exact, but according to the photo, said Mr Craddock, it was after 9.37 and well before 10.30. Anna said her mother likes to have a cuppa at around ten. She told the court that she could still feel the sensation of the hot tea in her hand when she recalled watching William play on the grass.

While Lindsay sat drawing, William became restless. He began jumping on and off the low deck, playing a game that Anna said was new to her – 'Daddy Tiger'. She believed it was inspired by 'Mummy Monster'.

'I don't remember how William came to be a tiger, but it may have been something he'd been doing at day care. He was saying, "I'm a daddy tiger". "Mummies and Daddies" is a game William and Lindsay played often, so by William saying that, it meant he wanted Lindsay to be the baby tiger. Lindsay didn't want to play with him, so he just ran around and played on his own.'

William was amusing himself by dashing around the corner of the house and roaring and clawing the air like a tiger. Nancy complained to Anna about the volume of William's roars.

'When he did this roar, my mother made a comment about him being so loud. That was just the way William was. He was full of energy. Mum said to me perhaps William had ADD [attention deficit disorder]. I told her that was not the case. That was just William.' Each time the little boy roared and ran a short distance around the side of the house, he'd pop back into sight again ... until ... he didn't.'

Anna tearfully told the inquest of her confusion about the timing of those final minutes. She and her mother could see William's little figure darting around the garden, the red on his Spiderman suit standing out brightly against dark green foliage. Then, he left their line of sight after rounding the northwestern corner of the house. But they could still hear him. An indeterminate period of time passed before Anna commented that it was unusually quiet.

The precise amount of lag between the sudden hush and Anna's search remains unclear. But she recalled that two inches of tea still remained in her mug when she noticed things had become too quiet.

'I heard him do one big roar. This roar was a ten out of ten in terms of volume. It had purpose. When William did it, he sounded like he was so close. Like he was literally just around the corner next to the steps. That's the last time I heard William. After that roar, there was just silence.'

*

From reading transcripts of Nathan's statements, we get a pretty clear chronology of what happened after he left Lakewood. While driving back to Kendall, Nathan made a phone call to a prospect in Sydney. The time was 10.23. He stopped at the roadworks at Kew. Waiting for the woman in the hi-vis vest to turn the red stop sign around, he remembered he'd promised to pick up Nancy's newspapers. He pulled up at the Kendall General Store and approached the woman at the counter.

'I said, "Have you got the papers there for Nancy?" and she handed them to me. I paid four dollars in cash. And it was at that point, I'm pretty sure, I sent Anna a text via Siri saying, "I'll be there in five minutes."' That message was sent at precisely 10.30 am. The time is beyond question. Call log records prove it. Nathan arrived back at the house about three minutes later.

By this time, both women had been looking for William inside the house, opening doors and cupboards. Anna went looking under the house, around the yard. She'd gone down to the front yard, perhaps as far as Ellendale Crescent, then back to the house.

Anna had her phone with her and when it pinged she read Nathan's message. She recalled being at the house at the time.

'I'm thinking I'm not going to reply. And I remember just going, oh I hope he's got him, I hope he's got him in the car.'

At 10.34 when Nathan returned, William must have been gone for at least fifteen minutes, to fit in all of Anna's searching activity. Police estimated William might have rounded the corner of the house for the last time at around 10.10 am. They could not pinpoint the exact moment – only the snatcher could do that.

*

At the inquest, Anna exhibited something of a tortured mother's tendency toward harsh self-judgement. She said she felt guilty for enjoying the silence, given William's usually noisy play. Anna estimated it was no more than five minutes before she got up and walked around the corner to check on him. She assumed he must have wandered off down the garden. But when she got to the corner and could see and hear nothing, no noise, no wind, no birds, something didn't feel right.

She scanned along the perimeter of the neat yard for a flash of red. *Oh, he's just gone down the hill looking for Nathan's car.* There must have been a just-perceptible quickening of blood flow, a tiny constriction of breath as she called out his name. But though her eyes must have strained to settle on that familiar little figure, the child wasn't in view. *Why can't I see him? Impossible. He was right here.*

Anna described the scene in her police statement, and numerous times afterwards.

'Everything was completely silent. It was so quiet it was eerie. There wasn't even any wind. I was standing at the top of the hill at my mother's house facing the eastern side of Benaroon Drive. I was looking out onto the road and was scanning all around me trying to see something red.' Panic rose in her throat, and an unwarranted guilty conscience began its assault. *How could I not have noticed him walking off?* Just a few seconds. But how many? Was it minutes? She recounted them as they thumped out in heartbeats.

'He was here just a minute ago,' she said out loud, rehearsing the conversation she'd have with her partner. But inwardly, she was already questioning herself, as mothers will. She counted and recounted her estimate of timing. *How long was it until I noticed?*

A portion of Anna's second police statement sheds more light on this question. In 2018, Anna told detectives she had some doubts about her recall of the timing of her last sighting of little William.

'I have thought so hard over the years as to how long it was between the roar and me walking around the corner to check on William and I just don't know. At the time, it only felt like about five minutes, but now I think about it, I know that I was relaxed at my mother's house – thinking the area is so secluded – so I wasn't focusing my undivided attention on William. I feel like it possibly could have been more like fifteen minutes after the roar that I went to look for him.' What has been consistent in Anna's testimony is her utter horror as the situation unfolded and the realisation set in that she couldn't lay eyes on her son. My heart races every time I re-read those statements taken in September 2014.

'I was calling out "William" quite loudly. I could not see red or William or anything … I was calling out "William". I was talking to him saying, "No more hiding, William. I can't see you. You need to come out. William, it's Mummy. You need to talk to me." I was saying this very, very loudly while still trying to remain calm so he wouldn't panic.'

Anna said before she had time to decide what to do next, she saw Nathan's car coming up the road. Wishful thinking made her presume that perhaps the child had met up with him. After all, William was expecting him back soon, and she had been asking them whether they could see Daddy coming yet. Before Nathan had the chance to get out of the car, Anna gestured to him urgently and he wound the window down. She asked if he had William.

'Of course not. Why would you think he's with me?'

'Because he's missing. He's gone.' The moment she uttered those words, Nathan got out of the car and took off running.

6

OUT OF LUCK

Laurieton is home to one of the Camden Haven's two tiny police stations. It's the beat of Senior Constable Chris Rowley, the first officer on scene on 12 September. A Kendall resident himself, Rowley was in Lakewood when he was dispatched to answer Anna's emergency call for police assistance. Australia was able to listen in when it was aired at the inquest in 2019.

'Police Emergency, this is Simone.'

'Yeah, hi. My son is missing. He's three-and-a-half.'

'Okay. What's your address?'

'Ah, ah, ah, 48 Benaroon Drive, Kendall.'

'All right. I'm just going to bring that up on my map. I won't be a moment.'

'Thank you.'

'How long has he been missing?'

'Ah, well ... I think ... we've been looking for him now for about fifteen or twenty minutes, but I thought ... it could be five or could be longer, because he was just playing around here and we heard him ... then we heard nothing.'

'Yeah, okay. Can you describe him to me? How tall? Obviously not very tall.'

'No. He would be … he would be about two and half feet. He is wearing a Spiderman outfit. He's got … um, dark, sandy coloured hair. It's short. He's got really big, browny-green coloured eyes.'

'Okay. What's he got – any kind of shoes on or any other distinguishing features?'

'Umm, umm, umm … he has … oh, he's got a freckle on the top of his head when you part the hair on the left hand side. You'll see a freckle on the top of his head.'

'Okay. All right. Do you know where he might have gone?'

'Umm, yeah. We actually live … well, Mum's property is near a state forest and they are on huge blocks. We've walked up and down Benaroon Drive and we can't find him.'

'Okay, what's his name?'

'William.'

'And what's William's surname?'

'Tyrrell. T-Y-R-R-E-L-L.'

*

I mined police reports and witness statements to determine what happened next. This is what I pieced together between the presentation of the first and second tranches of evidence in 2019.

Senior Constable Chris Rowley arrived at 11.06 am. He saw neighbour Anne-Maree Sharpley's signature long blonde hair. They knew each other from around town. Further up the road was a woman he didn't recognise. Ms Sharpley pointed to Anna and told him, 'That's the mother.' Rowley drove further up the road to speak with Anna Wyndham.

'I'm the mother.' Anna gave her details and he noted them down.

'Okay. Where do I go?' Rowley inquired. Procedure dictated that he begin at the beginning. Anna pointed up to the right at her mother's house, number 48, a single-storey blond brick home perched on a large corner block. She hurried up the slope on the front approach to the house and met the police officer on the driveway.

Nathan told the court at the inquest that while Anna spoke to the policeman, he was sprinting around, searching all over in a frantic state and calling loudly for William through the street and yards. Nathan testified that he'd remained outside the whole time after Anna made the call while they waited for police, madly dashing around the area and calling out. Anna said the same thing.

'When Nathan got home, did he go into the house?' Detective Chief Inspector Gary Jubelin asked her in 2016.

'No. He just took off and I didn't see him for ages. He just went straight into the bush.' She indicated on a map some bushland around the Millers' house. But in Rowley's report, and in footage captured by his body-mounted camera, the officer encountered Nathan in a mess of tears and shock, holed up in the bathroom. In his 2016 interview with Jubelin, Nathan was still confused about these events.

'I was running back to the house, and then I saw him arrive,' Nathan said, speaking of Rowley.

'Were you in the house when Chris arrived?' Jubelin asked him.

'No. I was outside.'

'It's come to my attention that when Chris arrived, you were in the bathroom,' Jubelin told him.

'Quite possibly.'

'And, an explanation for that ...?'

'I was looking through the house.'

Jubelin persisted in this line of questioning in Anna's interview. He was interested in Nathan's precise position at 11.06 when Rowley arrived.

'So maybe Nathan's gone around and then come back inside and got changed,' Anna volunteered. 'That would make sense to me.'

'From my point of view, I wouldn't be getting changed,' Jubelin replied.

After the worst two years of their lives, surely we can excuse Anna's and Nathan's faulty memories of that day.

Chris Rowley was determined to search Nancy's entire home. He wrote in the operations log that he searched the whole house. Nonetheless, Rowley would later testify at the inquest that the 'whole house' didn't include the roof space or the garage. But the cupboards and even the drawers had all been opened and the spaces under furniture checked. After this initial search, Anna asked Rowley whether she should notify FACS.

'No, not yet,' he advised her. His experience handling missing persons reports told him they'd most likely find him soon. Rowley headed off to the house next door and began a search of the yard. These neighbours, the Millers, were away on holidays. The officer's attention was immediately drawn to an underfloor space below the verandah. He shone his torch around the cavity but it was empty.

After Nathan ran off searching, Anna focused on what might have drawn William's attention. Children's play equipment was high on her list. There was some at Anne-Maree Sharpley's home, diagonally across the road and to the south of number 48. Ms Sharpley had dropped her children at preschool earlier that morning and was enjoying the peace and quiet. Anna saw her near the rubbish bins around the side of her house. She had a cigarette and a coffee mug half-full of Coke. The two women didn't know each other. Anna called out to her.

'Have you seen a little boy? His name is William. He's wearing a Spiderman suit.' Ms Sharpley hadn't seen him, but she told Anna she'd come and help her look. By this time, panic was setting in and Ms Sharpley could see that Anna was crying. She hugged her.

'Don't worry, we'll find him,' she said. Ms Sharpley would later speak of her sense of guilt at this effort to reassure the foster mother, considering the way things turned out. No one ever imagined William wouldn't be found.

Anna went back to Nancy's and got her mother's car, a dark grey Mazda. She explained her rationale at the inquest.

'In case he had gone down the hill, I thought that would find him quicker in the car. I got my mother's car keys which were on the kitchen bench.' She went on to say she drove out onto Benaroon Drive towards Batar Creek Road while Nancy stayed near the house, looking after Lindsay. She said she had a gut feeling that William had been taken, that he wasn't lost in the neighbourhood or the bush.

'I said right at the beginning, "Somebody has taken William." It was absolutely screaming at me.' Anna told the court of her search of the street, despite her strong belief that he was long gone.

'I went into every single property,' she said, then added, 'but not inside the houses.'

She recalled telling Anne-Maree Sharpley of her thoughts while they were out looking for him. 'William has either hit his head and can't answer me or somebody's taken him.' Ms Sharpley confirmed this at the inquest. Anna would emphatically reiterate to Jubelin two years into the investigation that she was convinced this was an abduction. 'My immediate thought was someone has taken him.'

At the inquest, Mr Craddock asked Anna the question that was on everyone's minds.

'If you were so sure William had been abducted and taken away by a vehicle, why did you bother searching people's yards?'

'I had to do something. I had to keep searching.'

The neighbours told the inquest that Nathan was racing around like a madman, searching the yards, although one observer recalled that his efforts struck her as inadequate and ineffective.

'This man moved very quickly through our property. It appeared to me that he wasn't looking very hard … He wasn't looking anywhere properly. He was just running around, not stopping to listen or to really look. He didn't part the bushes or poke around in the scrub.'

The witness went on to describe her impressions of William's foster father that day. 'I would say the male was assertive. He walked through the garden looking, rather than searching with his hands in the garden and shrubs, which is what I would expect him to do. It was unusual that the male was looking for his child and did not ask for help, provide a description or let us know where he was from or his name.'

Already, suspicions were setting in. But other neighbours were kinder in their evaluations. Anne-Maree Sharpley told of seeing Nathan running to and fro and calling out William's name. To her, the man seemed heartbroken and frantic.

Another neighbour, Judy Wilson, told of Nathan's continued searching late into the night. By her account, he was the picture of total devastation, wandering the yards crying. He kept asking if there was anywhere else William could be hiding. That remark made me wonder, did William hide from his foster parents often? And if so, how far did Nathan think the toddler would push it, realistically?

In their police separate walk-through videos, Anna and Nathan formed different conclusions about what William might've been doing when he disappeared. Nathan resorted to guessing.

'I think he was running … Anna was so sure that he wouldn't go far, but I felt in the way he was running he could have gone down there to Batar Creek Road. He could have. He's strong as anything. Strong, active, only three – but he could have got down there,' said Nathan.

Inquest testimony and witness statements from 2014 revealed that Ms Sharpley suggested going to Lydene Heslop's house in Ellendale Crescent because she had a cubbyhouse that might've attracted the toddler. Anna told the court she didn't remember searching that cubbyhouse.

Ms Heslop opened her front door to find Anne-Maree Sharpley there with a woman she didn't know. 'This lady's little boy has gone missing,' Ms Sharpley explained. Ms Heslop remembered the haunted expression on the foster mother's face. She called out to her children, who were in the backyard playing. They'd seen and heard nothing.

Ms Heslop strapped her young daughter into a stroller and joined the women, scouring the front, back and side yards of houses, down between the houses and through the bush of all the properties on the two streets. Ms Heslop had her own young daughter call out William's name, thinking a toddler's voice might be less intimidating and encourage him to answer if he was hiding.

Soon, other neighbours were searching and yelling out for William. Chris Rowley asked Anna to return to the house. Police might want her to provide more information. She wanted to keep searching, but complied with his request. Wauchope-based police, Senior Constable Tanya Smith and Senior Constable Dean Magennis, were hot on Rowley's heels. Within an hour, several more officers had arrived.

When detectives spoke to Nancy Wyndham about where she thought William had gone in those early minutes after he vanished, she recalled thinking that he had gone to see the grave site of her dog, Cassie, whose resting place was specially marked out in the garden. She'd shown it to the children before.

In her interview, Nancy spoke of her relief when William dashed around that corner.

'I remember thinking, oh, there's peace and quiet. I remember that.' The detective asked Nancy about her reaction after they discovered William was missing.

'Anna told us when she said she couldn't find William you said, "Oh, the little devil." Do you recall?' the detective asked.

'That's the sort of thing … that's the sort of thing I'd say, yes.'

'Where did you think William went?'

'Well, afterwards, my personal thoughts were … he was running. He got down to Batar Creek Road and was picked up somewhere down there. He could've been running to meet his daddy. He loved his daddy so much. After the children were rolling the dice, there was a point where Anna did say, "Why don't you see if Daddy's home yet?" And William went to have a look.'

*

What the foster parents had to say in court was interesting, but I discovered that you find out almost as much from the reactions of others. And after four years, I'd become super-sensitive to details. I'd read so much material. Everything seemed relevant. Anything could be a clue. I was all ears – and eyes.

I took extensive notes throughout, writing down statements that could later be quoted. I also diarised small observations, which made for entertaining reading when I returned to my hotel each afternoon. My task, as I waited for the slow turning wheels of justice to grind out some answers, was not merely to distinguish truth-tellers from liars. I don't know about liars, but there were lots of errors. Witnesses made gaffs in this case that were entirely unintentional. The real job was to strain the known facts like tea leaves – trap the relevant details, rinse away the trivial – and examine the residue for patterns.

When Mr Craddock called Anna Wyndham to the witness box, I was seated directly behind two Kendall women who were best friends and neighbours – Anne-Maree Sharpley and Lydene Heslop. They were due to give evidence that day, but first we had to hear from William's foster mother. I saw them exchanging glances in response to certain things she said. They'd whisper behind their hands and shake their heads, making me wonder if they disputed her answers. I put all the seemingly contentious details into my metaphorical tea-strainer.

My headmasterly nickname for counsel assisting the Coroner – The Boss – felt particularly apt as he questioned Anna about her search along Batar Creek Road that Friday in 2014. He displayed a photo taken in 2018 showing a bus shelter on that road. He noted that when William went missing, it had been white. But Anna testified she was sure it was blue in 2014. She looked confused, defensive. The Boss deftly took the reins and used his best school principal's tone to keep her on task. Both Anne-Maree Sharpley and Lydene Heslop shook their heads at the bus stop business, evidently puzzled by Anna's evidence.

Anna testified that Senior Constable Chris Rowley was the first responder. She couldn't recall whether he'd arrived in an unmarked police vehicle. Yet she'd been anxiously looking out for it. These comments elicited undisguised reactions from Ms Heslop and Ms Sharpley. But there was no malice in those responses, just confusion. No doubt they remembered seeing Rowley's fully marked Mitsubishi Pajero with the call sign 'Laurieton 18'.

To pinpoint distances and directions, Mr Craddock asked Anna which way she'd turned onto Batar Creek Road. Initially, she said left, toward the Riding for the Disabled centre. But that landmark lies to the south, a right turn. Anna became flustered, telling our learned friend she wasn't good with compass point directions.

Mr Craddock replied in a measured tone, 'I'm simply asking you to indicate whether you turned left or right.' I couldn't wait any longer. I sifted what I had in my tea-strainer of facts. Then I looked inside at the tea leaves, and there was the pattern: the woman was obsessed with unnecessary details and she presented them with exaggerated certitude. These two inclinations undermined her credibility on the stand. Even worse, they gave onlookers the impression that Anna Wyndham couldn't be taken at her word.

I experienced a sudden rush of sympathy for her. She had been wrung out like a dishrag, publicly and very cruelly. And I was impressed by her air of defiance in the face of a veritable firestorm of fury emanating from one side of the courtroom.

In her singularly self-assured manner, Anna told the court that while she was searching along the road, overgrown in places with tall weeds and spiky bushes, she hadn't looked inside any drains. Why? Because she didn't believe William would have gone into them. Two large drainage tunnels open out onto Batar Creek Road. They are of a sufficient diameter to admit an obese wombat who's just had his Christmas dinner. They gape invitingly right at toddler height. The fact that Anna didn't look into them greatly concerned some people intent on looking into her. They wondered – *wouldn't a distraught mother search absolutely everywhere?* I wondered what I would do.

Another place Anna searched was an area of reedy grass. Her next statement would send journalists into a flurry.

'I thought I heard something. It was a scream, quick, sharp and high-pitched.' Then she added, before anyone could dash from the courtroom to stop the presses, 'But even at the time I heard it, I knew it could be a bird. Or I could have imagined it.'

Folks around Kendall know the familiar call of the catbird. It's often mistaken for the sound of a crying child. But it's a startling sound to visitors. We can be quite sure Anna had dismissed that noise almost immediately, since she didn't even mention it to police until 18 September. Nevertheless, this titbit would provide the fodder for magazines' headlines: 'William Tyrrell inquest told of terrifying high-pitched scream';[9] 'It was like a scream: William Tyrrell's final moments revealed at inquest into his disappearance'.[10]

These headlines, and the outrageous stories under them, put me in a terrible temper. They taint the truth with poison, reminding me of the Green Goblin. In his quest for perfect power, Spiderman's nemesis injects himself with manipulated DNA and venom. But he goes too far with his experimentation. He corrupts himself, though like most journalists and commentators, he starts with the best of intentions. In the end, he's doomed. He can never, ever come back to our side. He's not just tainted, he's ruined.

Confusion remained about the timing of Anna's Batar Creek Road excursion. She told Mr Craddock that while in the car, she wound both front windows down to listen for William. Driving slowly, she made her way up Batar Creek Road as far as the property on which volunteers ran a Riding for the Disabled program.

When Anna pulled over to the verge to allow a large truck to pass her, the driver acknowledged her, as if she had pulled up for his sake. But she'd only stopped to give herself a chance to listen more intently to any sounds coming from the bushland. It was a rustling mass of green. She kept looking for red. Anna said it made her realise William wouldn't have gone down to a road where trucks were rumbling past. Again, the neighbours reacted with head-shaking and quizzical glances because locals know Batar Creek Road isn't commonly used by large trucks.

Anna said she turned around and drove back to the house. She knew she had to get help. Mr Craddock asked her which telephone she'd used. Anna told the court she grabbed her mother's house phone and took it outside to the carport. Nathan would testify later that he remembered seeing her standing there and signalled to her to go ahead and make the call. At 10.56 am, Anne-Maree Sharpley waited with Anna while she called 000.

'I remember thinking, I have to call the police,' Anna said, sobbing in the courtroom. 'He's not here.'

After Anna was excused from the stand for an adjournment, she broke down in tears and had to be assisted from the witness stand. She recovered sufficiently to walk over to where I was sitting and express her gratitude toward Lydene and Anne-Maree. The two women seemed shy as Anna embraced them and thanked them for all they'd done to help find William. Then Anna Wyndham received hugs from other supporters and friends, a few of whom quickly spirited her away into a back room.

So far in the proceedings, the foster mother's witness account was a dog's breakfast. It wasn't fuzzy though. Intricate detail was there, even if the whole thing was contradictory and wildly non-linear. I could imagine she would have felt absolutely devastated that her testimony left this impression. I was to learn in due course, however, that although it makes the evidence more difficult to interpret, recounting a jumbled narrative is consistent with truth-telling witnesses.

At an inquest, messy statements are considered a given. Some recollections are irrelevant; others will trigger emotions; still others will unlock new insights. Eyewitness testimony is frequently given out of its logical order, because the witness is not aiming to create a cohesive story. Rather, they are remembering and reliving a series of traumatic peaks and troughs. And for Anna, these troughs must have felt bottomless.

Near me were two women I had dubbed 'the Black Sheep' because they wore identical black wool coats. The women run a public relations firm engaged by Anna and Nathan soon after William vanished. They sat in the foster family's camp to demonstrate their support.

No doubt the Kendall locals present at the inquest felt intimidated by the aura of the Coroner's Court, and dwarfed by the magnitude of the occasion. I blush admitting it, but caught up in the sense of occasion, I too found myself a bit at a loss. I recovered my composure by pooh-poohing every city contrivance I encountered, from Opal cards to bubble tea, indulging my inner country-bumpkin. Scarily, these things were new to me in 2019.

By the end of the second week, I was getting the hang of court protocol. I obeyed the Reserved Seating signs. I remembered to bow when the Coroner entered. I was pretty sure I'd turned off my mob— (insert six seconds of loud Calypso music). At least I wasn't alone there. Gary Jubelin's phone went off too, and he handled it as coolly as I imagine Clint Eastwood would have. When my cheeks had faded back to their usual colour, I risked a glance around. I locked eyes with the Black Sheep, Jack Reacher and Colonel Mustard and gave them a small smile.

When she returned to the stand, I pondered on the dramatic way in which Anna Wyndham spoke. She over-enunciated her words. To describe it as theatrical might be an overstatement. 'A touch forced' is closer to the mark. It could come down to a personal quirk and nothing more. Or it could be a side-effect of having the entire nation's gaze fixed upon your every twitch.

I watched Ms Heslop's and Ms Sharpley's reactions as The Boss expounded on the possible significance of the two cars that no one else had seen parked near Anne-Maree Sharpley's property. Anna was the sole witness and, because of those peaks and troughs mentioned earlier, her descriptions appeared to have become embellished by the time of the inquest. But, it could also be argued that the desperate plight of the woman compelled her to wring more detail from her memory – anything that could help find William.

Anne-Maree Sharpley told police that her Friday morning routine was to reverse from her driveway at around 8.40 am when taking her children to Kendall Preschool. She would look up to the right behind her to check for cars, then reverse out onto Benaroon Drive. On 12 September 2014, Ms Sharpley told police she'd neither seen nor heard those cars or any other strange vehicles.

At this point in the proceedings, I filed two facts for a later sifting session: Ms Sharpley and Ms Heslop claimed they didn't see those particular cars; and, they were quite sure the street was empty that day. Mr Craddock pressed on, telling the court that Anna had said to Chris Rowley there was no way William would have gone into the thick bush near the Crabbs' home.

Anna went on to agree with The Boss that rescue workers were emerging from the scrub with ripped clothes because of all the prickly lantana bushes there, but when I looked at the women for their reaction, neither seemed to concur that the bushland there would be off-limits to a little boy. But they didn't know that little boy like Anna did.

When it was her turn to take the stand, Anne-Maree Sharpley told us Anna Wyndham had looked absolutely frightened, worried and lost when she'd first encountered her that morning.

'The look on her face said it all,' Ms Sharpley testified. She said it compelled her to help the poor woman find her child. Mr Craddock asked Ms Sharpley about the bus stop. She said she too went to the bus stop near the end of Batar Creek Road. In fact, she had directed Anna there, because she knew it was decorated with paintings of animals which she thought might attract a toddler. Since Ms Sharpley was able to recall the detail about the painted animal figures, I elected to take her word about the bus stop's colour. I decided it must've been white in 2014.

When Mr Craddock called up Lydene Heslop, she described herself proudly to the Coroner as 'Kendall born and bred'. (She would introduce herself to me in precisely these words early in 2020.) She came across as earthy and genuine; the quintessential can-do soccer mum. With her shoulder-length brown hair pulled back into a ponytail, Lydene's bright eyes gleamed with energy, as did her tanned skin. Friends in Kendall told me this was a woman who exercised like a demon.

The contrast between Ms Heslop and Anna Wyndham was inescapable. Lydene was educated at Kendall Central School and had volunteered in her community her entire life. She's a no-nonsense, salt-of-the-earth tigress of a mother, a family person. This woman is someone you want with you when you've run into trouble out in the bush. One local wag who'd travelled down from Kendall to court commented to me that Ms Heslop was 'Mrs Bear Grylls'. Knowing Lydene as I do now, I'm sure she'd take that as a compliment.

In the first hour after William went missing, Lydene Heslop launched an online appeal that led very rapidly to the marshalling of numerous local volunteers. This force for good would search for William on foot. Ms Heslop told Mr Craddock that police had good-naturedly scoffed at the idea that such a force could be raised in so short a time. Within the hour, they were eating their sceptical words and drinking her coffee. The resourceful Heslops generously provided food and gallons of free hot drinks for everyone on scene from their mobile food van. From my questioning of people around town I could see this was not out of character – the Heslops are forces of nature, good Samaritans and highly respected in Kendall.

Later that week, the court was shown a walk-through video of Nathan Thomas describing his movements at the scene. Afterwards, Nathan took the stand and gave testimony about his thoughts, feelings and movements at the time of William's disappearance and during the initial search.

'I was thinking so many things all at once,' he recalled. He emphasised his priority – the need to cover as much ground as quickly as possible. According to Nathan, William was not a wanderer. Yet in other statements to police he has said William was adventurous and that he'd 'definitely' have attempted to sneak away from adult supervisors given half a chance.

Earlier, Anna had spoken of William's sense of adventure with greater reservation. She said he had a good sense of fun but was reserved and clingy when it came to exploring independently. She'd told the emergency operator it was 'very out of character' for William to wander off, and in court she mentioned that 'he liked to stay within my line of sight'. Although Nathan initially testified that William was adventurous, he then modified that statement, saying fences would likely stop him wandering.

'He wouldn't even cross the street by himself. He wouldn't go far.' But in his earliest police statement, Nathan agreed William might purposely run away and hide, just for fun, in the hope that Mum or Dad might give chase. He admitted that, like most little children, being out of the line of sight of his parents wouldn't stop him from 'giving it a shot'. When asked whether William was a walker or a runner, Nathan replied that he could be either, depending on the situation and the mood William was in at the time. If he was excited, he might run.

According to Anna, William was often 'engaged in fantasy play' – another curiously academic expression to describe kids' stuff. He liked acting out the part of a tiger, so he certainly could have been running. The line of questioning in Nathan's walk-through video then turned to a very plausible scenario: could the toddler have done an uncontrolled 'gravity run' downhill, and before he knew it, was too far away to see or hear his mother anymore? Nathan nodded. That was certainly a possibility. In such a scenario, it was estimated that twenty seconds could take him to the southernmost corner of the yard – or even beyond.

Nathan seemed to invest a lot of confidence in the good judgement of his foster son.

'He had this sense about him. He knew where there was a danger or ... a risk. But he also knew his boundaries. He was a very good judge of understanding ... things where there's caution that's required, you know. Getting near a pool or something like that ... But sometimes he'd push the boundaries.' On the video shown to the court on a big screen, Nathan grabbed the fence wire as he spoke, lifting it up to emphasise the relative ease of William's passage through to adjoining yards. Some of the fences were no more than a single slack wire, which would prove no barrier at all.

'See? That's just easy. He could easily go through that.' He contrasted this with the difficulty of tramping through prickly bushland, tangled with lantana. It's something he believed his foster son would never attempt. Nor did Nathan believe William capable of climbing over or under other fences strained more tautly than the others.

'Too hard, too hard,' he repeated. He appeared to firmly believe that the little boy went to the road. He had quite sharply defined views as to which areas would have attracted William. He also had strong opinions on where the boy would not have ventured: terrain too steep, too rocky, too distant, too difficult to access through fences and prickly barriers. At this speculation, my thoughts turned back to our search for Tyler Kennedy. He'd been found in a place it was impossible for him to be.

*

For a child abduction to occur, two elements are needed: an offender and a temporary window of opportunity in which a capable guardian is absent. These stars certainly aligned to enable the abduction of little William Tyrrell.

Yet Anna Wyndham's vigilance that Friday was demonstrably strong. The children played in a safely enclosed area of the house's high balcony. They did supervised bike riding, helmets on, only on the driveway; tree-climbing, hands-on backs and bottoms; outdoor exercise, with shoes on to guard against sharp sticks, stones and bindis. They'd had a solid, healthy breakfast, probiotics included; then teeth-brushing and personal hygiene. She could hardly have been more vigilant and proactive.

Then, just before 10.30, in a silent, safe space in the country, she allowed her energetic little boy to explore and run free for a few short minutes. Anna's tragedy is the most heartbreaking aspect of this case for me. Because it could've happened on my watch – or yours – very easily.

My own children have grown up under the shadow of the William Tyrrell mystery. They were six and seven in 2014 and although they're now almost teenagers, we're still searching for Spiderman. Each evening when I say my goodnights, I think about how much it means to me that they're safe; that in that moment I can guarantee their safety, their happiness and well-being. It's in my power. It's within my control while we're at home. But when they go out, it's a different matter.

Those minutes in which I temporarily lost my son – aged three, like William – were torturous, but mercifully short. I wouldn't presume to compare that experience with the horror these people have lived through, but those few uncertain minutes when I lost sight of my little boy were very instructive. For the parent on duty, the emphasis is on *you*. The child didn't become lost – *you* lost him.

When I think about that, I'm struck by the sense of defensiveness I felt, even on such a small scale. Guilt compelled me to insist upon the shortness of the interval in which I wasn't watching him. I'd said it was less than a minute – under sixty seconds.

In my own mind, I believe it could have been more, but by the time I'd framed my response to others it'd become thirty seconds. Because it sounded intolerably irresponsible to admit that, as a parent, not only had I let go of my toddler's hand and turned my back on him for a whole minute, I'd walked into the next aisle of the shop without him. Two steps forward into the next aisle started the countdown. I was there for a period of time that I still cannot put my finger on.

'Come on,' I'd said, and rocked back on my heel, glancing back into the aisle where he'd just been. It was empty. But I didn't believe he'd have left the shop. 'He isn't a wanderer,' I remember telling people. 'I like to keep him in my line of sight.' I quickly worked my way through each aisle until I reached the front door. I realised with a sick feeling that he wasn't in the shop. Outside was a busy carpark and the deep canals of Settlement City. Could he have left the shopping centre?

Fifteen minutes later, we were reunited. He was safe. A woman found him wandering in the carpark, on the edge of a canal. She escaped before I could kiss her. My heart resumed its regular beat pattern within an hour or so. The terrible high-pitched ringing in my ears ceased the instant I saw his familiar red hair, his little green t-shirt. That experience comes back to me forcefully when I think about Anna Wyndham's description of searching for William in his little Spiderman outfit. Not the contradictions I heard in court, not certain befuddled details. Just her harrowing description of desperately looking for her lost toddler.

'I was just walking around in circles trying to find him. All I wanted to see was red.'

7

SPINNING

Much has been written about protocols in missing persons recovery operations. The key priority being called for in Australia right now is to have uniform standards across jurisdictions. Currently, different states use different data entry processes, which is staggering. We obviously didn't learn our national lesson from the rail gauges of last century. Railway lines across the country were laid according to three different widths, so no single train could travel interstate. It wouldn't be until 1995 that all the state capitals were joined by rail. Whether we're talking trains or information, transferrability is vital to efficiency. And there are few greater needs for efficiency across the nation than in rescuing missing persons and solving crimes.

Here's what happens when a missing person incident is reported to authorities. First, the reporter must physically attend the closest police station to make the report. Don't believe the myth that you need to wait twenty-four hours – that's a furphy. And sadly, it has led to needless deaths. You can report anytime if the people who know the missing person best become worried. Police pay close attention to loved ones' inner alert systems. They are often spot on.

After a report is made, the countdown timer begins. Police will conduct a risk assessment to help them prioritise the investigation. Local Area Command will then make inquiries with government agencies. If a missing person is a foster child, FACS take steps to preserve privacy. During this early stage, support is offered to families in the form of briefings to explain police operations and crisis counselling.

The Officer in Charge will assess what is achievable in terms of resources. A Strike Force is created on the policing data management system, Eagle I (pronounced 'eagle eye'). Then a command post is established, with all reports created in the field going to the local police station. A database of evidence is created from reports gathered at the scene. Sometimes, it is shared across jurisdictions. Data is forwarded to the national Missing Persons Unit. The Strike Force will refer to this repository throughout the investigation. The State Crime Squad or the Major Crime Squad may get involved.

Assistance may be sought from the media, provided it doesn't compromise the missing person's safety. A recent photo is filed, along with a physical description. Health records may form part of the data released publicly, if relevant. Dental records, DNA profiles and surgical histories may be accessed. Currently in Australia, authorities are working to establish a national database of unidentified bodies to which this data can be cross-matched.

Police are alert to any suspicious circumstances within the family circle of the lost person. Any discrepancies in stories told to investigators are scrutinised. The last people to see the missing person alive are of particular interest and are often required to make multiple statements. Typically, the premises where the person was last seen will be searched. Evidence will be photographed and bagged. Cars will be forensically tested and checked for prints. The surrounding area will be searched and sometimes swept by tracking and cadaver dogs.

After all of that data has been processed, doorknocking begins. The neighbours will be canvassed, door-to-door as well as hotels and motels, pubs, caravan parks and privately let accommodation.

Video and still imagery captured by cameras attached to businesses and local council infrastructure will be harvested and reviewed. CCTV footage is obtained from highway cameras.

Video footage is extremely valuable to detectives. It can confirm and refute alibis. But cameras aren't infallible. The number of cameras in use, their angle and area of coverage, their mounting, the lighting, their speed of image-capture in frames per second can affect the usefulness of data collected.

Meanwhile, media releases will be coordinated to publicise the missing person's profile. When making media alerts, police are cautious. Each announcement runs the risk of desensitising the public to the importance of every individual case. And, as we've seen in this case, some receive more media attention than others. After the three-month mark, a missing person's case is reclassified as 'Long Term'. Hospitals, clinics and morgues are checked periodically for any unidentified bodies.

Search and rescue operations commence very early, often concurrently with the earlier steps of the investigation. Police have told me the first seventy-two hours are critical. Evidence must be collected as early as possible. Witnesses need interviewing quickly, before their memories fade, or before they become tainted with media reports. It can be very difficult to tell truth from false memories that the witness believes to be true.

Other evidence-gathering operations occur in an organised manner, with investigators' movements and actions diarised while working in the field. These notes are then firmed up as they are digitised, along with any photographs, before being logged in a centralised bank of data.

Forensic evidence degrades outside the seventy-two hour window. Footprints, fibres and hairs, blood spatter and finger and palm prints are delicate and must be collected early. Bullet casings and weapons, grass seeds, soil, clothing scraps and solid objects are collected.

Sites are examined for trace evidence of routes taken through brush which may be marked by broken twigs or disturbed foliage and cobwebs. In the outdoor environment, these won't exhibit tell-tale signs forever.

DNA proteins are very vulnerable when exposed to rain, wind, heat and humidity. Samples may be too small to return a result, and profiling is time-consuming and labour intensive. Australia currently has no central DNA database, which means forensic cross-matching can only be done on an ad hoc basis where detectives request tests against particular suspects.

Mobile forensic tools extract evidence from digital devices – phones, tablets and the like. Police examine the devices of the missing person's loved ones and the last people to have seen them alive. Data retrieval techniques such as Cellebrite technology can hand police call and text logs and lists of contacts, emails, photos and internet browsing history.

Cell phone towers can establish a device's position in time and space, if not yours personally. Smart crooks leave their devices at home. But on the positive side, smart parents can now buy GPS-dependent units that children can wear on their clothes or person. When I discovered the existence of this tech, I wondered why most people don't use them. I am seriously suggesting parents consider it.

*

If a child wanders off into the bush in the Camden Haven area, a few possible fates can befall them. Falling or sustaining an injury could send a victim into shock or unconsciousness. Thirst, uncontrolled bleeding and hypothermia are frequent causes of death among bushwalkers, and our little bushwalker was only three-and-a-half years old. Lantana bushes exude a powdery substance that can trigger an asthma attack, and William was an asthma sufferer.

Then there's drowning. The Camden Haven River is by no means a mighty waterway but it is twelve metres deep in places, varying from serene to fast-flowing. It's no more than two kilometres from Benaroon Drive as the crow flies. Obvious dangers in the bushland are rocks, cliffs and waterways. Then there are the hidden hazards of abandoned mineshafts and well-holes – death-traps, thirty metres deep or more. A small child could very easily fall in. Obscured by vegetation covering the surface, their depth would prevent cries being heard, particularly in an isolated spot. If a child survived the fall, chances are they would drown in the water at the base of the shaft.

Then there's wild animals. Wild dogs and dingoes are prolific in the Middle Brother State Forest. I've seen the damage wild dog attacks do, ripping out the throats of three-day-old calves. These animals are ferocious predators. Encounters on Fraser Island reveal some dingoes are prepared to have a go at older children and even unaccompanied adults.

These key dangers set the parameters for the initial search operation. On scene that Friday, the Mid North Coast's Police District Commander, Superintendent Paul Fehon, was in charge. Fehon is a cop through and through, and if I had to guess, I'd say he wears his policing shoes on social occasions even while off-duty. He's such a cop that it's hard to notice the man inside the uniform.

At the beginning, the New South Wales Homicide Squad led the investigation, headed up by Detective Inspector Hans Rupp. Detective Sergeant Justin Moynihan was Officer in Charge. Senior Constable Dean Magennis arrived not long after Chris Rowley. At about 11.40 am, Inspector Aldridge and Sergeant Hardwick arrived.

Senior Constable Wendy Hudson – a Kendall resident from birth – was also there by this time. Hudson is a redhead who I feel sure will get the top job when gingers take over the world. She's a short lady with short hair and very possibly a short temper. She looks very practical and down to earth, straight as a die. My Kendall friends tell me that's an accurate assessment. I'm sure she takes her job seriously, particularly the moral responsibilities that go with it. Watching her at the inquest, I saw she had a determined expression on her face much of the time, as if she was expecting opposition or attack at any moment and was ready to beat it down with her baton.

Aldridge assumed the role of Field Commander. A log was commenced and the search of houses and yards began. The interior of number 48 was searched and re-searched, although Wendy Hudson noted in passing that the foster father's car was not searched that day. Still, it was an appropriately thorough search that left little to chance. Later, Nancy's car would be tested for fingerprints, as would Nathan's. Both vehicles were forensically examined. The results of those tests confirmed the foster family's statements about the use of the vehicles and didn't yield anything significant.

The land search coordinators were specially trained and had hundreds of successful missions under their belts. Gibson Engineering in Kendall assisted police by handling the printing of maps. SES personnel searched all the water drains. At 12.40 pm, Senior Constable Tim Williams of Laurieton Police assumed the role of Land Search and Rescue (LandSAR) Coordinator. Line searches were initiated, with participants going over ground in an organised configuration just metres apart, to ensure nothing was missed. Over the next fourteen days, line searches would be conducted across an area of eighteen square kilometres.

*

At the inquest, Senior Constable Wendy Hudson told of a trip she'd organised to the beach with the foster carers and Lindsay, as a means of getting them out of the house. It was on Tuesday 16 September. They drove through Laurieton to Diamond Head beach, making some impromptu stops to ensure media helicopters weren't tailing them. They made a sandcastle and searched for shells to take Lindsay's mind off things. They were joined by a neighbour from Sydney, who had been brought up to Kendall – a playmate for Lindsay.

On Friday 19 September, Superintendent Paul Fehon arranged for Wendy Hudson to meet him at the Kew Country Club. When she arrived, she saw Anna, Nathan and Lindsay in their vehicle, ready to return home to Sydney. Hudson was tasked with following them down the highway to ensure they weren't being tailed by media or anyone else. She continued her escort until they reached Johns River.

Detective Sergeant Shane Guymer of Taree's Forensic Evidence and Technical Services Command conducted a forensic investigation with the consent of William's foster grandmother. Photographs were taken inside the residence and in the yard and surrounding area. Tanks were searched with cameras where possible and drained if not. Permission was granted to conduct extensive searches of the neighbours' homes and swimming pools.

Technical data was retrieved from the electronic devices of the foster family, the Roads and Maritime Service and from cell phone towers. The police helicopter PolAir Two was deployed twice to search the overall area. The priorities were any local bodies of water, roadside drains and bushland nearest Nancy's house.

The biggest barrier to the search were the thick red lantana bushes that choked the forest's edges. Some patches couldn't be traversed. But the lantana also gave them a lucky break. Wherever it was found in abundance, it signalled to searchers that a child simply couldn't have got through the mass of prickly branches. Still, they didn't read the colour red as a stop sign. They pushed through, determined to be thorough.

Tim Williams is a specially trained land search coordinator. Dog handler Paul Burg of the SES had worked with Tim Williams on previous land searches. If I were about to plunge to my death off some remote escarpment, I reckon Burg might just be solid enough to cushion my fall. He looks like he permanently lives outdoors, with Chuck Norris. When I saw him at the inquest, I half-expected to see he'd left a Panzer tank, or at the very least, a Hummer in the carpark.

To begin their planning, the coordinators followed the protocols detailed in the *National Land Search Operations Manual*. Search zones of interest were identified on topographic maps and sectioned up under the command of accredited land search experts. Foot patrols fanned out from Benaroon Drive in all directions. Line searches involved numerous SES volunteers. Tim Williams' methodical approach left no stone unturned, and search sessions went well into the night for several days until all the target areas were covered. Dams were pumped out and those that were too large were searched by police divers.

Search coordinators lifted the covers off drains and used cameras to check inside. A local resident, James Opdam, had career experience in search operations and checked some uncapped drains that had been awaiting council approval since the subdivision was created. At the inquest, I watched the footage taken inside the drains and wondered if I was looking at a possible escape route for an abductor. It seemed unlikely, given the amount of undisturbed cobwebs and leaf matter that had settled inside.

On Sunday 14 September, a single strand of what appeared to be human hair was found clinging to a barbed wire fence at the intersection of Benaroon Drive and Batar Creek Road. The search yielded precious little else. From 16 to 19 September rain had fallen, washing away trace evidence.

A campsite off the Lorne Road was searched. A pair of men's underpants was found there and was photographed and bagged in evidence. Various other finds were noteworthy, including a child's stuffed animal toy, four marijuana plants in a planter vessel (literally 'pot plants') and a bloody rabbit carcass in a bag.

On 16 September, the search perimeter was expanded to a radius of three kilometres. SES volunteers used brush-cutters and chainsaws to clear undergrowth, fallen branches and trees. The inquest heard about the difficulties of operating in extremely steep terrain, and of some mishaps with running chainsaws in the search's early days. Searchers were also plagued by bees, with one officer being the target of a sting operation of a different kind.

False reports have circulated that no scent traces of William Tyrrell were ever found at 48 Benaroon Drive. Actually, his scent was detected all over the property, but the trail didn't extend beyond the perimeters of the yard. Metal probes were used to release any odours from under the soil and cadaver dogs sniffed over the area. In this case, timing was a factor. By the time dogs had arrived on scene, numerous people had been walking around the site, potentially contaminating scent trails.

Dog training focuses on two specialisations: ground scent trails and airborne scent (known as 'tracking' or 'trailing'). Each dog specialises in one or the other, rarely both. Viable human scent trails can be composed of skin and hair particles on the ground or on vegetation, while air scent comes from gases. In both ground and air tracking, the longer a person has spent in a particular area, the more strongly their scent will be retained. A viable trail can vanish after just twenty-four hours, but usually not before that. Sometimes, the process involves linking together scent found in disparate locations to piece together a trail. This is problematic when the search area is large.

A dog's ability to detect scent varies from one animal to another and depends upon whether they're trained for finding airborne scent or tracking particles along the ground. A ground-tracking dog needs a starting point to work from. But air-scent dogs can pick up human scent carried in moving air currents, so no starting point is required. The dog will move toward the area where the scent is at its greatest concentration. Air-scent operatives include cadaver dogs trained in sniffing out human decomposition gases and trace amounts of blood.

Scent doesn't cling to the exact path a person took. A walking or running person wearing shoes may not leave any scent on hard surfaces that they've stood on, but they'd still leave a cloud of odour in the air in the vicinity. Contrary to popular belief, wet weather doesn't wash scent away. In fact it can have the opposite effect, refreshing the odours left by the person being tracked. It's for this reason that scented particles are easier to track in moist, cool, oxygen-rich places, but these conditions are also ideal for decomposition and as material degrades, the odours degrade.

The authorities threw every resource into the effort to find William or to determine what had happened to him. Apart from the Dog Squad, these resources also included the police's Operation Support Group, the Public Order Riot Squad, the Police Air Wing (PolAir), the Marine Area Command, the Diving Unit, the Mounted Police, the Trail Bike Squad, the Rescue and Bomb Disposal Unit, Search and Rescue, and Police Search Advisors. These police resources were employed in addition to those of the State Emergency Service (SES), the Rural Fire Service (RFS) and a veritable army of more than three hundred untrained volunteers.

The day came when police delivered sad news to the public. It was no longer possible William could still be alive if he was lost in bushland. Before the search officially wound up (two weeks after he vanished) the zone had been extended to the Middle Brother State Forest. It took in an expanse of dense bushland within a ten-kilometre perimeter of Benaroon Drive. I've seen the maps police used, marked with concentric lines that fan out in widening circles, fittingly, like a spider's web.

Under the Coroners Act 2009,[11] a suspected or confirmed death that has occurred under suspicious or unusual circumstances warrants an inquest. No less than thirteen massive folders packed with material were tendered to the inquest as the brief of evidence, and that was only the first of three tranches. Mr Craddock told the inquest that such an extensive search was not wasted because it was able to virtually rule out the idea that William was still out there in the bushland somewhere, waiting to be found.

'William didn't fall down the drain or get lost chasing a wallaby in the bush,' he said. The assessment Mr Craddock presented to the Coroner was that the search was thorough and comprehensive, suggesting that had William Tyrrell been lost, he would certainly have been found.

*

There were hundreds of alleged sightings of William reported to police in the first months of the investigation. Tips from the public poured in, stretching police resources to breaking point. Over six years, Strike Force Rosann would capture no less than 2750 alleged sightings of William Tyrrell. Early on, these reports were given significant priority and were disseminated to all police in the state, as well as law enforcement agencies across the country.

Residents were canvassed and provided statements about their movements and observations. Strike Force Rosann took the unusual step of publicly appealing for anyone within one kilometre of 48 Benaroon Drive on the morning of 12 September 2014 to come forward. Jubelin's message was clear: if you weren't prepared to speak to police about your reason for being in the area at that time, they would assume you had something to hide. And they'd track you down.

Kendall was canvassed by way of media releases, letter drops and door knocks. They also called on hotels, motels and caravan parks within a ten-kilometre radius to identify possible suspects. A significant number of residents had their properties searched.

Police records record 263 residents being interviewed and 364 questionnaires being distributed.

On 19 September 2014, vehicles coming in and out of Kendall were being stopped and details of the occupants and owners recorded. Local businesses were canvassed and CCTV footage obtained from twelve premises. The only footage of interest was retrieved from the Kendall Tennis Club in Graham Street, which showed images of vehicles entering and leaving the village. Unfortunately, the imagery captured on this footage displayed only the side panels of the vehicles, making identification difficult. The time period interrogated was 5.15 am to 11.00 am.

Images of these vehicles were displayed publicly for locals to examine and identify. Because there are numerous roads leading to Benaroon Drive, it's possible that any abductor's vehicle may not have been captured on CCTV footage at all.

When police examined the Child Protection Register, they concentrated their efforts on people living within thirty kilometres of Kendall. These persons were investigated, and police came up with nothing that proposed they had any involvement in William's disappearance.

The media made appeals to the public for any information that may assist police. As a result, the Strike Force was inundated with information from people claiming to have psychic or clairvoyant powers, visions or dreams. To reach those of us without supernatural insight, William's public relations team created the 'Where's William?' campaign and used specific milestones including William's birthday and the anniversaries of his disappearance to attract public interest. A new initiative, 'Walk for William', gathered momentum and saw thousands of people join in. This community event involved thousands of participants dressed in red and blue joining an organised walking rally. The aim was to bring public attention to the fact that William's case remained unsolved.

Then, on 12 September 2016, the New South Wales State Government announced a reward of one million dollars for information leading to the recovery of William Tyrrell.

*

Early in the investigation, a Persons of Interest (POI) list had been generated from a variety of sources. Some of these people were directly nominated as having knowledge of William's disappearance. Some have remained unidentified, as they were mentioned to police by description only, not by name. Police developed 440 investigative packages containing relevant information on these POIs, including profiles, photographs, maps and suggested interview questions.

A number of Vehicles of Interest (VOI) were also identified, including a much-discussed black Toyota Camry. Just a few days after William vanished, I remember hearing veteran 2GB radio broadcaster Ray Hadley had taken a call from a local truck driver who claimed he saw a woman in a black Camry acting suspiciously in the Kendall area on the day William vanished. She had been parked at the Kew service station at the same time as the truckie stopped there to wait for pick-up instructions from a client he was to meet in Kendall. When the truck driver proceeded to Kendall forty minutes later, he again encountered the woman in the Camry. This time, she was loitering near the shops in the main street, seemingly without purpose. The conversation sparked a good deal of local interest. The truckie had called the station in response to an appeal for information Hadley made on-air.

Hadley urged anyone who might have been in the Kendall area the previous Friday before eleven o'clock and seen anything suspicious to call Crime Stoppers. He concluded the segment by noting the enormous odds against a child being snatched from Kendall in broad daylight. Despite the black Camry story lighting up social media

116

forums across the country, police said they investigated the report and had already discounted it as being irrelevant back in 2015.

Adding to the soup of information, in August 2019, the inquest heard some interesting testimony from Kendall man Tim Palmer. He told of a conversation he'd had with his friend Michael McInally in 2018. Apparently, McInally wanted to unburden himself over a secret he'd been keeping since 12 September 2014. Palmer was all ears.

McInally told him of seeing a man in a white Commodore driving 'crazily' down Batar Creek Road that morning. McInally said he saw the driver reaching across the passenger seat with his left hand, pushing something down into the footwell. He struggled to steer with the other hand to keep the car on the road. Palmer said when his mate related this tale, he believed he was trying to get something off his chest. But he knew McInally would be angry at him for reporting it to police.

'He said if I was to tell anyone this story, he would deny it.' Palmer admitted that his friend was quite drunk during this conversation. But it haunted Palmer to the point where he let his sister persuade him to make a report. Apparently McInally hadn't wanted to tell police because he was scared of getting into trouble for not reporting it sooner. But Palmer explained the most compelling reason for his silence – McInally had taken ice that morning. If true, that fact casts doubt on his recall.

McInally was sullen as he gave evidence, contradicting Palmer's story on multiple points. First, he said the driver was using his left hand to hold up his phone as if to improve reception while driving. The Coroner interjected with a perceptive question.

'Why, after four years, would you tell a story about seeing someone trying to get phone reception? How would you even remember something so trivial?' Recovering his composure, McInally also disputed the location he'd mentioned to his mate, changing it from

Batar Creek Road to Comboyne Street, the main road in Kendall. I wondered if he knew the driver and was scared of implicating them. But it's doubtful what McInally saw was William Tyrrell being driven away. Perhaps it's just what he thought he'd witnessed.

The Palmer–McInally conflict illustrates the way in which suspicions among the people of Kendall festered, as the weeks since William was last seen turned into months, then years. Inevitably, folks took sides. Minor disputes between neighbours blew up into ongoing feuds, where once they would've been quickly settled and forgotten. Close friends still knew they could trust each other, but they were more hesitant to accept newcomers. It was harder to break into established groups.

Kendall residents are a tight-knit crowd who have built their community on trust and openness. The contrast of dealing with the tragedy of a child abduction from this place was particularly difficult for parents of youngsters. One Benaroon Drive mother I spoke to said her family couldn't rest easy at night until they knew for certain they weren't living down the road from a child killer. As a mother myself, her words to me in 2019 really resonated: 'I have a daughter who still can't go to sleep in her own bed,' she said some five years after William vanished.

At the shops, conversation skirted around the elephant in the town. No one wanted to talk about William Tyrrell, because everyone had different opinions and diversity divides in country towns. There was no common ground even in this familiar territory. There was no way of knowing whose side you were on. If you were speaking to someone, they could be a friend of Nancy's. You couldn't share your suspicions about her daughter and son-in-law – it might get back.

Locals also disagreed about whether life in Kendall had changed. Some swore they were unnerved and no longer let their children play outside. Suddenly, your neighbour's eccentric habits took on a darker significance. Old men helping kiddies on their bikes gave pause for thought. It wasn't as easy to catch a lift with someone you didn't know. Risqué stories and even harmless jokes became reinterpreted.

I remember one afternoon in the summer of 2016, my husband and I took the boys to Kendall swimming pool for a sports carnival. People were set up at the barbecue area when we arrived and the sausages were already sizzling. The William Tyrrell case wasn't on our minds that day, until one of the guys wielding the tongs made a joke.

'Hey, what do you call two crows sitting on a fence? An attempted murder.' No one laughed. An awkward silence fell on the group. No one knew whether there was a child abductor – a killer even – living among us.

But others pooh-poohed this notion, saying there was no discernible difference to life in Kendall at all. For every pessimist who lamented that the tragedy tore the town apart, there was an optimist who declared it brought the community closer together. Some tight friendships remained, while others soured. Some parents took their children out of the local school, while others stepped up their voluntary work to help it survive the departures. Whichever side of the fence you were on in Kendall, you could expect opposition. And those who sat on the fence became decidedly uncomfortable. The only common enemy was the media.

It was tough sitting through the inquest, for obvious and not-so-obvious reasons. The case was harrowing. We didn't need anyone to tell us what little William might have suffered. Our imaginations filled that gap. In the absence of information came speculation.

I observed through gritted teeth the minute-by-minute scramble to post fresh details online. I became heartily sick of that ugly bloodsport – the race to snag a front page, extra column space, a prime bookshelf spot. Commentators did the chat show circuit, going with the noble angle – we need to keep William's name before the public so the case can be solved. But we've had half a decade of that. William's case has rarely been out of the news for long. For a country girl, it was an unpleasant introduction to the cut-throat business of news making. I was learning that people intent on hacking out a meaty story tend to leave a mess on the floor. And we're all complicit, whatever our intentions.

8

SWEEPS

I returned to Sydney in August 2019 for the inquest's second sitting. This time, I decided to break my expensive cab habit. Online, it looked straightforward enough: board the M92 bus at Lidcombe Station and ride it right to the court. I followed those steps and, after the bus deposited me at Parramatta, I realised I'd boarded at the wrong bus stop. The one I wanted was directly across the road. Sighing, I took a train from Parramatta back to Lidcombe Station in a parody of *Groundhog Day*. This time I crossed the road. I arrived fifteen minutes late, but didn't miss much.

On the second day, I had the bus situation nailed. In fact, my confidence was so high as I alighted that I felt sure I could navigate a shortcut through the court complex's vast carpark and save myself the walk around the block. I set off. A black metal fence with an automated security gate blocked my passage.

But I was in luck – a maintenance van approached and as the gate slid open to permit access, I nipped through. I realised my mistake when I saw that the few doors into the building were all locked with pass card readers. There'd be no entry through those for me. I turned back in time to see the gate locking me in with a clang that sounded rather final. Sheepishly, I pressed the intercom button, which must have been put there for country mice like me.

'Hiya. I've managed to lock myself in your carpark,' I said brightly.

'No problem, ma'am. I can unlock the gate from here. One moment …' Click. The gate remained shut.

'It's still closed. It didn't work.' She tried again, and again. Clearly, the gate was punishing me for breaking the pedestrian rules. Her tone changed ever so slightly as she informed me she'd need to send the security guard to let me out.

'Thank you. Sorry for the trouble.' I reminded myself of Bill Bryson fumbling his way around some foreign city. When the guard arrived, he looked friendly, so I pretended that it was a security drill and that I was timing his response.

'Ninety-six seconds. Not bad. You pass,' I told him, and slunk through the gate. I gave him a little wave as I trudged all the way around the block to the front of the building where city people enter.

After court on Tuesday, I'd gone into the Sydney CBD to meet a friend for dinner. At roughly the same time, a man had gone on a rampage nearby, stabbing a young woman to death then brandishing his knife at random people in the street. He kept slashing before some heroic bystanders crash-tackled him to the ground and forced a milk crate over his head. File that idea away in your self-defence arsenal. They managed to disarm him and passed him into the care of police. I was wandering the food stalls at Town Hall Station, just a block away. I feel that whenever I enter that city, the universe sets something in motion to have me expelled.

After my two false starts, on the third day of the inquest I finally conquered the public transport and the pedestrian route to the courthouse. But I was on the train home by Wednesday. A health problem called for my return. I didn't miss a great deal. An early adjournment on Thursday was followed by a closure Friday. I caught up by watching the news. As I did, I received a call from a Channel Seven newsman who kindly filled me in with the backstory.

The second and third weeks of the August sitting were moved north so the local senior citizens who'd been subpoenaed would have easier access to the court. I was delighted. I didn't have to be in the city and I could go home every night. I drove down the Wingham Road to Taree through gritted teeth as the corrugations permanently altered the Peugeot's auto electrics. Actually, it's a winding dirt track generously called a road. I live at one end of it and you can drive on it for forty minutes and reach its namesake at the other – the town of Wingham, just west of Taree. It's quite a trip, but anything's better than staying in Sydney.

Taree is a two-hour drive north of Newcastle. Situated on the banks of the Manning River, it's an important dairying and logging area. I was amused watching the city lawyers picking their way through humble Taree. It's a farming town, very laid back and unaffected by frivolous city fashions. You can find reasonably good coffee, fine dining and gluten-free options but you have to look pretty hard. I treated myself to a riverside lunch at Sailo's, a yacht club on the north bank of the Manning River, when I couldn't face another sandwich.

I've lived on the Mid North Coast for most of my life. Raised on a farm west of Taree, I learned the ubiquitous rule of country life pretty early: everyone knows everyone. I have many connections with Kendall. My children attended Kendall Community Preschool. They have a lovely vegetable garden there, a sandpit and timber play equipment, and best of all, a hive of wild bees. I have been assured they are mild-mannered bees.

I have friends and business associates in community groups like the Country Women's Association and the Camden Haven Show Society. We have our own agricultural show in Comboyne and it was in my role as secretary that I first met Ronald Chapman. He's been the flower judge at the Show from time immemorial and is a life member at Kendall.

I caught up with Mr Chapman after he gave his testimony in Sydney. He was delighted to see a local in the Big Smoke and we talked about our mutual friends from the local show circuit. Being a small town resident, I discovered he also knew Nancy Wyndham and had crossed swords with her before, over begonias.

Waiting out yet another adjournment in the garden area at the front of Taree courthouse, I also recognised a friend of mine from Kendall. Rheannon Chapman operated the bottle shop, Kendall Cellars, in 2014. And, of course, she's related to Ronald Chapman. I've known the Chapman family for some years. These are highly capable, practical and community-minded people. I recall Rheannon shaking her head in despair as we talked about the way Kendall had been demonised by the media. Worse still, social media vultures had descended on the village, feeling it was their right to hound and interrogate strangers on the street simply to satisfy their own curiosity. It had caused a great deal of misery, and achieved nothing.

'See all these people?' Rheannon said, indicating the public gallery at the courthouse. 'Not one of them was even there. *We were there.*'

*

In August 2019, at the inquest in Lidcombe, Ronald Chapman made a stunning claim. He said that around 10.45 am on Friday 12 September 2014, he'd seen a boy fitting William Tyrrell's description being driven away at high speed in one of two cars that seemed to be travelling together. Chapman said the leading one was a fawn-coloured four-wheel drive. He'd seen a similar car some time afterwards – an old Toyota Land Cruiser.

According to his testimony, the car following behind was an iridescent blue Ford sedan, a six-cylinder model. Ronald Chapman has lived in Laurel Street for forty years. Laurel Street intersects Batar Creek Road about half a kilometre from Benaroon Drive. On the day in question, Mr Chapman was standing on his verandah, about to check his mailbox for a delivery note.

Anxious to collect an order of daisies and bromeliads so they wouldn't be stuck in the post office over the weekend, he'd been listening out for the postie. He heard the distinctive metal sound of his neighbour's letterbox lid, looked at his wall clock, then went out to check his own box. That's when he saw the cars.

The four-wheel drive came from Batar Creek Road and it was shifting. The driver was a fair-skinned, plump woman of thirty, blonde hair up in a bun on top of her head. She almost lost control of the car as she rounded the corner, sending loose gravel down the embankment and onto Mr Chapman's lawn. Apart from the speed, what caught his attention was the unexpected sight of a child standing without a seatbelt on.

'In the back seat was a young boy with his hands up on the window, palms outwards on the glass and his face in between.' Ron Chapman estimated his age to be three or four. As the car passed, he saw the boy wasn't crying, but looked bewildered. His clothes were red, with royal blue under the sleeves and a thin black pattern of lines all over.

Mr Chapman said he was outraged at the speed and recklessness of the drivers and at the fact that the little boy in the back was unrestrained. He told the court that he uttered a profanity to describe the woman's foolishness.

'Under my breath I called the woman a stupid "b",' he confessed sheepishly at the inquest.

About fifty metres behind came the other car, rapidly accelerating. Mr Chapman said it would have had a head-on collision if there'd been an oncoming car. The windows were heavily tinted, but sunlight illuminated the driver through the windscreen as the car cut the corner. It was a man. He couldn't give further details. The view had been too fleeting.

The cars were travelling east, turned onto Orara Street, then presumably continued out of Kendall. But Mr Chapman couldn't determine whether they turned left, towards Lorne and Logans Crossing, or right, towards Kew and the highway.

When Mr Chapman saw the evening news, he concluded the outfit was a Spiderman suit. He'd seen the five-year-old kid next door wearing one before, immediately making the connection between the boy missing from Kendall and the child he'd seen in the car. He said when he saw the picture on TV the boy's appearance – fair complexion, light browny-blond hair – gave him a start. He had no doubt it was the same boy he'd seen that morning, he told the court. Everyone was spellbound.

Detective Sergeant Laura Beacroft had made a walk-through video in which she tested his ability to hear the neighbour's mailbox lid closing, as he claimed. When we saw the footage at the inquest, the sound could be heard loud and clear.

I spoke to two lawyers at the inquest about Mr Chapman's credibility as a witness, explaining that two of my good friends had known him all their lives. One friend – who was born and raised in the town – is president of the Kendall Country Women's Association; the other – born and raised in Comboyne – is an accomplished botanist. I would name them, but I fear they will come after me with a big stick or force me to ingest some sort of bush tucker as a punishment. These people emphasised his honesty, integrity and his eye for detail and description. Ronald Chapman, they told me, is a stickler for exactitude when assessing colours, shapes and sizes of flowers and plants. It's what he's known for in Kendall. But one thing still troubled me: was it possible to make out thin, black lines on such a rapidly moving Spiderman costume? Because Mr Chapman said he saw them, which was how he recognised the superhero it depicted.

Mr Chapman has good vision and only wears glasses for reading. Still, I could see the general consensus was that he meant well, but was mistaken. He may have seen a woman and child but later conflated William Tyrrell's disappearance with this unrelated sighting.

Mr Chapman testified that he went to the Kendall Club that night for dinner and told locals what he'd seen. He had his niece and her husband staying with him that weekend. They'd been out that morning. At the club, he had sought out Senior Constable Wendy Hudson, whom he's known since she was 'a babe in arms', he said in court. But Hudson wasn't there that night, so he told her sister-in-law, Allison Kennedy, about it and asked her to pass the information on. Apparently, Kennedy forgot and Hudson was never alerted.

Ronald Chapman explained that because he'd passed on a message to Hudson, he'd decided to wait for detectives canvassing the area to follow up. No one ever knocked on his door. He kept waiting, but as time went on, he came to believe that police were following more substantial leads or perhaps had been tipped off about those cars by other witnesses.

While he testified, I overheard Young Hope's Michelle White – whom I'd dubbed the Awkward Bridesmaid – whisper to Anna Wyndham, 'He's so cute!' Anna wore an inscrutable expression while Mr Chapman testified. Perhaps she was thinking along the same lines I was: *why didn't he tell Nancy what he'd seen?* I waited for this crucial question to be put to him. Eventually it was. I suspected I already had the answer, which he confirmed in his reply.

'Er … I didn't get on very well with her.'

Ron Chapman stood in the foyer of the Taree courthouse. I approached him and said, 'Back again for another round of questions?'

'Yes,' he replied. 'Although I don't know why they bothered. No one believes me.' I really felt for him. From what I'd heard, he was right. Investigators had dismissed his sighting, or at least diminished its importance over time. I took the opportunity to broach a burning issue.

'I presume they are struggling to believe you because they can't explain why you didn't come forward right away.'

'Yes,' he agreed.

'Why did you delay reporting what you saw for so long?' There. I'd asked the critical question.

'I agonised over it,' he told me. 'For days, then weeks, I just wasn't sure whether they'd believe me.' That was ironic, since their disbelief was founded primarily on the delay in reporting.

'I felt they'd think I was just a silly old goat,' he went on. 'And I was right in the end.' Mr Chapman told me he was warned that police would prosecute him if he was found to be wasting their time. He assured me he took the steps he felt necessary to inform the local police. Evidence from numerous local witnesses verifies that he told at least a dozen people of the sighting within days of the incident.

Then Ron Chapman made a stunning revelation. He told me his visiting nephew, Danny Connell, and his wife, Kathy, had telephoned Crime Stoppers the next morning, on 13 September. News of the sighting had so unnerved his guests that they reported it to police, Mr Chapman said. I was intrigued. I wondered why the police had taken so long to act on that report. Then, our conversation turned to the recent Comboyne Show at which Ron had officiated as flower judge. We indulged in a little local gossip before Mr Chapman was whisked off to give evidence.

When Ron Chapman told the court of his nephew Danny Connell's timely phone call to police, there was a collective gasp. But he couldn't account for how his nephew knew about the vehicles he'd seen, as he hadn't mentioned them at all that day. Mr Chapman had told me he wanted to keep his relatives 'out of it' and he used the same expression on the witness stand. I wondered how Danny Connell could've known about the sighting unless his uncle had mentioned it.

I watched Jack Reacher and Colonel Mustard react with wry smiles at each other and realised something wasn't right.

After the court took a lunch break, we returned to hear what that something was.

Danny's and Kathy's testimony would reveal that Ron Chapman was mistaken. Danny Connell had called Crime Stoppers more than a year after their visit to report a minor incident they felt could be important to the Tyrrell investigation – but it was nothing to do with the supposed sighting of a little boy in the back of a vehicle. It happened on Friday 12 September 2014 just after 10.30 am.

The Connells had seen an old white ute hit a roadsign at an intersection in the main street that day. The driver was an elderly man with thick-rimmed glasses. Both witnesses saw him, but only the woman remembered he was wearing an Akubra hat. They'd wondered whether the incident might have been related to the suspected abduction, since it occurred around the time of William's disappearance.

The Connells both testified that Uncle Ron had never mentioned his supposed sighting of William Tyrrell to them. If he had, they certainly would've told police, they assured Mr Craddock. I walked away not sure what to believe about Mr Chapman's evidence.

*

At the time Detective Vanessa Partridge made a walk-through video with William's foster grandmother, she was perturbed. 'I just had this feeling that things weren't right. There's something wrong. William's not missing,' she said. The detective I'd dubbed the School Prefect relied on her policing instincts. She felt sure they were looking at an abduction. But common sense tells us lurking around a private home and snatching a noisy child is a very risky manoeuvre. How is it the perpetrator wasn't seen or heard? How would they lure William away noiselessly? And how would they make their escape from Benaroon Drive?

These questions haunted investigators, none more so than Gary Jubelin. In 2015 he told the *60 Minutes* program's Michael Usher that it was 'extremely unlikely' there was a stranger in the yard the day William vanished.[12] Instead, Jubelin favoured the theory that the little boy ran away from the house and yard, further down the road.

'I can understand how a three-year-old might think, "Dad's coming home", waiting for him, knowing he was due home soon, then coming down the roadway and looking for him. Then ... someone who has the propensity to commit an evil act like this decides, "This is a situation I'm gonna take advantage of ..." We call it an opportunistic crime.' Jubelin posed the possibility that Spiderman provided a convenient ruse by which the perp approached William. 'I think the Spiderman suit plays a part in this, in that ... any stranger could come up and you could get a rapport happening with William straight away by calling him Spiderman,' he said.[13]

Nancy's closest neighbours, the Millers, had been away since late August in 2014. They returned on 13 September, after hearing the news about Nancy's missing grandson. I filed this snippet away in my rapidly expanding pink-paged dossier.

Recently, I was lurking around Benaroon Drive taking some photos for this book when I noticed that the Millers' house would be an ideal vantage point for someone to watch the little porch where William had been playing. I wondered – as you probably are now – whether there'd been a lookout posted somewhere around that empty house that morning. Because if so, that would make the impossible task of snatching a child out from under the noses of two reponsible adults very possible. Easy, even.

Before the official search had wrapped up, Anna and Nathan faced the heartbreak of returning home without William. The nil finds of the search made things crystal clear: he wasn't in the bush. He wasn't anywhere. Yet, his things were everywhere – his room, his clothes and toys, his little bed, his cup and cutlery – all serving as reminders of their loss. And Spiderman – the superhero they would come to hate. In the *60 Minutes* television interview, Anna struggled to put into words how the couple dealt with the experience.

'We wake up, we just relive it. I just can't believe it's happened. We just don't have our boy. His sister no longer has a brother. We have to watch his sister learn to play on her own, learn to be an only child. It's heartbreaking.'[14]

Before the tragedy, the couple were in the process of gaining approval for house extensions, in part to make more space for the children. Sometimes, when I read through their statements and watch recorded interviews, the full weight of the foster parents' burden becomes palpable. They speak of their recollections of William's excitement at the prospect of watching excavators, construction workers and tradies complete the project. I can picture them as they recall his favourite songs and television shows. They look at his little drawings and photos of happier times, family videos. And they try not to think about certain things, desperately.

Particularly, they try to avoid thoughts about what he would've been going through when he was snatched away. It tears their hearts out … but it's all they think about. Everything else pales into nothing. They think about him crying every time Lindsay does. They think about his screams for help when their little girl wakes up with nightmares. They think of the pain he might have suffered every time she hurts herself. They picture him struggling to free himself, to run away, to open a locked door, calling for help – calling for them to come and rescue him. It is a living horror movie. And it never ends.

Anna has shared some of her private thoughts with interviewers, impressions that come to her when she casts her mind back to that terrible day in 2014. Doubtless, they resonate with parents everywhere.

'He would have been beside himself. He would have been petrified.' She told of a night time ritual she followed in the early days of the investigation. 'I'd lie in his bed ... and I'd just pray that he wasn't scared, that somebody was loving him.' She told reporter Michael Usher, that she used to go into William's room as if to say goodnight to him.

It's hearing about these moments that brings the horror into sharp focus. And through the years, there's been no respite. Is their little boy alive and suffering or dead and oblivious? At the *60 Minutes* interview in 2015, there was still hope, evidenced by Anna's words. 'If somebody has him and if he is alive I want him to be safe. I want him to be feeling loved and I want someone to be looking after him. We need to know what happened because we cannot live like this.'[15]

At that time, detectives said publicly that they hadn't closed their minds to the possibility that William may have been abducted by a person hoping to raise him as their own son. They said he may still be alive because no evidence had been recovered that would rule it out. But privately, I suspect the Strike Force leaders didn't want to let these people down by seeming to be giving up on little William.

When Gary Jubelin asked Nathan what he thought in 2016, he answered with optimism, but not conviction: 'There's always a chance.' I would guess they realised by then that, in all likelihood, William was dead.

When Nathan attended the last week of the March 2020 inquest session, I observed a man who'd significantly aged since I'd last seen him. His hair was now more salt than pepper. His face was gaunt; eyes alert and suspicious. He used to offer an acknowledging smile if I'd catch his eye as we took our seats. But this day, he wasn't leaving eye contact to chance. He seemed shut down. Nathan sat, legs crossed, twisting his centimetre-wide wedding band around and around. In sync, his suspended foot made impatient circles in the air.

Trouble brewed on the inquest's final day in March. Someone had noticed a silver vehicle parked close to the courthouse, its occupant armed with a camera. I overheard police saying that messages had been posted by someone onsite in Taree, promising pictures of the foster family. I could see Nathan wasn't going to let that happen, not on his watch. His body went rigid at the news; a coiled spring. He disappeared for a few minutes then returned with pictures of the spy. The detective I'd previously named The Duchess had also taken some snaps. I read undisguised anger in the faces of William's foster parents, which turned to triumph as the culprit's identity was revealed. And who could blame them?

Over the course of the months after William disappeared, I read, in devastating detail, various police accounts of the foster father's involvement in the search operation of September 2014. Reports showed that Nathan became more desperate with every passing day of the search. Understandably. He struggled to contain his emotions as police and organisers gave him updates at the scene. I thought about what he had told police on the second day of the search.

'There are hundreds of people here. Why have we not seen something? I'm worried that as every single minute goes by, we're losing. We're losing time. If he hasn't eaten, if he hasn't had anything to drink, you know. I know he can deal without food but water is priority. You know, if he doesn't have that … I'm worried that he's lying out there somewhere and if he's not already … you know … he might be incapacitated, might have hit his head. Someone told me there was a two-year-old little boy at Johns River. I don't know where that is in relation to here. It's not far though. A little two-year old boy had gone missing. And he'd crawled or walked … middle of winter, but you know, the stories – I'm sure they've been embellished …'

9

EVERYBODY LOSES

Whenever I talk about William Tyrrell, I encounter people with a keen sense of personal ownership over his story. It is mostly their online interactions that have formed this feeling. Taking it personally appeals to our instincts as adults – we are the protectors of children. The case has saturated the news, leading to a nationwide 'fostering' of this little boy. Australia fell in love with him through two pictures – *that one* and the snap of him in a blue-checked shirt.

The nation's response must first have been reassuring, then later, disturbing, and finally angering for his loved ones. We weren't there when his parents and carers were struggling, before he went missing. We never changed a bedsheet or prepared a breakfast for him. We didn't go through the shock of sudden bereavement, the endless not knowing. We weren't pouring our resources of time, energy and money into the investigation. Heck, we weren't even out foot-slogging in the bush. Whose child was this, really?

The tale of how William Tyrrell's birth family disintegrated is filled with pathos. Brendan Collins met Karlie Tyrrell in 2008 through her brother Tom Tyrrell. Tom's statements paint a fuller picture of the family situation in which he, Karlie and their younger brother, Ashley, grew up. Their parents separated when Karlie was eleven. Domestic violence, addiction and mental health problems took her mother away and young Karlie and her brothers would stay with their dad until they grew up.

The Tyrrells and their neighbours called their Department of Housing estate in Northern Sydney 'Smurf Village', or 'Lego Land' or 'The Ghetto' – all equally apt names. It was composed of long rows of blue townhouses that looked like Lego bricks. There was only one road into the neighbourhood. Kids hardly out of nappies roamed the streets at all hours, wreaking havoc, and regular people were too afraid to drive in. Their parents seemed unconcerned about safety – they knew Houso kids were tough, and they were battling their own problems.

Smurf Village was afflicted by chronic unemployment and was overrun with crime; gang wars, theft, prostitution, family violence and a thriving drug trade. You either grew up streetwise or you didn't survive. Substance abuse, fights and unprotected sex kept teens occupied, perpetuating the cycle of unwanted pregnancies, family violence, joblessness and hardship. These kids had seen far too much sex, violence, addiction and imprisonment to be interested in receiving an education. Targeted bashings, break-ins and suicides were everyday events.

An ugly mound of earth and debris on the estate became a popular meeting place. Christened 'Ayers Rock', authorities had promised it would be turned into a park. But when it eventually did receive its makeover, it merely provided a hangout for bored youths to gather and brew up trouble.

By his late teens, Brendan Collins was in the habit of riding his pushbike to Smurf Village to visit friends, including Tom Tyrrell. They would enjoy a few drinks together. One day, Karlie was walking her dog when Tom suggested they go over to Brendan's place. This was the first time she met him. Karlie's previous boyfriend was in prison at the time for armed robbery. Not long after this first meeting, she began dating Brendan. Soon afterwards, Karlie became pregnant.

After Lindsay's birth, they set up house together in Meadowbank. They needed practical support but neither family was in a position to provide that vital help. Karlie's father, David, struggled with his own addictions and had no resources at his command, financial or otherwise. Money was scarce and, although Brendan was employed, the pair struggled to balance their desires with their new responsibilities as parents. The young family sometimes visited David's house. The unit was always a shambles, and so was its occupant.

Destructive patterns set in early and the couple were barely coping with the unfamiliar demands of child-rearing. With the naturally volatile Karlie under this pressure, things routinely erupted into explosive fighting. When Karlie's younger brother, Ashley, got out of jail, he was under a strict curfew. Police cruised past to check that Ashley was complying with the curfew one night when they encountered Karlie.

The fallout from a fight with Brendan had prompted Karlie to get extremely drunk. When police saw her erratically pushing the baby's stroller down the street, they were concerned. Tom Tyrrell stumbled upon the scene just as his sister was being arrested. She'd punched a police officer who had attempted to protect the baby. This led to FACS stepping in for the first time and taking Lindsay out of Karlie's care.

Karlie Tyrrell is no stranger to violence. Before she was even twenty, she'd dished out her fair share. At eighteen, Karlie had a serious assault on her criminal record. On her twenty-second birthday, she celebrated by punching a female police officer in the face.[16] Having her children removed didn't seem to change these patterns of violence.

Just six months before William went missing, Karlie was charged with assault occasioning actual bodily harm and destruction of property when she flew into a violent rage and gave Brendan and his townhouse a beating they wouldn't forget. She was handed a twelve-month good behaviour bond and a community supervision order in August 2014. Her rap sheet would later list two convictions for shoplifting and also noted that Karlie Tyrrell had a number of aliases known to police.

But in 2018, Karlie turned the tables on Brendan Collins, claiming that it was his violence that led to the children being unsafe in their home. As she told one journalist, 'It wasn't working and my kids come first, so I had to leave. I don't want him in their life.'[17]

*

When Gerard Craddock narrated how Karlie and Brendan hid William from authorities back in 2011, I saw the Coroner intently watching the birth parents. I wondered if she meant to gauge the degree of guilt they felt over flouting court orders. I saw no discernible trace. It's hard to call this action by its legally appropriate name – unlawful abduction.

I can imagine myself shielding my own child from the clutches of a seemingly faceless system and I was grateful to hear the Coroner express that very sentiment. Her humble, generous empathy with these young parents revealed a deeply human face in that system – one that despite its failings and flaws, aims to protect our nation's most vulnerable little people. Even if too often, those little people grow up and repeat the destructive cycle all over again.

Uncle Ben reminded Peter Parker of an important truth when he found out he was Spiderman. Both sets of William's parents and the Department of Family and Community Services know it only too well: 'with great power comes great responsibility.' When we intervene in the lives of children, we must have the end-goal in mind at all times: helping people break the cycle. We need strong scaffolding around vulnerable people to help them cope with substance abuse and with families disrupted by domestic violence. Karlie and Brendan found themselves acting out their own anger after finding themselves ill-equipped to face the challenges of just living, let alone parenting.

In police interviews following William's disappearance, Tom revealed that Karlie would get emotional and 'fire up' whenever anyone spoke about the kids being in care, so he avoided bringing it up. When she did speak about the children, Karlie told Tom they were 'doing good' in their foster home. But she'd complain that their clothes and haircuts made them look 'geeky' and felt the foster parents were too strict about food choices. Tom has said that he never talks to Karlie about William's disappearance because she gets worked up in anger, then becomes really sad. He told police he was puzzled by his nephew's disappearance and was certainly not involved in any way.

Tom said he would stay away from his family, because he was sick of their 'bullshit with drugs etc'. His et cetera presumably meant criminal activities. Tom's younger brother, Ashley, has spent much of his adult life in jail. As for Brendan Collins, Tom said his drug problems worsened after William disappeared. Tom Tyrrell told police he had to deal with his own bouts of depression over William's disappearance.

Moreover, he did not believe that anyone he knew took William. 'None of my family members have given me any reason to suspect them as being involved. I am a very truthful person and if I knew something, I would have told the police straight away.' From my reading of his statement, Tom Tyrrell seemed a credible witness. In 2014, he was in a long term relationship with his partner and had stable employment and a company vehicle. He seemed to have his act together and had perhaps broken the intergenerational cycle of dysfunction that has plagued his family. Nevertheless, I wondered why we hadn't heard from him at the inquest.

Before William was born, Brendan Collins had lost his way and was dabbling in petty crime. He found himself in a destructive cycle, putting him at odds with family and on the wrong side of the law. These circumstances led many sleuths on social media to point the finger at him as the likeliest abductor. *After all, he's done it before*, was the implication. This is an unfortunate consequence of having the unsavoury aspects of one's life splashed across the news pages – unfair, but understandable. But Brendan always maintained he was not involved, as he told police in his 2014 statement.

'I do not know where William is and I have not taken him or organised anyone to take him. If I was going to take William, I would have also taken Lindsay as well. I wouldn't take one and not the other. I have been praying that the police find him safe.' Going by the friendly and supportive manner in which detectives greeted Brendan Collins at the inquest, it appears they believed him.

Brendan Collins' statement was taken by police two days after William vanished. He was thirty-two years old in 2014 and living with Karlie Tyrrell and Francis, then eighteen months old. The couple were expecting their fourth child's arrival. In his statement, Brendan gave a watered down explanation of why the other children were removed by FACS. 'Both Karlie and I at the time were going through issues and as a result, DOCS believed that Lindsay wasn't safe in our care.' In a masterful understatement, Brendan went on to say FACS believed he had anger management problems.

Reading the statement, it was clear that Brendan Collins loved and missed his children. But his statement also betrayed a simplistic grasp of a child's most basic need: to feel safe in their own home. He appeared not to comprehend the impact of anger and domestic violence on children, a roadblock to reunification noted in FACS' earliest assessments. Brendan complained he found it hard to get to access visits because of his work commitments and because he didn't have a driver's licence.

He admitted he hadn't seen his children for four months before their last access visit. He truly didn't appear to realise that his infrequent attendance came across as ambivalence – work and transport arrangements shouldn't be factors when you're fighting to have your children returned.

The court orders initially granted Karlie regular, supervised access to the children, but when it was discovered that she was still living with Brendan, access visits were limited to six times per year. At the 2019 inquest, Brendan admitted that he missed a couple of visits, and Karlie missed some as well. He also said he had never met the foster family and didn't know their names or where they lived.

During her inquest testimony, Karlie maintained she had never met the foster family either and didn't know anything about them. She admitted she once saw the foster mother when she turned up early to a visit and spotted her talking with the Salvation Army case worker. But she didn't speak with her. Karlie said she had no idea where the family lived, what the foster father looked like or what car they had.

Despite losing custody of Lindsay and William, the couple were able to retain care of their son Francis for a while. A new assessment gave them the green light to keep Francis and his newborn sibling. Sadly, by the end of 2015 both of these children had also been placed in the permanent care of others.

Brendan's mother, Natalie Collins, has always insisted it was the children's mother who was violent toward her partner, and the aggressor in the relationship. In 2019 she told me of a time when Karlie smashed Brendan's head into a window. According to his mother, Brendan preferred to leave the house rather than fight back and escalate the violence. But it seems unlikely that all the domestic violence was one-way traffic in that household.

Natalie was married for twenty-six years to John Collins. The couple had a son and a daughter. After they split, Natalie had a five-year relationship with Darryl Clifford, and the couple welcomed

ABOVE The house on Benaroon Drive. Note the neighbouring window with a view to the back patio. The front yard slopes quite steeply toward the road. This is the view from where the two strange cars were parked the morning William disappeared.

BELOW Strike Force Rosann used satellite imagery to assist in their search. This diagram I have drawn shows the key sites of interest and a possible route an abductor could take.

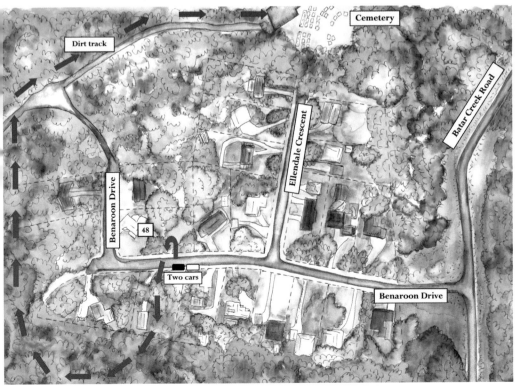

THIS PAGE, TOP The tennis club's security camera captured imagery of traffic heading out of Kendall village. After crossing the North Coast railway line, vehicles head east toward Kew and the Pacific Highway beyond. The 'Keep Left' sign in the foreground is the one hit by a driver in a white ute on the morning William disappeared.

THIS PAGE, BOTTOM The Royal Hotel at Kew was frequented by Frank Abbott and Ray Porter. This is the view from outside the nearby coffee shop where the men often met.

OPPOSITE PAGE, MIDDLE LEFT The restored chapel at Herons Creek where Frank Abbott and Geoffrey Owen were involved in voluntary work. The owner's intention for the heritage project was to provide a hub for community activities.

OPPOSITE PAGE, MIDDLE RIGHT The quaint and quiet main street of Kendall, looking east toward North Brother mountain. It's hard for urban dwellers to grasp the quietness of this little village. While Kendall has its moments of thriving activity, there is often no one about at all.

OPPOSITE PAGE, BOTTOM I made this watercolour map of the Camden Haven area for a local tourism brochure back in 2014. It provides a good overview of some places of interest.

The cemetery is a two-minute walk from the Benaroon Drive home through a bush track. It's a lonely place that few people visit. A central carpark lies to the left of the brick structure, and could have been used as an easy escape from the area via Albert Street.

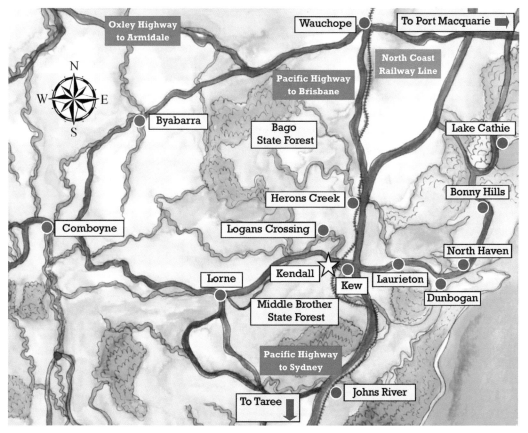

The swamp in which two-year-old Tyler Kennedy was found in May 2013. A dense pine forest ends at the edge of this stretch of marshland. When this photo was taken, the ground had dried out considerably and new grass was growing. It's a mosquito-infested place and so impenetrable that I couldn't reach the precise rescue location through the trees.

This wooden bridge on Logans Crossing Road is not far from the Misty Way property where Geoffrey Owen lived at the time William Tyrrell was taken. William's abductor could have escaped via this isolated bushland. The road is rarely troubled by traffic.

The inquest into William's disappearance began at the NSW Coroner's Court at Lidcombe in March 2019. The second sitting was in August 2019 and evidence was heard in Sydney and Taree. The third sitting in Taree was suspended on 17 March 2020 due to the COVID-19 crisis.

ABOVE This farm machinery shed is located on private property directly behind Kendall Public School. There's vehicle turning space and the area is screened by bushland. This may be the shed referenced in Ray Porter's death-bed confession.

BELOW Now no strangers to media intrusion, Bill and Margaret Spedding face the cameras outside the NSW Coroner's Court at Lidcombe in August 2019. Bill made a statement in which he expressed his sympathy for William's loved ones and his relief that he was no longer considered a person of interest in the William Tyrrell investigation.

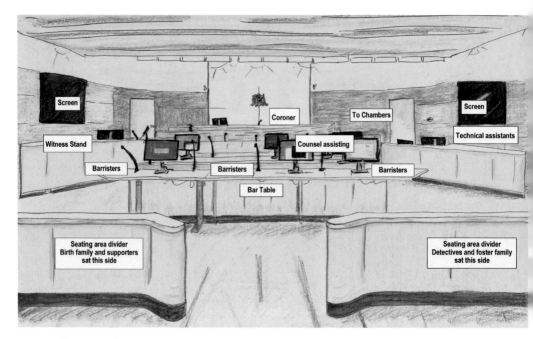

ABOVE Photography is not permitted in NSW courts. I sketched the NSW Coroner's Court at Lidcombe to illustrate the layout and the relative positions of people involved in the proceedings.

OPPOSITE PAGE, TOP I made sketches of each person of interest who appeared before the Coroner in 2019 and 2020. Clockwise from left are: Paul Savage, a Benaroon Drive resident who came under the suspicion of Detective Chief Inspector Jubelin; Robert Donohoe, another convicted paedophile who was known to be in the area on 12 September 2014 and who joined the search for William Tyrrell the same day; Tony Jones, a local convicted paedophile who had given false alibis and whose vehicles were of interest to police; Danny Parish, part-owner of the Herons Creek property where Abbott resided and owner of a number of vehicles of interest to police; Frank Abbott, who is serving a sixteen-year prison sentence for paedophilia (a friend's death-bed confession and a child-abuse victim both pointed to Abbott's involvement in the abduction and murder of William Tyrrell) – this sketch was taken from a photo, since Abbott was barely visible when he appeared by video link at the inquest; and Geoffrey Owen, Abbott's one-time neighbour and fellow church member. All six men deny any involvement in the crime.

OPPOSITE PAGE, BOTTOM Strike Force Rosann police onsite at the forensic search in Kendall, July 2018. From left: Senior Constable Daniel Dring (NSW Police Public Order and Riot Squad); Detective Senior Sergeant Mark Dukes; Detective Sergeant Andrew Lonergan; and Gary Jubelin. (AAP IMAGE)

ABOVE Kendall hosts the annual Camden Haven Show, one of Australia's longest continually running agricultural shows. The pig race always draws a big crowd. (FAITH BELL PHOTOGRAPHY)

BELOW Boating, fishing and water sports attract seasonal visitors to the Camden Haven. The river is home to a multitude of fish, dolphins, oyster colonies and a huge variety of birdlife. This image shows the view from the southern bank of the river at Dunbogan. (FAITH BELL PHOTOGRAPHY)

Brendan. Darryl Clifford has another son, Michael, who is well known in Australia as a member of the band 5 Seconds of Summer.

Natalie has another son, Mitchell, to a different father. Mitchell and Brendan are to this day good mates and lived together in Ryde before Karlie came on the scene. Natalie took care to inform me that Brendan's life was positively rosy before Karlie Tyrrell came along. Natalie is a loyal mum, no doubt about that.

When she moved in with the brothers, it wasn't long before Karlie demanded that Brendan throw Mitchell out. When the pair began living together as a couple, Brendan was earning good money as an excavator driver. Natalie said he made sure his family had a decent roof over their heads, nice furniture, good food and clothes.

In conversations with Natalie, I was told fights initiated by Karlie would escalate until she or Brendan would storm out. If Brendan took off, Natalie said Karlie would lock him out. Once, she allegedly had her brother and his mate ambush Brendan at a railway station. They gave him a bashing, leaving him partially conscious on the railway tracks.

Natalie said Brendan would come home to find their two children had been left alone in the house. Throughout this time, Natalie and her daughter would go over two nights a week. They'd cook dinner, change the bedsheets, clean up, play with the children, bath and change them and put them to bed. Natalie told me it was the only way they could be sure the kids were getting enough to eat each week.

Natalie remembers Karlie telling her in 2013 that she and Brendan spent more than $2000 on Christmas presents for William and Lindsay. On the next access visit in the new year, they asked the kids about how they were enjoying their new toys. According to FACS reports the conversation went something like this.

'Have you tried playing the guitar we got you for Chrissy?' Karlie asked her daughter.

'No. Mummy threw it out.'

'What about the toys?' Karlie asked William.

'I don't know where they are,' he replied. 'I haven't seen them.'

On one access visit, the children turned up in costumes. Brendan wondered whether they might feel more comfortable wearing normal clothes like the other kids at the play centre, so he went to Big W and bought them ordinary clothes. The children put their new outfits on and Karlie threw the other costumes in the bin. For Natalie Collins, William's costume was a symbol of his 'spoiled life' in the care of rich people.

When I spoke of wanting to meet Karlie, Natalie warned me that she's not an easy person to get to know. She said Karlie tends to alienate everyone in her life. She has no filter. When people tried to help, they were either shouted at or used, then discarded. When Natalie and a friend visited Karlie in hospital, another patient said hello to the women when they entered the ward. Karlie shouted angrily at her.

'F**k off. Don't talk to them. They're my visitors!'

Karlie Tyrrell stayed home all day on Thursday 11 September 2014. Police statements reveal that Brendan was with her all morning. His shoulder was sore and he'd meant to call in sick, but he fell asleep and forgot. He awoke in the afternoon, made the call to his boss and said he'd try to get to work the next day.

Brendan took Francis out for a walk in the afternoon. They ended up at Woolworths, returning just before dark. The couple had no visitors. Karlie said she and Francis played in the backyard while Brendan cooked honey mustard chicken and rice for their dinner. Karlie recalls going to bed before midnight, leaving Brendan up alone.

On Friday, Brendan rose early, threw on his signature hoodie and headed to the McDonald's a few blocks away. He sat at a table beside a long window. The place was all but empty at this time of morning;

it was 5.00 am, just before sunrise. Closed circuit television cameras captured footage of Brendan choosing a table, ordering hotcakes, which he neglected to collect from the counter for some time. He messed about on his tablet using the free Wi-Fi service. He'd been there for quite a while before making the decision to call in sick. He still wasn't feeling up to going to work.

Brendan said when he got home, his heavily pregnant partner was still sleeping, as was their young son, Francis. He told police he texted his boss to say he wouldn't be at work, but later admitted he's not a hundred per cent sure he ever sent a message.

Natalie Collins told me that Brendan rang her before dawn that morning and told her something didn't feel right. She later wondered whether he'd had a premonition of the trouble to come. Brendan said he stayed at home all day, which wouldn't be easy to verify, since he was there alone.

Karlie slept in until 9.30 am Friday morning. Brendan had already been up and told her he'd been to McDonald's for breakfast. She wanted to go to the Blacktown shops, but Brendan didn't want to go out again. So Karlie took Francis in a small stroller, walked to the railway station to get a train to Blacktown.

Karlie made a call to her brother Tom while she waited. Just before she boarded the train, she texted Brendan. 'We're going to Blacktown. Meet us there if u want.' She visited an ATM and various shops, then called Brendan, but he didn't answer. Karlie told police he had a mobile phone and frequently changed the number. Her bizarre explanation for this was that he 'always loses his sim card'. Brendan didn't have an email address or a Facebook account as far as she knew.

Karlie's police statements describing her movements on 12 September 2014 have been verified by CCTV footage captured in various public places, including shopping centres and railway stations. We know that Karlie shopped for baby items, ate Red

Rooster takeaway for lunch and bought Francis a pizza. The little boy fell asleep after his lunch and because he couldn't lie down properly in the small straight-backed stroller, Karlie went to Big W and bought a new pram. She assembled it in the store and put Francis in it.

Brendan was still at home, and he answered Karlie's next call and said he wouldn't be coming to the shops. Karlie shopped at Best & Less at around two o'clock for baby clothes. Then, she took a train back home, arriving about 4.00 pm. Brendan had the music up loud and she turned it down because Francis was asleep in the new pram.

When it was Karlie's turn to testify at the first inquest session in 2019, Mr Craddock asked her to recall what happened when she found out her son had vanished from Kendall. Karlie described how police came to her house. The police initially thought her son Francis was William when they knocked on Karlie and Brendan's door. The children look very much alike. They wanted to know if William was there.

'What have you done?' the police asked her. Karlie said she didn't know what they were talking about. They told her William was missing from a town near Port Macquarie.

'Missing? What do you mean "missing"?'

'He's f***king what?' Brendan recalled that when he heard the news, he believed at first it was a joke. Then came confusion, shock, disbelief and anger. He went out the back to have a smoke while police searched the house.

In her police interview on 14 September 2014, the twenty-six-year-old mother told police she was confused when the police had initially arrived at her door, thinking they may have had a warrant out for her. When they told her William was missing, she remembered thinking he might just be missing from day care, she told police. But after they asked her about her movements that day and took her shopping receipts, she started panicking. She realised immediately that if police were tracking her movements, and Brendan's, they must believe that William had been abducted, not just lost in the bush.

'I got upset and started crying because I was worried about William.' Police reported that, as the news sank in, she began to move around the house as if in a daze. She alternated between disbelief and inconsolable sadness. Then anger.

Three women from the Salvation Army came to the house after the police left. Brendan told the court that it felt like the Salvos were the only ones who were trying to help. That evening, the couple saw the news on television. That's when the full reality began to sink in.

Karlie was concerned for Lindsay, testifying that the two children were very close, like best friends. She believed if Lindsay was with William, she wouldn't have let him wander off.

'She always looks out for him. That's what I don't understand,' she said to a detective during an interview. When asked directly whether she had any involvement in William's disappearance, Karlie was adamant.

'I definitely don't know where William is. I didn't take him. I had nothing to do with it. If I took him, I would be gone and I would have Lindsay as well. Plus, I just wouldn't do that. I want my kids back, so I wouldn't do anything that would stop that happening. I want a normal life. I don't want to be hiding away with them somewhere. If I did something like that, I could lose Francis and the baby that I'm about to give birth to. I didn't have a clue that they were near Port Macquarie either. I just want my son found.'

Karlie didn't leave the house for some time after she received the terrible news. She said at the inquest that police only contacted her after that first visit on 12 September 'when they felt like it'.

When Karlie was asked on Channel Seven's *Sunday Night* program where the fault lies in this tragedy, she made her view crystal clear: 'I don't want to blame the carers, but they were responsible for looking after him and they failed.' Still, in that interview she revealed that she was carrying a load of guilt herself. Karlie told the reporter she felt like 'the worst mum in the world'. She said she knew people would assume she didn't care about her child.

'I'm not a bad person. I'm not a bad mum. I didn't want to go on news being angry or anything, making anything worse. It didn't mean I didn't love him.' Karlie said she'd made some 'bad choices', which in her words were related to 'domestic violence and drugs, alcohol and marijuana'.

'I feel like whoever has him needs a bullet. Just let him come home. Please. It's not fair. This isn't fair.'[18]

*

In 2017 Karlie assaulted another female police officer. Mall security guards were trying to quell her aggression toward customers, but were forced to involve police when she refused to simmer down. Marks on her toddler Francis' legs drew questions from one of the female officers. She was told it was none of her business, but far less politely. Her tirade at the police went on.

'Ryde coppers lost my son!' she yelled. She used an element of the female anatomy to describe them. Then she concluded by spitting in the policewoman's face twice and shouting obscenities that expressed her extreme disapproval of the officer's red hair.

'F**k off, you ranga c**t!' The insult rang out across the Top Ryde shopping centre and with that, a good deal of public sympathy for Karlie Tyrrell evaporated. She was convicted of assaulting a police officer in the execution of duty. In a later interview, she claimed that a sudden panic attack had precipitated this assault.

Nonetheless, Australia has felt sorry for Karlie Tyrrell. As if having her precious young child going missing wasn't bad enough, it seemed the young mother's name had been thrust into the headlines against her wishes, exposing her to scrutiny. But in fact Karlie made no attempt to conceal her identity. Unlike William's foster parents, neither Karlie nor Brendan sought court orders to suppress their names. On the contrary, Karlie is an avid Facebook user and continued posting selfies and comments that identified her as William Tyrrell's mother very early in the investigation. Perhaps she wasn't given timely advice about how to deal with the inevitable queries that would come, the Facebook stalkers and the 'new friends' who hoped to ingratiate themselves with a young woman whose life was now considered public property.

When I met her in 2019, things didn't go so well. It was on day five of the inquest. I thought perhaps Karlie might be willing to talk to me. On her way out of the courtroom, she was surrounded by a small group of supporters, some of whom had accompanied Brendan, Natalie and I at the café during adjournments. They fended off photographers, ushering her to the outdoor courtyard. All the way there, I heard her talking loudly, as if to herself. She was sounding off about the media, the police, the fact that she felt the proceedings were a waste of time and all manner of other observations she wanted to air publicly. Karlie makes no secret of her dislike of rules, of police, of FACS, and pretty much anyone in authority. Her conduct at the court made it clear that you'd better stay out of her face or else. But it wasn't calculated or staged. It was just ... Karlie.

As I exited the foyer via the revolving door, I saw Karlie was seated on a garden bench outside. I noticed some scarring on the lower part of her face. She looked simultaneously world-weary and child-like, as if she'd had to grow up too quickly. Her shoulder-length dark hair had auburn highlights. She was distracted, fiddling with her white button-up blouse. Her support crew had drifted into two clumps some distance from the café, smoking and muttering among themselves.

I went over to Natalie and asked her to introduce me, which she did. As we approached, Karlie rummaged through an oversized handbag. I noticed she had petite hands, like a child's.

'Karlie, this is Ally.' So much for the introduction. Even though I'd been warned, I had underestimated Karlie's volatility. She glanced up at me as she lit a cigarette. I saw so much of little William in her brown eyes and dark lashes.

'Hi. I just wanted to let you know how sorry I am about William and what you've been through.' I told her I was writing a book and that I'd like to talk about her family and what they've suffered. No response.

Then, I added a detail I instantly regretted mentioning.

'I'm also a friend of Bill Spedding ...' and before I could say any more, she replied, 'Get away from me!' in a deep growl, startling in its ferocity. I felt she might leap at me at any moment, and took an involuntary step backward.

'I'm sorry. You don't understand. He's been wrongly accused. I've known Bill for ages.'

She cut me off. 'You don't know nothin'. They're all in it together!' she yelled in my face. And that was the sum total of my exchange with William Tyrrell's biological mother.

As I took the train home, I thought back to the thirteen massive ring-binders of evidence laid out in the courtroom. And that was just the first tranche. Ninety per cent of it was useless, pointing neither to the perpetrator nor the answer. But when you're trying to solve a baffling mystery, everything seems potentially important. Karlie Tyrrell thought 'they're all in it together', meaning FACS, the police, the neighbours and Bill Spedding, which is illogical. But she could be forgiven for reading connections into the mystery that simply weren't there.

Over the past five years, if you'd asked me what I believed happened to William Tyrrell, on any given week I'd have given you a different answer.

Five years after her son's disappearance, Karlie needed desperately to know the truth. She didn't know who to trust. She couldn't turn to the police – she'd burnt her bridges with them. She wasn't William's primary guardian anymore, so she couldn't turn to FACS. Then there was the foster family. Her communication with them had been limited to letter form. She'd been forbidden from approaching them personally. She must have been keenly aware that she lacked the education and empowerment to risk writing a personal letter. So Karlie Tyrrell went it alone all those years. Her mother was mentally unwell and her father passed away in 2018, not long after he accompanied Karlie to court after she spat at police. On reflection, I feel I got off lightly during our encounter – I only got shouted at.

*

Brendan's life unravelled further after William disappeared. He'd been homeless and unemployed and did a stint in Parklea prison for drug offences in 2017. According to his mother, he would go on rampages in his room, smashing up the place and swearing and threatening her as he raged about his inability to protect his children.

Brendan stole other people's mail, some credit and identification cards and a range of items from shops, including some children's toys and a set of clothes for himself. In 2018 he hadn't removed the security tags and was easily nabbed by police. Over these years he entered guilty pleas to a raft of theft and drug charges.

Arrested three times in three months when he was at his lowest ebb, Brendan's ice habit left him looking like a wild-bearded derelict. His nickname, 'Bones', had never been more apt. He was, according to his mother, acting very strangely. He wasn't eating. He'd walk down the street kicking at brick walls. He'd root through rubbish left out in council pickup piles and bring random things home. He was found to have stolen some odd treasures: an Asian religious figurine, a souvenir magnet of Sydney, a Star Wars toy, two Maglite torches, Kodak photographic paper, a stationery set and boxes of hayfever tablets. Police also found two bank keycards and some bagged cash in his pockets when he was arrested in January 2018.

He didn't resist arrest, and was cooperative and polite to police and the magistrate who issued him with a sentence. He told the court he'd been promised excavation work, which he'd take up after his release, and that he intended to use his income to pay for psychiatric help to enable him to stay off illicit drugs.

Meeting Brendan in 2019, I was impressed by his composure given the immense pressure and scrutiny he must have felt at the inquest. It was day five and I'd been awake most of the night suffering food poisoning from a suspiciously warm chicken Caesar salad. I'd barely survived the taxi ride without needing an unscheduled stop and doubted I'd last until the first adjournment. I was right. I had to make a hasty exit and attend to some urgent bathroom business. Then, I navigated groggily to a padded bench and, succumbing to temptation, stretched my sorry self out on the seat. 'Just for a few minutes, while no one's around,' I told myself, and promptly fell asleep.

When I next opened my eyes, I saw Brendan Collins coming out of the courtroom, taking a break. He was staring at me. I clutched my stomach and mumbled, 'Food poisoning.' He nodded sympathetically.

'You should get your head down,' he said. Then he got himself a drink at the water fountain and went back inside. Brendan looked like a lost soul, clearly out of his comfort zone but unable to avoid the spotlight. I feared he'd make a bad impression on the witness stand, inviting criticism and suspicion from people more privileged than he. I needn't have worried.

Brendan Collins is no stranger to the court system, even though his previous appearances have been as the defendant, not as a witness. During Brendan's testimony, Tracey Stevens gaffed by inadvertently naming Karlie. Brendan told her magnanimously that he excused her for that. Some barely suppressed smiles lit up the bar table. On the stand, the impression Brendan left was one of quiet dignity and strength. He assured the court he was fond of his children, despite the circumstances.

'I was the number one person who didn't want to let him go,' he said of William's handover to FACS.

Ms Stevens had to ask Brendan to speak louder and more clearly. He tends to mumble when overwhelmed by a formal occasion. It was clear that he wanted onlookers to know he was a father who genuinely cared about his children, despite the life of disadvantage he'd led. Brendan's key message to the court was that those who'd placed themselves in authority over his child had failed in their duty of care. He expressed a simplistic but impassioned view of where the blame should be laid – and he was certain there was blame to be laid.

In his police statement, Brendan took pains to note William had been hospitalised as a result of some serious bouts of asthma and that he'd had a fall resulting in a black eye while in foster care. He said in court, 'I don't think the foster mother and father really care about the kids as they aren't their kids. They don't love them like we do.'

Brendan Collins has not for a moment wavered in his view that William was never lost in the bush. But his view of where the responsibility for the tragedy lies is contradictory. He says he doesn't blame the foster parents, but in the same breath said he feels that had FACS never become involved, he and Karlie would've been able to keep William safe.

'They f***ed up,' he said to the court. He expressed a respectful apology to Her Honour and to the court that his vocabulary 'wasn't up to scratch'. But he came across as genuine – a battler from a family whose struggles with dysfunction were entrenched across three generations.

In the hours before Brendan was due to testify, Anna Wyndham asked for a private meeting with him. Details are sparse, but Natalie Collins told me the foster carers wanted to grant Brendan more access to his daughter, now that William was gone from her life. Brendan told his mother Anna produced a photo as a means of illustrating just how close their family had become. It showed Nathan cuddling Lindsay in a display of father–daughter togetherness. Then, according to Natalie, Anna remarked, 'I hope seeing that doesn't upset you.'

When this anecdote was shared with me, Brendan's supporters expressed outrage at what they believed was Anna's cruel reminder of all that Brendan had lost. But I saw it differently. I believe she was motivated by kindness. I think her gesture to include Brendan in Lindsay's life was in recognition of his importance in her world.

Perhaps through that photo she hoped to show Brendan her desire to surround the child with love. It was evidence that his daughter was happy, in a loving and stable home, and that she would be supported by loving parents as she dealt with her bereavement. Surely that is the best hope any parent has for their child. Surely, past hurts can be left behind for Lindsay's sake. If parents like Karlie and Brendan, Anna and Nathan – and you and your partner and me and mine, and all those single parents and grandparents out there – can rise to the challenge of being the best versions of ourselves for our children, society wins. If we can't, everybody loses.

10

THE GAMBLE

Ocean Drive is the main road through Laurieton and North Haven, small fishing towns on the Camden Haven River. It runs through Bonny Hills and Lake Cathie and on to Port Macquarie and is linked to the highway by a shortcut known as the Ghost Road. In 2014, Bill and Margaret Spedding lived at the eastern end of it. Officially named Houston Mitchell Drive, the road's local moniker delighted sensation-hungry journalists. It was nicknamed for the tall ghost gums that flank it – a fact that disappointed those who were out to paint Bill as a child killer. But they published headlines about ghosts anyway.

Bill Spedding is an electrical contractor and, among his other trade pursuits, repairs washing machines and whitegoods. When police discovered a number of telephone calls and text messages between Bill and 48 Benaroon Drive, they immediately took interest in this seemingly unassuming gent. Nancy Wyndham explained that she'd called Bill out to the house to quote on fixing her washing machine the Tuesday before William went missing. And that he was due back before the weekend.

In January 2015, Bill Spedding's Laurieton business premises, his Bonny Hills house, his Wellington address and the family's three vehicles were all subjected to an extensive forensic search. Incongruously, although the news media were all over it,

Superintendent Paul Fehon appeared on-camera saying he wouldn't describe executing the search warrant as a major breakthrough. Fehon explained, 'We searched a number of premises in the Laurieton and Bonny Hills area yesterday as part of the ongoing investigation and the search for young William. This is a line of inquiry we're taking.' Those premises all turned out to be connected to Bill. Detectives searched an office in Laurieton's main street that Bill used as his business headquarters. In the window was a sign reading *Speddo's Pawn Brokers,* although he never ended up launching that business.

Much was made of the fact that detectives removed some items from Bill's upstairs office unit, among them a mattress and computer gear. The implications of these items when taken together could hardly have been clearer if they'd drawn a picture for journalists. They waited, eagle-eyed, to swoop. Police would later say that nothing of interest was found during those searches. Nevertheless, the mud stuck.

To compound suspicion, Bill had posted about William's disappearance on Facebook. He shared a message posted by another user: 'Today, somebody is keeping a secret. They got up this morning. Had breakfast. Realized they need to pick up some more milk. Wasted time on Facebook. Made some calls. All the while maintaining a poker face.' Bill posted his own message as well. 'Don't give up looking.'

On the surface, it was just an off-the-cuff comment. But to some, it sounded like the gloating behaviour of the kind of psychopath you sometimes see depicted in movies. It appeared Bill knew something.

Another post had come to light, this one from a Facebook page called 'Bring Little Spiderman William Tyrrell Home': '*Where is he?*' These three words struck people as chilling – people who were suspicious of Bill Spedding, that is. The highly publicised searches that had turned Bill's life upside down had people thinking, 'Where there's smoke, there's fire'. Neither they, nor Bill, nor I could explain how police had been able to obtain such invasive warrants without compelling evidence of wrongdoing. It would be some time before there was an answer.

Adding fuel to the speculation around Bill Spedding was the revelation that he and Margaret were FACS-appointed foster carers for three of their grandchildren. The news kept following the search story. An excavator was used to sift through a woodpile and tree cuttings at the Bonny Hills property. Sniffer dogs were used around the yard.

A septic tank service truck was called in, emblazoned with the memorable tagline, 'Number 1 in the Number 2 Business'. The police reported they'd received a tip-off via the Crime Stoppers hotline, precipitating the devastating forced removal of Bill and Margaret's three grandchildren, but they remained tight-lipped on its source. I wondered whether the media feeding frenzy had been whipped up in a deliberate strategy by investigators to manufacture a result for the William Tyrrell case.

Bill Spedding's basement became the focus of the cameras for the next few days. The cavity under the rented house was said to be 'a carbon copy' of the layout above. It sounded bizarre on the news because viewers weren't thinking logically. It's a brick home, so naturally the load-bearing sub-floor spaces follow the same pattern as the rooms above.

Much was made of the existence of this 'subterranean dungeon', as one ambitious journalist put it. But all that greeted police when they explored the dark recesses of this basement room were big huntsman spiders and a colony of miniature bats. Years later, I remember Bill telling me how chuffed he had been about their encounter with the bats. They went looking for horrors, and they got more than they bargained for!

*

One August morning in 2016, I had an interesting encounter with a fellow I'd called to the farm to pump out our septic tank. I watched as he connected a wide pipe to the outlet. Within minutes, the pump started making gurgling noises. The operator unhooked the pipe, gave it a shake, and out fell three plastic toilet freshening canisters. I hurriedly assured him they hadn't come from my family, as we never used them. The previous tenants must have been the culprits.

This mundane find sparked an intriguing conversation with the pump-out man about the strangest items he'd found in septic tanks.

'What's the worst thing you've ever found in a tank?' I asked him.

'A horse's head,' he replied.

'Really? Well, I don't suppose they flushed *that* down the toilet,' I joked.

'Nope,' came the reply, as if I was being serious. 'People put dead animals in their tanks to kick-start the action of bacteria. Breaks everything down.'

'Hey, I might try that next time we have to dispatch a rooster.' He didn't answer, but bent over and fiddled around with the hose. Then, straightening up, he stretched his back then lit up a cigarette.

'Tell you what, though. The worst thing I ever looked for in a tank was a little kid.' His gaze told me he was genuinely haunted by the memory. I wondered at the odds. *Could this guy be the operator who'd pumped out Bill Spedding's tank?*

'You mean William Tyrrell?'

'Yeah. Little fella who went missing from Kendall,' he replied. 'Washing machine bloke who lived at Bonny Hills.' My mind raced with a dozen questions for this man. But I elected to play it cool. I didn't want to show too much interest in case he suspected I might want to use him as a source – which of course, I did.

'Ah, so *you* did that job. I remember it being on the news.' I heard my feigned nonchalance sounding unconvincing.

'Yeah, that was me.' I searched my mental question list for the top priority one.

'So, how sure do you reckon the cops were that he was in there?'

'Bloody sure,' he answered. 'To me, it looked like they were certain. And when they didn't find anything, they looked bloody pissed off, I can tell you.' He went on to describe the media's determined efforts to conjure a story out of even the most insignificant of details.

'There was this stick in the tank,' my companion recalled. 'You should've seen the fuss they made over it. A bloody stick! The way they were acting, you'd have thought it was the murder weapon.'

'So you think the little boy was murdered?'

'Well, he hasn't shown up, has he? Seems to me some bastard has offed him pretty quickly. Probably straight after he was taken.'

'So you don't reckon he just got lost in the bush?'

'Nah, mate. Someone took him for sure.' I could see from his reactions that the operator had been permanently affected by his role in the search for little William. His next statement precisely echoed my thoughts.

'Anyway, I'm just glad I didn't have to be the one to find him. It's not something you'd ever get over, finding a little kid's body in a septic tank.'

*

The search warrant was enacted on the basis of credible suspicions that Bill Spedding had something to do with William Tyrrell's disappearance. A perfect storm of circumstances had brewed against Bill. A tip-off from a family member with a vendetta set the Strike Force alight. They were onto something big. The caller had told police about historical allegations of child sexual assault against Bill Spedding. But, like a stick of dynamite with too short a fuse, it would blow up in their faces.

Despite the search uncovering nothing incriminating, police kept the pressure on. On 22 April 2015, the media were camped outside Bill's house from dawn. Someone obviously had plans in place. Something big was going down that day. Detectives descended in the early afternoon and arrested Bill Spedding on charges unrelated to the Tyrrell case.

But most onlookers were thoroughly confused, and believed that a washing machine repairman had been arrested on suspicion of involvement in the William Tyrrell matter. It would be a win-win for Strike Force Rosann, unless of course those charges came to nothing. And after three long years, that's precisely what happened.

With the search warrants proving fruitless, investigators dug into Bill's background and made what they thought was a crucial discovery – there had been some allegations of child sexual assault raised against him in the past. In the blink of a screen-dazzled eye, unfounded 'allegations' turned into 'convictions'.

During an acrimonious custody battle in 1987, Bill had been the target of a woman who elected to take the low road to bring her ex-husband down. Two weeks after Bill had cared for the couple's two children on an overnight stay, she levelled accusations of sexual abuse at him. Suppression orders at the time prevented Bill being identified as one child's father and the other's stepfather. It sounded odd that a grown man would have two young children staying with him in a caravan, until it became clear it was a routine parental access visit. Up until a few months prior, they had all been living together in the family home.

Highly respected Family Court Judge Richard Gee once branded Bill's accuser 'compulsive, obsessive and bizarre' as a witness.[19] Nevertheless, Bill was imprisoned for three months in 2015 while we all waited for the wheels of justice to turn. In a remarkably well-timed coincidence, just before the date of Bill's bail application on 10 June 2015, police revealed that they'd found a Spiderman toy in

Bill Spedding's work van. They'd found it months before, of course, when they'd executed the search warrants.

But the police persisted, bringing charges against Bill in both New South Wales and Victoria. After three months in prison, public humiliation and a cripplingly expensive trial, on 7 March 2018 Bill would ultimately be declared not guilty. The judge noted that the Crown's case relied on 'facts' already discredited and dismissed by authorities back in 1987. There was no case to answer, the judge said as she acquitted Bill and ordered costs to be paid in his favour by the prosecutors.

When the allegations were first raised, investigators had interviewed Bill and his accuser, and spoken to the children. Immediately, his accuser was advised not to pursue the matter further due to a total lack of evidence and, I suspect, a lack of credibility in the eyes of the police. Despite her best efforts, there was no medical evidence suggesting sexual assault. There was no explanation for the long delay between an event that supposedly caused such physical damage that it required medical treatment and the eventual assessment by a doctor who found nothing amiss. Conveniently, the crucial files that supposedly contained evidence had been 'lost' by the time Bill's case came to trial.

The two complainants themselves were reluctant to appear. On the stand, both supposed victims confessed that they had no memory of any such abuse. Further, they retracted their earlier statements, some which ran to forty pages in length, which had described in detail events of which they now admitted having no knowledge.

Because of the collapse of the New South Wales case, the Victorian case, which rested on the same faulty evidence, was withdrawn. Although journalists revelled in reporting stories about 'the 1987 charges' and 'previous convictions', there were no charges brought against Bill in 1987. He had never – and has never – been convicted of any crime. In fact, FACS had satisfied themselves that there was no case to answer back in 2009 when they'd looked into the matter before granting Bill and Margaret custody of their grandchildren.

Strangely, after the outrageous allegations levelled at Bill were proven false and he was completely exonerated, the Australian media took zero interest in reporting the fact of his acquittal. Bill would go on to launch an action for wrongful arrest and imprisonment against NSW Police. He also sued various media agencies for inaccurately describing him as a 'convicted paedophile'.

When Bill was first named as a person of interest in William's disappearance, I felt sure he was innocent. But I didn't really have a good reason why – it was just a gut feeling. During the time Margaret had lived next door to us, I'd got to know her. But because Bill had been juggling his Wellington business with his new set-up in Laurieton, I had never seen much of him. So, naturally, the new revelations shook me. *Am I on the wrong side?*

I'd heard reports that Marg had visited a clairvoyant to check whether Bill was telling her the truth. *Hey – wasn't their morning tea together the basis of his alibi?* I heard whispers around town that people knew Bill was involved in kids' after-school sports. *Did that mean anything untoward?* I started to wonder why the police were able to obtain such an invasive search warrant. And I wondered why the Speddings seemed to have people in their circle who hated them.

Bill must have been super-sensitive to people believing the worst of him. The media picked up any slack to make sure of that. So, already defensive, his speech and behaviour were always going to be coloured by the elephant in the room, no matter whom he spoke to. And so was the listener's perception of whatever he'd say. That kind of pressure can make people appear a little strange.

In addition, when someone pushes the nuclear button of child sex abuse, everyone runs for cover. It is arguably the most damaging form of allegation you can face. People would tell me that despite my feelings and beliefs, I just could not know what went on behind closed doors.

Before Bill's 2018 acquittal, after his release from prison on bail in June 2015, we met up by chance. I'd been shopping in Laurieton and happened to see him at an automatic teller machine. Margaret waited in the car, a 1999 maroon Ford Fairlane she affectionately called Myrtle. Bill went back to the car and got in. I followed, and tapped on the window to get his attention. His first facial expression said it all. This was a man under siege. He looked ready for a fight, until he recognised me, and even then he remained guarded throughout the conversation.

He rolled down the window and I expressed my sympathies. They were cautiously received. Margaret told me they were getting some support from people who knew them, but copping a lot of flak as well. She told me she was extremely worried about Bill, concerned for his safety. They had endured numerous threats, including phone calls from anonymous vigilantes who told them they were being watched. I told Bill if ever he wanted to access a document trail on the case, I'd been amassing material that he might find useful. Bill already knew I was a textbook author and commercial writer, so our chance meeting that day gave him a bright idea.

A few months later Bill approached me with the idea of writing a book to tell his story. He wanted to proclaim his innocence. I offered to do it in the capacity of a ghostwriter. I wanted to do the book free of charge, as a means of helping him and Margaret out – they were in deep financial distress because of the costs of Bill's defence. I saw this as an opportunity to help them recoup some of their financial losses. The Speddings would become more than $200,000 indebted to Bill's brother, who had mortgaged his house to help Bill raise bail and fight the child sexual assault charges.

Suspicious-minded people have asked me why I offered to work pro bono on such a project. All I can say is it's been a part of my professional life as a teacher, a tutor and a writer for as long as I've been working. Countless people do this as a matter of course in their professional lives. When you've written dozens of books over your life, as I have, ghostwriting someone's life story isn't such a mountain to climb as it might seem to someone who hasn't done it. Granted, I hadn't anticipated the massive job his book would become when I made my offer. But I didn't think it was a big deal to do some writing for a person I considered the victim of a terrible injustice.

Most fortnights for the next three years, I would meet with Bill and Margaret, at my place or theirs. Marg would serve tea cake and sandwiches and we'd sit around the table or on the couch and get into it. He would tell me about key life events and I would write the material up for the book. The book is written in Bill's voice, from his point of view. It includes Bill's experiences in jail, at the trial and after his eventual acquittal. When the time came to seek a publisher for the book, it was treated like a hot potato. No one quite knew what to make of Bill's story.

*

'Is he still outside?' Bill asked as he looked through the curtains of his front living room window on one of our storytelling afternoons.

'Yep. Hiding behind the yellow wheelie bin.' Bill kept watching him until he finally emerged. 'Idiot!' Photographers and junior reporters had been outside the house since five o'clock that morning. They would camp out frequently, hoping to catch the Speddings in the act of doing anything that could ignite suspicion.

Margaret was talking animatedly and fussing with tea and the ubiquitous iced tea cake that she'd proffer at every meeting. Reporters were either camped outside their house or calling their unlisted phone numbers. They tried to get even the tiniest titbit of information to get the jump on the other journos following the story. I was furious at the demonising of this innocent couple.

After Bill's release from prison on bail, and during his trial – which had stretched over three years – we had maintained regular contact. But I worried that I may become unwittingly poisoned against Bill by what I was reading and hearing from other sources. The pressure really got to me. I'd spend night after night reading, researching and trying to join dots between all sorts of people. I tried to come to an understanding of why the police were so hot on Bill's trail. I asked Bill himself – he said he didn't know. All he could tell me was that the police gave him the impression that they were certain of his involvement in William's disappearance.

Playing devil's advocate, I tried to come up with a workable scenario for how he might've pulled off an abduction. None of it made sense, in light of the timeline of that morning in September. Would a tradie really drive out to a client's house in a quiet neighbourhood and steal their grandchild? In broad daylight? In a sign-written van, to boot? I tried to determine a powerful motive, beyond the usual. It seemed there would've been easier targets for Bill to stalk. Like many other people, I sleuthed the families and wider circles of the families. There were startling connections that freaked me out completely. How could one of the Spedding clan know some of the Tyrrells? Were they all in cahoots?

All the while, I kept working for Bill, looking down one trail after another, unaware that some of them would lead me down some very deep rabbit holes. In the end, I threw my lot in with the Speddings and set about doing whatever I could to help Bill clear his name. It was the right thing to do. I couldn't let unsubstantiated rumour and innuendo rule my conscience. I had to follow the evidence wherever it led, and it didn't lead me to Bill Spedding's door.

Meanwhile, some imbecile was sending Bill text messages purporting to be from William Tyrrell.

'Mummy. I want to come home,' said one message. These distressing threats were taken seriously by the police and they were investigated, in case they were linked to the real perpetrator. They were horribly sick pranks. The number couldn't be traced.

Pressure on Bill reached a crescendo when he was jumped and bashed outside a pizza shop in Kew one afternoon. The perpetrators faced charges over the assault, which began with a simple inquiry: 'Aren't you that Bill Spedding?' Bill and Marg would be refused service at food outlets and even at a local pathology clinic, whose staff seemed to suffer from a strange pathology of their own. And it was catching.

In March 2015, a tip-off from a local resident led to a fresh search being conducted, this time around Long Point Drive, a bush track off the Ghost Road that traverses some dense forest. According to a witness granted day release from prison to testify at the inquest, Bill Spedding's work van was seen exiting that part of the forest via a dirt track on 13 September 2014. The witness surmised that because his own vehicle was known to Bill, when he drove past, Bill ducked down beneath the dashboard to avoid being spotted. The inference was, of course, that Bill must've been up to no good.

Police filmed a video drive-through, and combed a significant area of bushland for clues. Although the media had a field day reporting irrelevant finds including animal bones, nothing relating to the disappearance of William Tyrrell was located. Bill Spedding categorically denied being there on that particular day, or on any other day before or since.

He was celebrating the end of the football season with his family at the Laurieton United Services Club, some twenty minutes' drive away. In 2019, the Tyrrell inquest was presented with a video showing Bill Spedding enjoying a beer at the club at the time in question, just as he'd always maintained. The witness was returned to prison and Mr Craddock advised us to disregard his testimony. Earlier, he had anticipated the man's malicious intent, saying that the evidence to be presented after the adjournment 'appears to contradict whether a person has any involvement in the case'.

From the start of 2015 until mid-2017, Bill Spedding was the media's prime candidate for the abductor of William Tyrrell. After all, he was at the house, wasn't he? No, actually he wasn't. The media had reported incorrectly that Bill was at the house the day William vanished. Later, they watered the story down a little, reporting that he was *expected* at the house that day. Neither of those assertions proved true. The truth about Bill's movements in relation to number 48 Benaroon Drive was entirely uncomplicated, as the truth often is.

I asked Bill to relate the details he remembered of his encounter with Nancy Wyndham in 2014.

*

On Saturday 6 September, Bill took a phone call from an elderly woman from Kendall. He'd written down the address, noting that Benaroon Drive was a street just off Batar Creek Road. But he'd misheard the name and wrote down 'Tar Creek Road' in his work notebook. The next Tuesday, he called into a shop on his way through Kendall to ask about it when that name failed to register on his satellite navigation system. The proprietor set him straight.

Bill drove out to Nancy Wyndham's house. She led him around the side pathway and they entered the laundry from an external door. He diagnosed the problem. The machine's printed circuit board had failed and it needed a new balance switch. Nancy had mentioned she'd hoped to have the machine back up and running before her visitors arrived for the weekend. She didn't specify who, but Bill assumed it was family.

Bill assured Nancy that he would order the parts right away and made an estimate on the cost for the repair work. As he packed up his tools, Bill arranged with Nancy Wyndham to call and let her know when the parts for the machine would arrive. They could then decide on a time to have them installed. Bill couldn't recall precisely when he placed the order, but told police that it would generally have been in by 1.00 pm the following day.

At his first police interview, Bill could not remember whether the parts had arrived on Thursday morning or Friday afternoon. It mattered a great deal, because if they were delivered Friday afternoon, he would be in the clear. He could not logically have gone to Benaroon Drive to fit the parts unless he had them in hand. However, if they had arrived on Thursday afternoon at his Bonny Hills house, Bill would have been in a prime position to arrive at the Wyndham house unannounced to finish the job sometime on Friday morning, before or after the school assembly he had attended that day. Anna's statements to police certainly seemed to float the possibility that her mother expected the repairman to just show up without calling.

At the inquest, Bill Spedding's lawyer Peter O'Brien accepted the Coroner's invitation to put some questions to William's foster mother. Anna's reaction to Mr O'Brien was defensive when he drew her attention to a portion of her police statement concerning the telephone call she'd made to his client, Bill Spedding. O'Brien explained that he knew Anna had placed a call to the whitegoods repairman at 9.03 am. He asked her why she'd made that call.

'The machine had been left partially dismantled and unusable,' she said, repeating what she had said to the police originally – that when she and Nathan first arrived, Nancy had told her daughter they couldn't do any laundry.

'I thought two weeks was an excessive time to have to wait, so I decided to check up on whether the parts had arrived,' Anna's statement reads. O'Brien wanted Anna to explain why her mother had told her she'd been waiting for two weeks when Bill had assessed the machine and ordered the part only three days earlier, on 9 September.

Anna didn't have an explanation for the discrepancy, insisting her mother told her she'd been waiting two weeks. I wondered if the mystery might be explained by the machine having been non-functional for some time before Spedding was called in. O'Brien reiterated that the parts had been ordered on 9 September. But Anna didn't do herself any favours with her reply when O'Brien asked her whether it was possible she or her mother was mistaken about the timeframe.

'Anything's possible,' she said curtly. Anna called Bill Spedding from her mother's landline, but she didn't remember whether she'd called his home or mobile telephone. In any case, the call only reached his voicemail. She said she didn't remember whether she left him a number to call back. O'Brien's questions kept coming:

'Is there a cordless phone at your mother's? Where is it situated in the house? Does it have an answer function? Does it record incoming messages silently or audibly if a call is missed?' The lawyer's line of questioning was clearly leading to the point that she didn't receive Bill's return call, and that telephone records show that Bill did call back that day. When he did, there was no answer at the house.

Anna said she didn't make many calls that day. Her mobile phone was in the house while she was out in the yard and on the verandah. She explained she wasn't diligent in checking messages and doesn't remember whether police checked messages left on any of the phones that day. O'Brien persisted.

'Can I test your memory?' O'Brien asked. 'Do you recall your mother listening to a message from Bill Spedding at about 2.45 pm about the washing machine parts coming in?' Anna said she believed her mother mentioned it one afternoon, but couldn't remember which day the parts had arrived.

'On these [telephone] records I can see that following the call to Bill Spedding, a call from a Geoffrey Owen was made to my mother's landline. I have no recollection of this phone call. I know that Geoff Owen is my mother's handyman, but I do not know anything else about him.' The mystery of the forgotten call was cleared up when Anna explained that the two adults were out in the driveway with the children at the time Owen had telephoned.

'I think we went out to ride the bikes shortly after the phone call I made to Spedding. The phone cannot be heard from where we were riding the bikes,' she said.

Geoffrey Owen was a qualified electrician and electronic technician who lived in Logans Crossing in 2014. The sixty-six-year-old kept a diary of all his work appointments. Owen had done some plumbing for Nancy back in June. On 8 September, Nancy asked Owen to quote on replacing some rotting boards on her deck. He came to the house, looked at the job and rang through a quote. Nancy gave him the go-ahead to repair the deck on Tuesday 16 September. Then, on 12 September, he received a call from Nancy Wyndham.

'Can we put off the job to a later date. It is my grandson that is missing. Young William is my grandson.'

*

The William Tyrrell inquest was dogged by privacy issues, stalling and set-backs throughout the twelve-month period between March 2019 and 2020. In July 2019, an order was made preventing an affidavit and an exhibit relating to a person of interest from being made public. The Coroner made special mention of the fact that during the application by Robin Bhalla, barrister for the NSW Police Commissioner, there was no contradictor. On 13 September the order was challenged by a lawyer for Channel Nine, who applied to have the closed court order revoked, citing the public interest. The application was unsuccessful, provoking outrage at the bar table.

Bill Spedding's lawyer, Peter O'Brien, reacted angrily, reminding the Deputy State Coroner that his client didn't have the benefit of a closed court when he was so publicly named as a person of interest. O'Brien had a point. Both FACS and the NSW Police had pushed for court closure and non-publication orders from the outset of the inquest. The brief of evidence was heavily redacted, prompting concerns about open justice. O'Brien and Swift were becoming fed up with being left out of the loop.

Both supported Channel Nine's application to have the secrecy orders lifted, explaining there was an appearance of actively opposing openness. This was clearly directed at counsel assisting the Coroner. O'Brien's frustration boiled over at what he saw as an arrogant disregard for fairness, prompting this mild reply from Mr Craddock, 'It's always frustrating to lawyers especially when there's something happening they don't know about.' Mr Craddock's tone was that of a school principal chiding a teenager. I felt the moniker I'd given him on the first day was justified – The Boss. 'If it were possible to broaden the scope of people who could be permitted to observe the evidence, we would do so,' said Mr Craddock.

O'Brien's real beef was in relation to applications he'd made to call certain witnesses that weren't listed. These people included former lead detectives Gary Jubelin and Hans Rupp. 'Each of these police officers did have significant involvement in the investigation at the highest levels,' he argued. O'Brien was irritated that he'd not been presented with statements from either Rupp or Jubelin. With Rupp's retirement and Jubelin's removal as Strike Force leader, it seemed no one with ultimate responsibility was available for questioning.

The public gallery shared his annoyance. He'd been limited to grilling Detective Sergeant Laura Beacroft, who could plausibly claim ignorance of certain machinations – such as media tip-offs that led to the Spedding circus – due to the timing of her involvement in the case.

Michelle Swift, representing Brendan Collins, added a plea to bring these seasoned detectives forth to 'speak to the overall narrative of the investigation'. For the birth family, and for more than a few impartial observers, the inquest did indeed come across as an exercise in storytelling.

Both applications to hear from these witnesses were denied. Rumours circulated that Jubelin was itching to get on the stand and that Mr Craddock was standing in his way. In fact, a slightly embarrassing scene had unfolded the previous week in Taree when Jubelin got in Mr Craddock's face as the courtroom was emptying for an adjournment. He was seen vigorously making his case to testify, but even though he got up close and personal, his argument hit a brick wall.

It must have been infuriating for the detective to watch his investigation being picked apart thread by thread without having any right of reply. The Coroner gave her reasoning that, since the inquest was such a long way away from making a ruling, if Jubelin did appear as a witness, focus on William would be lost at a crucial point. But O'Brien persisted. He reminded the inquest that Bill Spedding has never been convicted of any child sex offence.

'This has been a frustrating and damaging investigation for Mr Spedding,' he maintained. He went on to question why some persons of interest were identified while others stayed in the shadows. He spoke forcefully about the community's entitlement to know whether things could have been done better. But Her Honour was adamant: 'If there is a need to examine the adequacy of the police investigation, it is not now. Should we get to that point, it may be at that time I would consider any application made.' Addressing O'Brien's other concern, she added, 'I accept that Mr Spedding has suffered consequences as having been named as a suspect.'

In 2019, the day before they were scheduled to testify at Taree, Bill and Margaret invited me to meet them for lunch. I suggested Sailo's. It was sad to see the reaction Bill caused when he appeared anywhere in public, even after being completely exonerated. People's expressions darkened as recognition dawned, then they began whispering across the table, leaning forwards in conspiratorial postures. Bill brushed it off, but I could see Marg was upset. She forced a loud laugh as if enjoying herself.

My outrage at the Speddings' ill-treatment returned forcefully that day. After staying in a hotel in Taree for most of the week, it turned out that the Speddings would not be called to the stand until the inquest returned to Sydney. They had no choice but to drive the five-hour trip back to Wellington, before heading down to Sydney for the final week.

Bill has a lot to say, and he has told me his whole story. His narrative gave me a plausible explanation of his complete innocence. It was appropriate that as a ghostwriter, I became haunted by the story I wrote. But Bill will tell more of his story in his own time. He could genuinely be the unluckiest washing machine repairman in the world.

11

LONG ODDS

In some ways, this case delivered a masterclass to the Australian public in what *not* to do when your child goes missing. Attempts to 'manage' public perceptions usually backfire. The very fact that the foster parents engaged a public relations firm put people offside. Their obstinate refusal to be identified has plagued the investigation and stirred up suspicious minds.

We were assured that William Tyrrell's foster status had nothing to do with his disappearance. That was a big statement, and Mr Craddock wanted it established from the very outset. At face value, Mr Craddock was saying that neither Karlie or Brendan, nor their associates, abducted the child, despite having done so before – technically, at least.

The police considered William's foster parents suspects in the beginning, until at least the end of September 2014. But they were reassured that if FACS or Young Hope had any concerns, they wouldn't still have custody of Lindsay. Nevertheless, people made a sport of pointing suspicious fingers. William's foster family looked decidedly uncomfortable in the courtroom. They tried to ignore the icy stares and unmasked hatred coming from certain quarters. But from my seat behind them, I overheard Anna whisper to a companion.

'They keep looking at me.' 'They' were William's birth family. Seat shuffling shielded her from their steady gaze. When the foster parents took the stand, their testimonies only increased suspicion. Public indignation would be further inflamed as certain discrepancies came to light. Paradoxically, the less possible it seemed that these polite, well-to-do people could be criminals and liars, the more they were suspected of orchestrating a cover-up.

It was pretty easy for vindictive Facebookers to cajole working-class Australia into hating William's foster parents. Television journos also had a tilt. They seized on the way William's birth family were 'forced' to enter the court via the front door, exposing them to the cameras, while the foster carers were secreted through a private entrance. But I didn't see any forcing. And as far as I could tell, no one from the birth family made requests for special entry arrangements. Admittedly, Anna and Nathan made quite a splash early in the proceedings when they were ushered into court by the recently retired NSW Minister for Police, Troy Grant. The dignitary was booted and suited for the occasion, escorting the couple in an unmistakable show of solidarity with officialdom.

Online, journos made much of a formal complaint against a cameraman who'd tried to film William's foster parents leaving the inquest, in breach of court orders. Some newshounds paid for interviews that painted the gulf between the families in lurid colour. It showed up nicely onscreen. Public sympathy for a lost little boy highlighted a class divide, and we all took sides, even if unwittingly.

In September 2019, near the close of the second inquest sitting, someone posted a family photo of Nathan Thomas being silly with the children by wearing a pair of underpants on his head and pulling a face at the camera. No one knows how the photo was obtained. But it ignited a flurry of derogatory comments on Facebook.

'Something not right about that man at all.'

'Not normal behaviour at all. Whose undies are they?"

'Probably LT's.' [The initials refer to William's sister, Lindsay Tyrrell.]

'He's one sick man, that's for sure.'

'Dickhead! Needs to learn to tell the truth!'

'Captain f***kn Underpants.'

In 2020, we heard news that a woman was charged after making fourteen nuisance phone calls to Nathan, accusing him of various crimes. Some people went so far as to show up at the foster parents' house. One vigilante did a short stretch in prison for harassment. Undaunted, the moment he was released, he got right back to it.

During his time in the slammer, the man's outraged supporters continued to carry the torch for him. One magistrate called him misguided and a self-appointed 'avenging angel of justice'. It was an unfortunate choice of words that implied there was an injustice to rectify.

Whether starting trouble or inciting others to do so, the net effect was to make things intolerable for William's foster parents. In 2019, Anna had described the awful situation to the media:

'You're dealing with the trauma of a child missing, being right in the middle of an investigation, fighting to have your voice heard, trying to get your life back to normal … and then to be subjected to people driving past our house, taking photos, publishing it all over Facebook …' In spite of this, Anna and Nathan didn't take most of their troubles to police until months later, when they reached breaking point.

'We had many conversations where we just said, you know what, we don't want the police focusing on what's happening with us. We want the police to focus on what's happening with William.' Which wasn't much, according to the couple in similar media interviews.[20]

174

The foster family clearly knew that even well-meaning interference is still interference. Schapelle Corby wanted to use her highly publicised release as a convicted drug smuggler in Bali to focus attention on William's case. News footage showed her emerging from her Kuta home with William's picture prominently attached to her handbag. Anna and Nathan were unimpressed and their response was swift. In a case of 'get off our team', they hastily released a statement to distance themselves from the Corbys.

It's reasonable that the foster carers were uncomfortable with scrutiny. Anna cited Lindsay's needs as a key motivating factor. Her foster status and her identity as William Tyrrell's sister must not be permitted to affect her future. These were compelling reasons for them to stay out of the spotlight. And the vitriolic attacks they endured proved Anna's fears were well-founded.

But there must be a balance. Australians had legitimate questions that demanded answers. The more obstructed they felt in getting them, the more it seemed this mysterious foster couple were being over-protected. At first, people assumed FACS were responsible. In Australia, there's a technical term for that particular protocol: arse covering. But actually, the stonewalling had been initiated by Anna and Nathan on the day William disappeared. They had issued a directive. They were not to be photographed or named. Both made complaints to police that their privacy was at risk.

*

From the first hour of the search, Nathan Thomas was in a frantic state of alert. He testified in 2019 that he'd searched non-stop for the first few days. Anna also asserted that her husband was out searching before she made the emergency call.

'I cannot remember what I spoke to the police about,' said Anna. 'I was too stressed. When I was on the phone, Nathan was still out searching. I think my mother and Lindsay were at the house.' There were times in those first days when Nathan would suspend the hunt to fit in other pressing activities like interviews and scene walk-throughs. But the sporadic nature of his early search efforts struck some people as suspicious.

Once the initial shock wore off, however, Nathan was consistently active in the investigation. He was at the command post from 5.00 am, asking police for updated maps. He wanted to know what dams and waterways had been drained, which sections of bush had yet to be covered, what forensic results had been returned. He was searching on foot and keeping tabs on developments. Police records indicate that Nathan Thomas tirelessly pushed for information, pored over maps, requested frequent updates and campaigned for extra support on the ground, in waterways and in the air.

As for how Nathan was cleared as a suspect, a few factors were assessed. His car's location was tracked through point-to-point cameras, through the onboard satnav system and triangulation of his phone signals. He can be seen on CCTV at the Lakewood precinct, precisely where he said he was – when he said he was. His receipts and bank statements match the point of sale details at a pharmacy called Your Discount Chemist.

Nathan's business calls and the people he contacted all checked out. He was seen at the Kendall shops at exactly the time he said he picked up his mother-in-law's newspapers. His phone data tallies with his testimony except for some text messages he seems to have deleted some weeks prior to the trip north. He couldn't explain the lost messages, but put them down to a periodic dump that everyone does from time to time without a precise memory or motive. Everything police have in regard to Nathan Thomas puts him in the clear.

But it was a different situation for Anna Wyndham and her mother Nancy. When it came to their movements that day, we could only take their word for it. Their accounts differed at points, although the discrepancies were inside normal investigation parameters. Leaving aside the scenario that Nancy, a frail senior citizen, killed William in a fit of temper, the key claim that remained contested was Anna's report of seeing the two suspicious-looking cars. It was almost a year later – on 6 September 2015 – that the public would first hear about them.

The Nine Network's *60 Minutes* aired a special report and police released a recording of Anna's 000 call.[21] The timing of these releases suggested to some that there was a link between the two pieces of information.

In the heat of the crisis, Anna had forgotten to mention seeing two cars. We can understand that. But what are we to make of the police's decision to withhold the information for twelve months? Some felt it implied that police didn't initially believe Anna. But these are highly trained investigators, well used to taking evidence from unreliable witnesses. Going back over old media releases, I could see that Strike Force Rosann was looking at this information with great interest from the very beginning. In fact, in early public appeals for information, the focus of their inquiries became car parts that may have fallen off an old, beaten-up vehicle or vehicles.

Police knew the sighting of vehicles could pare down their lists of suspects, but with no residents seeing any cars, Anna's testimony could not be verified. So why did police decide not to push in this direction with the media? In 2015 Gary Jubelin fronted the cameras to explain that the decision was part of a carefully designed investigative strategy. Very few people involved in policing in Australia have had more pressure on them to get a result, so I'll take his word for it.

With police issuing multiple public appeals to anyone connected to the cars, it seemed incredible that the drivers – if they were innocent – never came forward. None of the neighbours said they had any visitors that morning. And no local person was able to shed any light on who might have owned them. That is, until 2019.

Imagine it's true those vehicles were there, and that no one else saw them. Let's accept this staggering fluke. Is it believable that you'd later notice specific details, yet not remember seeing the cars at all when prompted by the emergency telephone operator's question – was there anyone suspicious in the area – any vehicles?

'No, no. No, no. Not that I am aware of,' replied Anna. In short, this would be a very silly story to tell, told in a most unhelpful way – way after the critical time period. But it's not silly if it's true. Truthful witnesses do tend to appear unbelievable at times because they see no need initially to seem credible. They're simply relating facts, and remembering more as time goes on. There's no compulsion to persuade. They just presume they'll be believed.

In his second police statement, when asked for his thoughts on the two vehicles, Nathan failed to shine any light on the issue.

'Sometimes I can not notice things. I can't recall seeing them, but that doesn't mean they weren't there.' He did, however, reveal in a police statement that the cars narrative supported a gut feeling of his.

'I keep thinking and hoping there's an element of ... someone from the family.'

'You're talking the biological family?' the interviewing detective asked.

'Mmm.'

Most people report a child missing after they've been out of sight for three hours, sometimes even longer. The timing of Anna's call is way inside that average. To me, this speaks of the foster family's suspicion that William was targeted. No doubt they wondered whether it could be because of his foster status. There had been talk of finalising William's and Lindsay's status in their family through adoption. If so, perhaps the abductor was someone from his birth family. This was certainly the impression Anna gave when she shared her almost palpable impression that someone had grabbed him by the shoulders, lifted him up and spirited him away.

*

The parental cover-up idea rears its head every time there's a mystery around a child's death or disappearance. Some of the speculation arising around the foster family was purely fantastical, malicious and foolish. Sceptics cite statistics telling us that missing or dead children have usually fallen victim to an act of violence perpetrated by a loved one. That is true.

But overwhelmingly, these cases are murders, not accidents. They are premeditated, not hurried cover-ups. Even with premeditation, time and all the motivation in the world to cover up your crime, it isn't easy to get away with murder.

Was William Tyrrell an accident victim? Would they really have cooperated with a huge search when evidence could be uncovered exposing their guilt? Would they really trust an elderly widow to stick to the lie? Would their hopes of adopting Lindsay be sufficient motivation to justify the lunacy of a grand subterfuge? Would losing a child in their care be viewed any less harshly by FACS than failing to protect him from a genuine, unforeseen accident?

Why not go with a different story, one more plausible than a highly improbable abduction scenario? An opportunistic stranger who couldn't have known William was at his grandmother's house? A couple of passers-by whom no one else saw? Someone who followed the family without detection for hours along the highway?

Criminologists across the globe tell us that cases where loved ones cover up genuine accidents are rare. Plenty of accidental deaths occur within families, but they are not commonly concealed. I know what you're thinking – if a cover-up has worked, we won't know about it. Yep. Unfortunately, that's life. We don't know what we don't know.

What we do know is that accidents are common and kidnappings are extremely rare. We also know that while abduction can occur on the spur of the moment, it takes an awful lot of effort, an awful lot of commitment. But domestic accidents require no effort at all. Daily, parents of toddlers on every patch of this planet put their hands to their heads in breathless horror as they witness a wrong step, a close shave or a miraculous re-gather.

In other instances, we hear that a child was denied their near-miss – accidentally run over in the driveway; crushed by a toppled TV or shelving; drowned when someone didn't lock the pool gate properly. Cases where climbing, skylarking, pushing or play-fighting results in a death are also well-represented in the national statistics. But in most cases, even when someone may have neglected their duty of care, there's a common response. A child's family members tend to do what comes naturally: they call for help.

Loved ones are hard-wired to do anything they can to save their young. Seeing someone you love in serious danger, pain or distress is not something you can be cool-headed about, especially mere minutes or hours later. Trauma takes a toll. It creates panic. It distorts reality and confuses memory. These are not ideal conditions for hatching a plan to avoid taking responsibility.

Even in premeditated murder cases, it's difficult to overcome crime scene evidence that will invariably contradict the story told to police. We've all seen enough *CSI* and *Forensic Files* to know that. Blood spatter patterns, DNA, positioning, timing, conflicting statements, surprise witnesses and many other variables are too difficult to manipulate. Criminals need time to plan and prepare. Imagine how much harder it is for innocent people to compose themselves and cover their tracks after an accidental killing. Innocent people don't have any motivation to lie to the authorities.

According to global statistics, when people kill their loved ones, it's usually no accident.[22] There's a motive and somebody stands to benefit. But, despite all of this logic, the Foster Carer Snow Job theory just wouldn't go away. And that, Anna and Nathan's opponents told me, is because William was not their own flesh and blood. For years, I encouraged these people to look again at the stakes – to weigh the risk of failure against the small chance of getting away with it. Because those are some very long odds.

12

POKER FACE

Within just days of William Tyrrell's disappearance, residents in what were suddenly the two busiest streets in Kendall were turning on each other. Anyone was fair game. Could one of the neighbours be a child abductor? It seemed in that little estate in Kendall, the most mundane of observations could raise suspicion against someone. It could be a person's natural curiosity which tempted them to do some unwelcome rubber-necking. It could be a penchant for wearing woollen hats, movements to and from tennis or odd sleeping habits. Or it could be a long-standing vendetta. No one was exempt from being a potential candidate.

On the search's fourth day, Kendall awoke to a possible breakthrough in the case. And the nature of the find filled everyone with dread. A patch of red stuff that looked like blood had been located just a couple of kilometres from the place where William was last seen. Forensic testing revealed that it was blood, but it came from an animal, most likely a cow that had recently given birth. But police took interest for another reason.

A male in a white ute was seen sitting near Fox's Creek Road. The man was noticed intently watching police who'd just found the red patch, what they call a 'blood find'. He was viewed with suspicion because he seemed to take too much interest in the goings-on during a forensic operation. This man was later identified and ruled out. He was just a rubber-necker, they said.

Another local suspect came into view for a different reason. Neighbours had the impression that an Ellendale Crescent man was a bit unusual. They called him 'the Beanie Man' because he wore a knitted hat all year round. A local bus driver confirmed that the Beanie Man had been on the 8.55 am bus to Port Macquarie earlier that morning, ruling him out as a suspect.

*

Questions were also raised about a married couple in their late seventies who lived in Benaroon Drive. The woman recalled her surprise at her husband's early return from tennis that day. Her husband, whom I will call the Tennis Player, awoke around seven. He donned his tennis shoes in the garage, reversed the car, drove to the Kendall General Store for a newspaper and arrived at the Kendall tennis courts at 8.10 am.

From there, it gets complicated. The man said he played tennis until 10.15 am. He told police in his first interview that he left the courts and returned home. But in a second statement in 2015, he revised this timing after detectives presented him with CCTV footage in which his car was seen leaving earlier than he first said. Police recovered eight images timestamped between 9.32 and 9.34 am. The camera's timestamping was slow by nine minutes (an odd echo in this case), putting the Tennis Player's departure at no later than 9.43. The man swears he didn't reach his home, a two-minute drive away, until 10.15. 'My husband got home from tennis about 10.20 am and I remember thinking that he was early home because he usually doesn't get home until 11 am,' his wife told police.

Some people wondered where he was for that extra half-hour. Police certainly did.

When asked about his early departure, the Tennis Player had different reasons on different occasions. Police were particularly interested in his claim of seeing Senior Constable Wendy Hudson receiving a call, which the man inferred was about a missing child. Hudson was not at the tennis club in a policing capacity, but because she has officiated at the tennis club for years.

'The reason I came to leave the tennis club,' the Tennis Player said, 'was that Wendy Hudson, who I knew was a police officer, received a telephone call on her mobile telephone. I saw her using the telephone. I am not sure where she was standing where she took the call. After Wendy finished the call I heard her say something to make me think there was a child missing. I cannot recall if she said where the child was missing from.'

The difficulty is, the Tennis Player didn't mention Hudson's phone call about a missing child in his initial statement on 25 September 2014. No one knows why. In fact, the man couldn't have seen Hudson take a call about a missing child, and this raised the possibility that he had inside knowledge. Or, his recollections were simply muddled. Hudson's call needs to have occurred just before 9.43 am, when CCTV footage has him leaving the Kendall courts. But William Tyrrell was not reported missing until 10.56 am, meaning that the toddler was not the subject of the call. Neither the Tennis Player nor Wendy Hudson knew a thing about the drama while at tennis.

Wendy Hudson is a highly regarded police officer whose testimony seems watertight. She clearly recalled the timings in her statement.

'At 12.21 on Friday, I was at home when my sister in-law Allison Kennedy informed me a three-year-old boy was missing in Kendall and they wanted help to search. I contacted Senior Constable Chris Rowley on his mobile and he said there was a three-year-old missing in Benaroon Drive, Kendall.' Kennedy first heard the news when she called her friend Chris Rowley earlier that morning about another matter.

Wendy Hudson's phone records confirm she did make a call at around ten o'clock, but by the Tennis Player's timeframe, he had already left tennis by then.

Here we find another example of a witness who seems to have made two errors: he couldn't recall exactly when things occurred, which is understandable, and he conflated facts he knew before an incident with facts discovered afterwards. This was an infectious malady, it seems.

So far, there has been no closure on three issues. First, exactly why did the man leave tennis early? Second, where are the corroborating – or conflicting – accounts from other players? And third, why did the Tennis Player insist he arrived home half an hour after leaving tennis, despite claiming he went straight home, a two-minute drive away? Nobody seems able to offer explanations.

There would be multiple searches conducted around the immediate vicinity of the Benaroon Drive estate. The Tennis Player said that when police first searched his house he opened an access door under his verandah. But no one had opened any other doors or cupboards at the house. No one checked in the car. And William's foster father was met with open hostility when he asked to look inside the man's locked shed.

'The father of the missing child came back into my property,' the Tennis Player told police. 'He seemed agitated again. He didn't ask my permission and opened my roller door to my shed and went inside. He went through all the bins and cupboards and throughout my belongings in the shed.' The man and his wife both complained that Nathan was rude to them during his search of their property.

'I heard him say something to my wife along the lines of "You stuck up so-and-so". She said something back. I did not have any interaction with him and did not want to because he was rude to my wife.' Later, he added details of another encounter, this time starring himself.

'There was a man and a number of other people trying to get into the side of the shed. It was locked. He said, "I want to get in here". I said, "It's been searched, it's already been searched twice". The male said something like, "You high and mighty *%#! ... who do you think you are? You don't know what it's like to lose a child."'

*

When detectives asked Nancy Wyndham if there was anyone unusual in the area, she nominated one person – a neighbour who was a night owl. That's how I will label him to protect his identity. Nancy was hesitant to speculate about him when she made her statement in 2014.

'I don't know ... I feel a bit guilty but the police wanted to know anyone who was suspicious. I suppose if it was anyone it would be him ... He lived alone. He had these peculiar hours. I'd look out at night and the light would still be on at his place. He seemed to sleep during the day. I mean ... he was sort of like a hermit.'

A confusingly named off-duty police sergeant, Steve Kendell, went with another officer to the house after hearing information about the Night Owl. It's a small brick residence set in bushland. There are no near neighbours. The officers' repeated knocks at the door went unanswered. At first, they thought he must be asleep.

Kendell described an unusual feature of the man's house in his report.

'A wooden box had been fabricated and installed over a window. It completely covered the window, blocking out any light or vision.' Although no one answered the front door, Kendell said he heard running water. They looked through a gap in another window, this one ajar, and saw the occupant.

'Go to your door now, please. It's the police,' said Steve Kendell. The Night Owl unlocked the door and police searched his house.

Kendell said it appeared deserted, with few furnishings and a dirty kitchen sink. Police left him in peace, for the time being. His alibi seemed to make sense given his lifestyle – he was home alone, asleep.

Later that day, the Night Owl received another visit from police. They saw a step-ladder in the laundry that was set up to access the manhole. Kendell climbed it and looked around. The dust indicated it hadn't been opened for a while. He found nothing but a plastic owl used to scare birds and rats away. Fittingly for our pseudonym, they found quite a few plastic owls around the premises. Police poked around the yard and looked at the Night Owl's vehicle, but later it was discovered they hadn't checked the car's boot.

The third time police called on the Night Owl, they saw his television was tuned to a cable channel. The scrolling ribbon on the bottom of the screen was updating viewers on William Tyrrell's disappearance. The Night Owl had paused the program before police arrived and it was still frozen. Clearly, police saw, the man was watching for information on the story.

The Night Owl had been a taxi driver, which had left him with abnormal sleep patterns. He was described by neighbour Heather Savage in 2014 as being in his mid to late fifties. She described his hair as blondish grey in colour, and noted that his skin was pale and papery. The Night Owl was in poor health. He was an avid coin collector and traded them online.

When they first spoke to him, police noted the man had a small red mark on his right wrist, but when they asked him to remove his shirt to inspect his body, they found no suspicious markings. The Night Owl was questioned by police on 12 September and went to Port Macquarie Police Station on Monday 15 September, leaving his contact details. He'd decided there was too much activity in Benaroon Drive and was staying away from his home for a while.

Paul and Heather Savage knew that their neighbour slept in the day and was awake at night. Because he lived alone, they checked each night to see if his shadow was moving around the house. In the days after William went missing, Heather Savage had noticed that the Night Owl wasn't home very often. His entire routine had changed. Heather couldn't recall seeing his old white Toyota sedan parked in its usual spot out the front of his house. She had noticed over the years that if the car wasn't there, the Night Owl wasn't home.

On the Sunday and Monday after William disappeared, Heather saw that the Night Owl's car was no longer parked outside his house. She didn't see him at home on those days, but late in the afternoon on Sunday 21 September she noticed his car was home. At around 5.00 pm on Tuesday 23 September, Heather saw him drive into his driveway. When he got out of the car, he was wearing a backpack. The Night Owl walked around the house as if he was checking his windows and then disappeared out of sight.

Heather never saw his car after that Tuesday. Heather said that she saw the house lights come on each night, and presumed they were on a timer. Heather felt it was strange that the Night Owl had been back to his house but hadn't been staying there. A 2019 newspaper report informs us that the man was thoroughly vetted by investigators and ruled out.[23] But I found it interesting that just a month after William disappeared, the Night Owl sold his house and left the Kendall area.

As the police canvassed people in the estate, more names kept popping up that seemed worth a second look. The police spoke to another man, with whom Sergeant Kendell had had previous dealings, but he claimed to know nothing about William's disappearance. According to one investigator, the lantana around this man's yard was 'like 'Brer Rabbit's place'.

Brer Rabbit lived close to Benaroon Drive, in Batar Creek Road. He gave permission to police and they searched the house, inside and out, and underneath. The roof cavity was searched and nothing was found. Police obtained his consent to complete a search of Brer Rabbit's dam with a team of divers. A note I read in a police report suggested that it's a possibility other dams in the area could have been missed.

One of Nancy's closest neighbours, Judy Wilson, told police she'd heard the sound of children playing and laughing. She had gone into town that morning to run some errands and her husband wasn't home either. When she returned, William was missing.

'I don't think it was an opportunistic grab from someone who just happened to be here because we don't get strangers wandering around,' Mrs Wilson said in her statement. 'That's what I thought and that's what a lot of other people thought in the town.'

*

At the 2019 inquest in Taree, the media scrum outside the courthouse was hoping for some shots of Paul Savage. The footage showed a white-haired, craggy-faced man in his seventies, tall with slightly hunched shoulders. He attended court dressed in a tracksuit and sneakers, accompanied by his son and daughter.

Police interviews with Nancy reveal that Paul Savage had been helpful to Phillip Wyndham when he was ailing. Nancy had once called upon him for help when Phillip had fallen over. Both men were tinkerers: Paul enjoyed fixing up cars and Phillip was a former engineer. After Phillip passed away, Nancy would find Paul Savage at her back door from time to time, appearing unannounced and uninvited. At first, she took it to mean he was just checking up on her, having been recently widowed. But before long, it became a nuisance.

Nancy was never sure when Savage might appear on her private back patio. It began to unnerve her, but she couldn't pinpoint why. He'd walk through the carport and over to the back patio and just stand there. Nancy never invited him into the house, so they would chat through the screen door.

Nancy recalled that they had a bit of a tiff over Savage's dogged stance on climate change. Nancy describes herself as 'very much on the left, a left leaning politics sort of person'. Savage told her he believed all the scientists to whom she listened were crooked. Nancy described him in her police statement as 'extremely right wing and ignorant'. Having made that assessment privately, she made a conscious decision not to bring up the topic with her neighbour again.

Nancy felt it was a pushy thing to invite oneself to a neighbour's house. Sometime in 2014, after Phillip's death and before William went missing, she decided to approach Heather. She visited the Savage house to deliver her message. Heather didn't have much of a reaction, but promised to talk to her husband about his visiting habit.

Paul Savage then altered his usual walking route, which had previously taken him past number 48. Presumably this was to avoid Nancy's house. He was a regular walker of the bush tracks and, according to neighbours, knew the area like the back of his hand. Nancy told police she felt Heather probably hadn't known about her husband's visits. Nancy couldn't say whether she felt he had any romantic intentions.

Nancy recalled that she didn't see Paul Savage for a number of weeks after speaking to Heather about the unwelcome visits. Feeling she may have ruffled his feathers, Nancy made a point of telling Heather she wasn't holding anything against him.

'And he seemed to be normal after that,' she told police. 'He was such a loner,' she told police. 'Just awkward. Awkward with people.'

*

Nancy Wyndham told police that Paul Savage would have seen the Tyrrell children at her house a few times. The 2013 Christmas street party was held at Millie Jones' house. The Savages were there and so were William and Lindsay. The children both had their scooters. Nancy had told police Savage knew the children were being fostered. She had told people with some pride that Anna and Nathan hoped to adopt them.

Nancy didn't recall seeing Savage at all on the day William went missing. She told police that she'd assumed Savage wasn't home; she felt certain he would have assisted in searching the bush. But this is in direct contradiction to Savage's statement. He told the inquest he'd had a conversation with Nancy that day, after William disappeared.

Nancy described Heather Savage as 'a very withdrawn lady. Just very, very quiet.' Contrastingly, Paul Savage described Nancy as 'a pretty tough girl' to police. But he said that on the day William went missing, she was speaking in a higher pitch and at a faster pace than usual. She had tears in her eyes and was shaking. He recalled seeing Nathan inside the house while he was talking with Nancy. He said Nathan was crying and visibly upset. And, sensationally, he claimed that Nancy had told him that her daughter's impending adoption of William Tyrrell was to be finalised that very day.

At the inquest, Paul Savage's movements that day were fleshed out by various witnesses. On 12 September, Heather's brother Gregory Newton and his wife, Regina, were coming to stay the night. Paul and Heather had breakfast at around 6.30 am. Heather cooked a joint of meat and made a cheesecake lemon slice. She cleaned up the house in preparation for the visitors.

Paul went for a walk in the bush between 7.30 and 8.30 am. Heather usually accompanied him but, because she was expecting visitors, she stayed home to organise things. Heather Savage told police that on Thursday 11 September, she made up the spare bed for her brother and sister-in-law's visit. She remembered noticing red tail-lights in the carport of number 48 some time after 8.30 pm that night.

Savage said he remembered seeing Nathan Thomas's Land Rover at Nancy's on Thursday 11 September, parked midway along the driveway, nose in. He admitted he could only see the back of the vehicle from his place. But he contradicted Nathan, Anna, Nancy and his own wife by saying it was well before nightfall when he saw that vehicle. He knew Nathan's car by its colour, make and model, he said. But Nathan testified that he only bought the car twelve weeks earlier. Since that purchase, they hadn't been back to Kendall.

Contrary to his wife's statement, Paul Savage said neither of them knew visitors were coming to them that Friday. He felt Heather wouldn't have gone to bingo had she known. When Paul explained this at the inquest, his son and daughter frowned resignedly at each other. They could see their father wasn't helping himself. But he continued to contradict small facts from his wife's statement.

Regina Newton told police she and Gregory would never drop in unannounced. They'd telephoned Heather to arrange it. Regina recalled towels being placed on the guest bed and the room having been freshly made up with linen, indicating that Heather was expecting them.

On the day of William's disappearance, Paul Savage planned to pick up his brother from Lismore Base Hospital when he was discharged and take him home to Rappville, near Casino. Heather packed an esky with food for her husband to take along and got ready to go to bingo and lunch at the Laurieton United Services Club, as was her habit on Fridays.

Savage said that his daughter telephoned that morning. He also recalled telling Heather she'd be late if she didn't leave straight away. The time was definitely 10.35 am. He remembered looking at his watch, he told the court in 2019. Heather went to the carport, a makeshift structure covered with green shade-cloth. Their caravan was parked next to it. Both Paul and Heather Savage said that at around 10.38 Heather reversed out, did a three-point turn into Benaroon Drive, then drove off.

At this point in his narrative, I saw Paul Savage looking down at his hands. As he spoke about Heather's maroon-coloured Ford Falcon, he clasped, opened, reclasped and stared at his perspiring hands. Anna Wyndham picked up on it straight away. She whispered something to one of her seatmates and I'm pretty sure I got the gist of it. A scenario was forming in my head – which I'm sure it is in yours right now – involving a reversing maroon car and a little boy in a Spiderman suit standing in the driveway.

CCTV footage from the tennis club captured a maroon Ford sedan, model unspecified, leaving Kendall at 10.42 am, so the Savages' estimates were correct. In the images, the car's driver is not visible. It is beyond question that a maroon sedan was captured on CCTV that morning, leaving at approximately the right time to prompt some searching questions, and returning well after William went missing. But, it could've just been Heather going to and from bingo, as she'd said.

Another family with a maroon Ford – this one a Fairlane – is the Speddings. You'll recall my mentioning Myrtle earlier. It's highly likely that in their initial analysis, police thought the Savages' vehicle was Myrtle, which could've jangled their nerves sufficiently to seek a search warrant for Bill Spedding's property.

Paul Savage said he was quite clear about the timing of his movements on 12 September because he habitually checked how long his walks took him, to see if he was getting any faster. On his morning walks, he sometimes talked with a lady who lived in a caravan in the bush. She came to the campsite a few times a year. Savage said he found out later that the woman's name was Lynne. He felt she was a very honest person. He said he didn't see anyone else on his walk apart from Lynne.

On the morning of William's disappearance Savage returned home at about 8.50 am. What Savage didn't know was that Lynne was staying with a man who was listed on the Child Protection Register, having offended against adolescent males. Police had thoroughly searched the man's property and found all sorts of items – children's stuffed toys, underwear and household items. But they didn't find what they were looking for – William Tyrrell's fingerprints.

Savage testified that Heather was cooking when he came inside from his walk. He called Lismore hospital and made a few other calls concerning his brother. He remembered hearing children playing, and took it to be coming from Nancy's house. But he didn't see them. When Mr Craddock asked Savage about whether hearing the children that morning had annoyed him, he said, 'No. I didn't mind at all. Listening to kids play is wonderful.'

Paul Savage had two lots of tea and toast, he told us at the Taree inquest in September 2019. The first round was on the back patio before Heather left; the second on the front verandah after. Heather said when she'd left him, he was having a sandwich and coffee. A minor discrepancy. Heather reported that she didn't see any cars parked in the street, and her statement implied that she went out to the car alone. Savage disagreed, saying he definitely went outside with her, kissed her goodbye and waved to her as she turned the car around and drove off.

After Heather left, he locked the front door and listened to Ray Hadley's radio show, turned up loud. At some point, he called his brother, which going by the demonstration on the video played to the court, would've necessitated turning the radio's volume down. Savage said he then went to the master bedroom and bagged up some clothes.

He was planning to leave for Lismore at about 11 am. Phone records indicate that Savage did indeed call Lismore hospital at 9.02

and again at 9.59 am. Another call came from Savage's house to a diagnostic imaging centre in Port Macquarie. That call was made at 10.41, although Savage said he couldn't remember making it.

Savage remembers closing the holland blind in the bedroom, citing the need to block out the view from the Night Owl's house.

'He can see everything,' he explained. As soon as the Night Owl's name was mentioned, Savage seemed to seize upon it.

'He moved away within a matter of weeks,' he said to Mr Craddock at the inquest in 2019. Yet in the walk-through video played at the inquest, Savage doesn't mention his neighbour at all, nor the reason why he pulls the blind down.

Mr Craddock informed Savage that there was no phone call from his daughter to the house that morning. I studied him closely as he received this news. He looked blank. The Boss asked Savage to recount what happened when he heard a knock at the front door that morning. He told the court a blonde woman in her thirties was there. He recognised her as the woman who lived two doors down, but he didn't know her name. It was Anne-Maree Sharpley. She asked if he'd seen the little boy from across the road.

'He's missing,' she said. Savage told police he immediately went outside to help look for him. He said he saw Nancy outside and went over to talk to her. He could see by the way she was running around that Anna Wyndham was panicked. He saw the police arrive. Then he had a look in the bush across the road, but because it was really thick, he decided that William wouldn't have gone into it. Mr Craddock paused to let this remark simmer away while we held our collective breath, waiting to hear why else Savage might have drawn the attention of Strike Force investigators.

Savage said he walked towards the home of Peter and Sharelle Crabb and saw they'd been looking for the little boy too. They spoke briefly and then he cut through the bush and spent the next two hours searching alone. He claimed he became lost for a while, which neighbours found difficult to believe considering his familiarity with the walking trails.

But Savage insisted he got lost because he didn't stick to the trails. Eventually, he emerged from the bushland close to the back of his own house. He told Jubelin in an interview that he went inside for a cup of tea. Jubelin felt Savage's story was odd. To a detective, Savage's story amounted to one key fact: he didn't have an alibi for much of the morning when William went missing.

*

Heather Savage's brother, Gregory Newton, attended court in Lidcombe in August 2019. A striking figure, he reminded me of Ken Railings, the super-tanned dance champion from Baz Luhrmann's film *Strictly Ballroom*. He's very tall and wears an elaborate pinky ring. His white hair gives him a silver fox aura – like a man who's popular with the ladies in a Forties cabaret club. (In an interesting aside, Luhrmann got his start in film-making being the projectionist at Laurieton's Plaza Cinema. Now a national treasure we've lent to Hollywood, Baz grew up in tiny Herons Creek.)

In the early afternoon on that Friday, Gregory Newton arrived on the scene. He told police it might have been around 1.30. He parked his dark grey Isuzu utility in the Savages' driveway and saw Paul out the front of his house. Gregory helped his brother-in-law search, while Regina stayed at the house. Paul filled him in on the news of William's disappearance. 'Paul went on to say that William was a foster child, and that he was going to be legally adopted by the foster parents that day,' he told the court.

In her statement, Regina Newton told police what happened when they turned up. Mrs Newton's statement closely matched her husband's. 'Upon Greg and I arriving at Paul and Heather's house, Heather was not home. I knew Heather was at bingo but I didn't know when to expect her.' When Heather returned home around 2.00 pm there were people everywhere. Regina told her that Paul and Gregory were out searching for a missing boy. Police searched the Savages' house, including the roof space, the garage, the wood shed and underneath the house. They found nothing suspicious.

Paul Savage claimed he continued searching until seven that evening and participated in organised line searches. His brother-in-law told police they searched together at times, but he sometimes lost sight of Paul. He assumed he was still searching somewhere.

The next day, Savage woke at six. After breakfast, he and Heather saw off the Newtons, who were returning home. Then, taking a swimming pool net, Savage left the house, thinking he might check dams and waterways. But he had to abandon the search on Monday to collect his brother from hospital, a trip that didn't eventuate on Friday as initially planned. (We never heard testimony about this.)

In 2014, Paul Savage drove a silver Mitsubishi Pajero. That vehicle was parked in the front driveway of his house the entire time between Thursday 11 and Sunday 14 September. But it should be noted that the maroon vehicle belonging to the Savages was one of only two cars that left Benaroon Drive around 10.30 that morning. The other was only heard, not seen, and wasn't captured on camera.

Paul Savage was especially interested in William's history, because he too had been raised in the foster care system. In 2019, it was revealed that Savage had been haunted by an argument he heard between his divorcing parents when he was ten. They were at the railway station, fighting over which of them had to take young Paul. It seemed neither wanted him.

*

Miss Nellie's Café is just past the bridge as you drive into Kendall. Two women who were there on the morning of 12 September told

Sergeant Kendell that an unknown man with wavy chestnut hair and a two-day growth had asked for directions to Batar Creek Road. The man wore a maroon t-shirt and jeans, and looked to be in his early forties.

Another mystery man was described by Kendall General Store's former proprietor, whom I will call the Shop Lady. She told police that a 'well-dressed, well-spoken man' she hadn't seen before came in and may have asked for directions to Benaroon Drive. But the Shop Lady wasn't able to say exactly which day this occurred. She thought the person may have been driving a grey station wagon. She was annoyed that the police didn't seem anxious to speak to her, and that they'd been to speak to the bottle shop proprietor first. Evidently, this was viewed as a slight.

It seems the Shop Lady may have confused this memory with Nathan's mentioning of Nancy's address when he collected her newspapers. Another possibility is that the man was Heather Savage's brother Gregory Newton. It seems he did call into the shop that day before proceeding to Benaroon Drive.

Rheannon Chapman from Kendall Cellars had a security camera that would've captured images of people entering and leaving the General Store. Police emphasised to her the importance of retaining any CCTV footage captured immediately before and after the critical timeframe. They also asked Chapman not to discuss the 'well-dressed man' business with anyone. Odds are, they were simply seeking to avoid confusing people. Nevertheless, with Kendall being the tiny town that it is, and with local gossip an important source of entertainment, confusion reigned anyway.

13

DO YOU FEEL LUCKY?

I was absolutely floored when I first heard about Detective Chief Inspector Gary Jubelin's dismissal from the Tyrrell case. The news broke like a tidal wave over everybody who knew and loved William. Shockwaves also resonated through the ranks of the law enforcement teams who'd worked with the veteran homicide detective. Then, came even more startling news: his abrupt resignation from the police force. After I'd picked my jaw up off the floor, my conspiratorial mind entertained an intriguing thought.

'Oh, okay, nice play, Gary. I see what you're doing here.' He's purposely had himself put under the spotlight as part of a strategy to appear at odds with his team. He's made us think he's done something really wicked – recording a suspect without a warrant – that he followed a hunch that didn't find support within the ranks.

At first, the media remained quiet about the identity of the target he'd recorded. Hints came through that Jubelin might know who the abductor was, since he recorded that person without official approval. So now, anybody he'd ever questioned in the investigation would be wondering, *is it me he secretly recorded?* And that very suggestion would surely rattle those with something to hide. It would be a masterstroke of investigative strategy.

The alternative was unthinkable – that the operation dedicated to finding a missing child had descended into an egotistical cockfight among some of the finest investigative minds in this country. Incredibly, it turned out Gary wasn't foxing.

We soon learned it was Paul Savage who was the target of the allegedly illegal recordings that led to the charges of misconduct. Gary Jubelin went hammer and tongs for Savage from March 2017. He suspected Savage could have been involved in either abducting or accidentally killing William, or at least knew more than he was letting on. Savage's statements didn't add up. He couldn't account for some of his movements on 12 September 2014, and made assertions that were flatly contradicted by his neighbours.

Jubelin pursued the elderly man with vigour. He first recorded a phone conversation with Savage from police headquarters at Parramatta in November 2017. He recorded another at 10.30 pm just after Christmas in 2018, a third in May 2018 (which went for over an hour) and a fourth the following morning.

We discovered in 2020 that police had planted listening devices in Savage's house – all under the correct warrants. But the audio was poor in quality, and Jubelin didn't want to risk missing anything. He also wanted to cover himself legally against any false claims of harassment or ill-treatment that Savage might make later. So, on a visit to the house, he used his personal phone to record Savage close up. The wisdom of that decision was proven when it was revealed much of the audio captured by the bugs was inaudible.

One of the other charges hinged on the expiry of a warrant just a week before the illegal recording was made. Jubelin admits asking one junior officer to record a phone call made from police headquarters – hardly the actions of a man trying to cover his tracks. He also admits asking him to keep it off the system by passing two recordings off as captures from the official devices, not his personal phone. No doubt this was done to avoid the hassles that would come with working outside of normal operational guidelines.

Jubelin argued there was no criminal intent in it, telling the court that he had made no attempt to conceal the fact that he'd recorded those conversations. Jubelin's barrister, Margaret Cuneen SC, compelled Detective Sergeant Laura Beacroft to concede that the Strike Force were aware the recordings existed. She agreed it was no secret.

The fact that Heather Savage's maroon Falcon appears to have left Benaroon Drive in the five-minute window in which William was thought to have vanished was a compelling one to Jubelin. He led his team through an explanation of his thought process.

'Paul Savage – we know, he's a street stickybeak. His version of events was that he didn't hear any of the commotion [when William disappeared]. He went walking up into the bush uphill, got a little bit lost, and came back and had a cup of tea. That makes me suspicious. It's against his character. Someone invests so much time to look for [William] and simply goes into the house and has a cup of tea. That is strange.'

Jubelin didn't beat around the bush during Paul Savage's interview in 2017. When Savage claimed that he searched in the bush for half an hour, then came inside to have a cup of tea, Jubelin said, 'Well, that's a lie.'

'Why would I lie?' Savage retorted.

'You're covering up for Heather because there was an accident,' Jubelin said. 'Heather might have run over William.' Paul Savage vehemently denied it, saying Heather would've screamed the roof down had that occurred.

'Well,' Jubelin pressed, 'what if it wasn't Heather? What if it was you?' Gary Jubelin wouldn't back away from his recording of Paul Savage without valid warrants. He asserted that he had 'a lawful right and an operational need to record those conversations'.

In a recorded interview in 2017, Jubelin commented that Savage's car – a silver Pajero – was similar to Nathan's car. He suggests that perhaps William came running up to the car, excited to see his foster father, and was accidentally run over.

'There's no way in the world either one of us would hurt a child,' Savage replied. To Jubelin, that answer was evasive. It made a leap between a pure accident and malicious intent that Jubelin hadn't suggested.

Another possibility that no doubt occurred to Jubelin was that Savage took William as a means of exacting revenge against Nancy. Could Savage have ducked out with William and dropped him off at a pre-arranged location nearby, then left the car out the front for Heather to take to bingo? It's a possibility, considering that the Crabbs heard an approaching car perform a U-turn at the Savages' driveway at that time of the morning.

Jubelin wasn't done yet though. He went on to orchestrate an elaborate ruse in an effort to catch Savage out. He arranged for a Spiderman suit similar to the one William wore on 12 September to be placed out in bushland near the Savages' house. The idea was to shock the man into a state of confusion about what it was doing there. If Paul Savage had been involved in William's disappearance, the sight of the suit would be electrifying. To capture Savage's reactions, Jubelin had hidden cameras installed throughout the area.

As Jubelin poked the bear with some confronting lines of questioning, he felt he needed some insurance in case Savage came at him with allegations of mistreatment. So he recorded conversations using his phone.

'It was to have Mr Savage feel there was a degree of urgency to go and interfere with William's remains, potentially,' Jubelin told the court at his hearing in February 2020.

When Savage walked past the spot where the suit had been placed, he bent over and paused for about twelve seconds, looking intently at the site. He did nothing, said nothing. He just resumed his walk. Jubelin took this to mean that Savage needed time to think about what he should do. Others disagreed, saying Savage mustn't have seen the suit.

Significantly, the police had used a key detail about the suit William was wearing when he vanished. That suit – so famously photographed only from the front – had a large white spider motif on the back. But no photos of the white spider motif had ever been released. Police knew that no one but the abductor would have known about that white image.

To that end, the Spiderman suit planted in the bush had nothing white on it at all. It was all red and blue with a tracery of black lines. The next day, Savage came by again and this time reacted to seeing the suit. But he told police that he saw 'the white top with the stripes' on the suit. Why did Paul Savage say the white part of the suit had attracted his attention in the bush that day? Was he remembering something else he'd seen? We've not yet heard the answer to that question.

Then Savage changed his story. At first, he had insisted to Jubelin that he hadn't seen anything – even though he was video-recorded standing just five or so metres from the suit. But later, a phone tap captured an admission – he had seen the suit the first day, but said he'd thought it was a white cloth. Onlookers agreed that it's quite a stretch to mistake bright red and blue garments for a white cloth.

Another question that still requires an answer is where Paul Savage went for two hours after supposedly not seeing the suit that day. His absence was noted by police as particularly strange, given the fact that it occurred straight after he appeared to see the planted suit in the bush.

Paul Savage's daughter actually found one of the cameras in nearby bushland before the operation was complete, and handed it to her father. He didn't return it to police voluntarily until some time later, which further raised Jubelin's suspicions.

At Jubelin's hearing, Margaret Cunneen argued that because Savage's privacy had already been removed lawfully by warrants, there was no existing privacy for her client to have breached. It amounted to a technicality. Cunneen also strenuously opposed NSW Police's application for a closed court.

'There must be open justice in this case. Surely the application for suppression must be about specific parts of the evidence, not the whole proceeding.' Cunneen went on to explain that Jubelin had warned the NSW Police Force of the likelihood that these proceedings against him would derail the Tyrrell investigation.[24]

In 2015, before Jubelin became actively fixated on him, Paul Savage endured an immense loss. Heather Savage had died suddenly after severe headaches that were diagnosed as leukemia. According to his children, Paul took the loss hard and struggled to cope. Gregory Newton told police about how Heather's death affected Paul.

'I would describe Paul as going into severe depression as everything that they did they did together. He lost his reason to get up in the morning, and has been opening up to my wife. I haven't spoken to him myself about his depression but it's obvious to me from how much he talks about missing Heather.'

Jubelin's recordings captured some interesting audio. Paul Savage was recorded saying some odd things while walking around his empty house talking to himself. Margaret Cunneen read some of them out at the hearing.

'I'm not interested in your bullshit, mate. You're a little boy you're nobody. You're just a little boy. You're nobody. You do not tell me. I tell you. No way in the world.' It's unclear whether Savage was directing this at William, or equally likely, Gary Jubelin. Another grab captured Savage in threatening mode.

'I'm gonna run into your property too, in Gordon. This is my place. You do what I want.' When William's foster grandmother visited him in Sydney, she would take the Trainlink train to the North Shore station of Gordon. Paul Savage knew about that pattern. A third recording sounded especially damning. Savage was heard to say to his dead wife, Heather, 'Make sure you don't tell anyone love. They're after me, love. They're right after me. Sorry.'[25]

Savage insisted it was just a misunderstanding. He denied any wrongdoing. He denied having seen the Spiderman suit the previous day to reporting it. And he never addressed the issue of his strange mutterings. Although they were released in media reports, these matters were not discussed at the Tyrrell inquest for procedural reasons. But the developments certainly put Jubelin's intensive investigation of Savage in a different light.

*

As we know, Savage was of great interest to Jubelin because he claimed to have been lost in the bush in the search after William went missing. A keen bushwalker, Savage said he went on his own search for some hours right after William disappeared, only later joining an organised group. His testimony was incoherent at times, conflicting with his earlier statements.

Of course, the same can be said of Nancy Wyndham's statements. She stated she wasn't aware that Anna had taken the kids down to the front yard, twice. She didn't know about Anna's hand injury, she swore. She definitely didn't have morning tea before 10.30, and she said Anna took the pictures of William just minutes before he vanished, not half an hour. And at the inquest, lawyers never had the opportunity to straighten out all these flies in the ointment, because Nancy Wyndham – despite being of sound mind – was never put on the stand. We have never been told why. Paul Savage, on the other hand, who said his memory was deteriorating rapidly, had to answer for all of his muddles.

In the course of Jubelin's misconduct hearings in 2019, it emerged that Paul Savage had harassed a female postal worker in 2013 and was subject to a restraining order at the time that William Tyrrell went missing. Savage reportedly approached her vehicle and, taking hold of her arm, told her he wanted to spend more time with her. The woman described Savage's behaviour as 'strange' and said she was concerned about her safety when delivering mail to his house. Police were told that Savage had developed a fascination with her and had made romantic gestures and unwanted advances such as blowing kisses.

An Apprehended Violence Order was in place, which required Australia Post to terminate the delivery service of his mail to the house in Benaroon Drive. Savage had to collect his mail from Kendall Post Office. Undeterred, he visited the Kendall Post Office twice in a state of heightened emotion. He was crying and shaking as he asked to see the woman. Jubelin told the court at his hearing that witnesses heard Savage say, 'We can be together.' Although Savage said it was all lies, he never tried to contest the order made against him.

Then, in 2019, news emerged that Savage had found out the woman's date of birth from the restraining order documents served on him. Ill-advisedly, he approached her to say 'Happy Birthday'. Savage seemed to be making her business *his* business, as he had done with Nancy. The postal worker viewed Savage's comment as a thinly disguised threat that he was monitoring her and knew intimate details about her life.

In February 2014, Savage was charged with breaching the restraining order, after he approached the postal worker on her rounds. The outcome of that charge has never been made known. A little bird told me that there are other 'no bill' charges in Savage's background – which means they were withdrawn. These may have been discussed in a closed court session in March 2019.

*

Gary Jubelin's dismissal had a seismic effect. Doubtless, prosecutors took this under serious consideration before taking the unprecedented step of removing the lead investigator. What's compelling is the public way in which it happened, and of course, the timing – right before the inquest was to commence. It implied the Surveillance Act breaches were really serious. But even if misconduct had been proven, many believed that his goal eclipsed privacy in importance – Jubelin was trying to catch a child abductor.

Mainstream and social media commentators were left asking why we were not just giving this guy a quiet, in-house slap on the wrist. He was getting the job done. Surely whatever it takes is fair. Whatever means are required to capture child abductors should be open to law enforcement professionals at Jubelin's level. Far from requiring warrants, Dirty Gary should be armed with a shotgun and be permitted to blow the perp's brains out if he got half a chance. No doubt the police and the judiciary who elected to prosecute anticipated that the public would take this view.

The question is, why did they turn the public against the law enforcement establishment over seemingly minor breaches of protocol? On the surface, it stank of a cover-up, perhaps evidence of a boys' club Jubelin didn't fit into. The charges against Jubelin were halted by a global virus pandemic that stopped Petty Court proceedings in their tracks for some time. I saw sweet irony in the image of a minuscule-sized pathogen invading the giant organism of NSW Police, cell by cell, and shutting everything down.

Ultimately, Jubelin was convicted on all four counts of breaching the Surveillance Devices Act, and the court petulantly imposed fines of $2500 for each offence. Even so, Jubelin wasn't prepared to cop a criminal conviction on his record and launched an appeal. I feel the intention to bring Jubelin down a few pegs actually had the opposite effect. Not only did it elevate him to virtually heroic status, it also turned an uncomfortably glaring spotlight on what was a less than stellar police investigation. After the storm blew over and the dust settled, the state of New South Wales was all the poorer for the loss of a good cop.

A statement reacting to the decision to record criminal convictions against Jubelin was released by William's foster parents in April 2020. It aptly illustrated the tide of public outrage, thus:

> Overall, we hold grave concerns regarding the cavalier way in which police leadership have viewed William's abduction over the past two years. And, we hold deep fears for those families coming behind us and question how they might trust senior police to put their personal agendas, ambitions and bias aside to focus on solving these horrendous crimes. There needs to be greater transparency and accountability within NSW Police which can only be achieved through institutional change. Today, five years and five months on, we want to remind Australians that this is about a little boy called William Tyrrell. William is loved. He is missed every single day. William needs to come home.[26]

Jubelin is well known for his cowboy tactics, but he gets results. Some journos I've spoken to have downplayed his wins, reminding me he wasn't able to secure convictions in two infamous murder cases – Bowraville and Leveson. True, it's not right that two killers currently remain free as birds and are laughing in the face of the law. But that's life – homicide investigations sometimes go that way.

Nevertheless, Jubelin achieved a great deal in the puzzling death of Matthew Leveson – he found the body and an answer for the family, everything but a conviction. He had to do a deal with the devil to get that result. He personally participated in a staged role-play in order to catch person of interest Michael Atkins in a lie, though the ploy misfired.

Jubelin is a man prepared to take risks in the course of an investigation. And the Leveson and Bowraville families have continued to throw their wholehearted support behind the detective. Faye and Mark Leveson spoke publicly about how Jubelin's persistence enabled them to find their son's remains after years of digging in the densely forested Royal National Park at Waterfall, south of Sydney. The couple spent most weekends since 2007 conducting their own search for Matt's body and have expressed the certainty that if not for Jubelin's decisive action, they'd still be looking.

'His integrity and professionalism is beyond reproach,' they said publicly.[27] That surely counts for something. In Bowraville, he hasn't been able to put away the killer of three Aboriginal children whose families have suffered intolerable injustice. But, he says he knows who did it. As he's been famously quoted as saying, Jubelin takes homicide personally. Sadly, the Green Goblin steps in here with a message for the detective: 'They found you amusing for a while, but the one thing they love more than a hero is to see a hero fail.'

*

Jubelin came under significant criticism when he targeted Bill Spedding in the Tyrrell investigation. He was accused of having tunnel vision as he led the Strike Force, and indeed, his was a particularly dark tunnel.

Gary Jubelin was the arresting officer in the Jeffrey Hillsley case of 2003, in which Hillsley bludgeoned Michael Davies to death with a hammer while he slept on Christmas night. Not satisfied, Hillsley then turned his attention to the innocent man's ten-year-old stepdaughter.

After witnessing the unspeakably horrific murder of her sleeping father, she was tied up, tortured and brutally raped at knifepoint. Hillsley abducted the young girl, forced her to endure numerous counts of oral, vaginal and anal rape. She was certain he'd kill her when he dragged her to the deserted Chullora Rail Yards and perpetrated another violent assault. Hillsley later told police that Davies owed him $20 and, after he'd killed him for not paying up, he'd violently raped his stepdaughter because he knew it would have 'really pissed him off'.

The girl managed to escape from Hillsley and hid out in abject terror for sixteen hours before being found by police. Hillsley said it gave him pleasure to think about the father's horror had he known what he was doing to his child. It's almost impossible to see Hillsley as anything other than irredeemable, a true psychopath with no remorse and no hope of rehabilitation. He made a threat to a prison officer in 1991, telling him, 'The more that happens to me, the more the kids will suffer. They won't find me next time; it will be another Samantha Knight.'

While serving a twelve-year sentence for raping two five-year-old girls, Hillsley issued another chilling warning via the parole board. He wrote, 'A message for the community – I will be back. Thank God for little girls.' The message was signed 'Walking Evil'. Jubelin successfully had Hillsley put away for a life term. His file is marked 'Never to be released.' But the case stayed with Jubelin. He took this one very personally.

A decade later, while conducting routine inquiries in the William Tyrrell disappearance, imagine Jubelin's reaction when he discovered Hillsley's ex-brother-in-law, Bill Spedding, was at the house on Benaroon Drive the week William vanished. Bells would have gone off, loudly. He soon joined some dots between the two men and, suddenly, Bill was tarred with the Hillsley brush. When Bill's alibi couldn't immediately be verified, Jubelin's focus would turn laser-like onto this Spedding character.

Imagine the explosive effect of the aforementioned 'tip-off' about previous allegations against Bill. The Strike Force leader's heart would have been positively racing. This was the break he needed. He thought he'd got his man.

Bill Spedding told me that Jubelin appeared absolutely certain that he was guilty during his interrogation. He remembers the detective leaning over the desk, pointing his finger in his face and saying, with frightening venom, 'I know you did it. Every time that William Tyrrell's name is mentioned in this country, Bill Spedding's name will be mentioned right along with it.' That was his commitment, and that's precisely what he delivered. That doesn't make him a bad cop. It makes him an empathetic person who pursues a lead until it forces him against a brick wall.

I had occasion to speak to Gary Jubelin during the inquest. His willingness to listen made a striking contrast with other detectives I've met. I was also impressed by his shiny head, and by the fact that, unlike many detectives, he doesn't jingle when he walks. What is it about detectives, keys and small change? He wore his trademark black suit and thin black tie. His menacingly athletic physique and boxing-scarred face are at odds with the aura of Zen he gives off. I fear he'd happily punch some inner peace into anyone who he felt needed it.

I could see how Jubelin had developed a reputation for empathy. I'd had him pegged as arrogant and unapproachable and I was dead wrong. I'd presumed Jubelin had become sidetracked by the Spedding lead in the Tyrrell case. Again, I found I was wrong. Through my research into Jubelin's work on this and other cases, I came to realise he's not a man prone to distraction. He was just following the evidence wherever it led, and keeping question marks firmly inked over the contradictory or missing evidence that had prevented Spedding's elimination as a suspect.

Perhaps it was a combination of expediency and a sense of justice that motivated investigators to bring formal charges against

Spedding for thirty-year-old allegations, and we mustn't forget that the decision was validated by the NSW Director of Public Prosecutions' committal of Bill Spedding to trial.

Concurrently, Jubelin was pursuing other lines of inquiry. From the outset, Superintendent Paul Fehon had stressed that the search warrants on Spedding's properties did not represent a significant breakthrough in the case. Nevertheless, by the time supposedly 'fresh allegations' of child sex assaults from the past surfaced, Bill became the prime suspect in the public consciousness. Police didn't actively work against this perception.

The public's frustration at the lack of progress in the case boiled over on social media. People conflated the two separate issues: William's disappearance and the historic child sex allegations. Bill was positioned at the centre of the web that linked seemingly unrelated suspects. But that plan would backfire. Later, when Bill's acquittal diminished the likelihood of his involvement in William's disappearance, Jubelin faced criticism for having wasted time chasing the wrong man. This meant there had been less heat on the real perpetrator and therefore less chance of catching them. Or so the argument went.

By the time of the 2019 inquest, it seemed there was some evidence to support Bill Spedding's alibi. People had seen him at the school assembly, which was firmer in some people's memories than others. One local man distinctly recalled giving Bill's grandson a high five to congratulate him for his role in a particularly stirring choral rendition of Leonard Cohen's 'Hallelujah'. He remembered catching Bill's eye at the time, and Bill giving him an approving nod for affirming the child. Quite a few other parents mentioned the song and verified that it had indeed been performed on 12 September.

A dated school newsletter proved their recall was accurate; a receipt verified morning tea for two had been purchased at Café Buzz; a delivery docket proved Nancy Wyndham's washing machine parts weren't delivered in time for Friday morning. It was a bitter pill to swallow that it had taken five years to bring all this proof of innocence to light. Once again, the Green Goblin had it right when he warned his nemesis, 'No matter what you do for them, eventually they will hate you.' Our hero-making process is ruthlessly arbitrary.

On 12 September 2016, the second anniversary of William Tyrrell's disappearance, the New South Wales State Government, fronted by then-Premier Mike Baird, offered a million-dollar reward for information leading to the arrest of the person or persons responsible for William's abduction. This was the largest reward ever offered in the state of New South Wales. Enticements like these are designed to break up a group, or even a partnership. The cops know there's no honour among crooks. When the idea of a reward was first floated, a much smaller figure was on the table. But William's foster father told police, 'It's just not enough. It's not enough for our boy.' The man who pushed for the million bucks was Gary Jubelin.

'It's unacceptable that two years down the track we haven't found out what's happened to William,' Jubelin said. 'If he's alive, or if we find William's remains, as unpalatable as that sounds, we've said to the family we're going to do everything possible to find out what's happened to William.'

*

Gary Jubelin spoke at the Sydney Crime Writers Festival in September 2019, the week after the Tyrrell inquest's second phase wrapped up. I happened to catch his talk. Okay, it wasn't a coincidence. Two weeks before the event, a journalist friend told me Jubelin would be featured at the festival, so I had snapped up a ticket. Jubelin's session was so popular that when I tried to get a second ticket for my sister later the same day, they were already sold out. But in the end, we managed to smuggle her in when a few people failed to show.

The session took the form of an on-stage interview with veteran Australian journalist Jana Wendt. She introduced Jubelin as 'almost unique in being a detective who's also a stellar communicator'. With thirty-four years of policing under his belt – twenty-five of those as a homicide detective – Jubelin presented as an emotionally intelligent character.

'Policing attracts the best and the worst of people,' he said, noting that police must guard against the tendency to become corrupted by the power that comes with being in uniform. There's an arrogance associated with the job which he confessed went to his head in his early years.

'The first time I put on a uniform, traffic stopped for me when I went to cross the road. I wasn't even at a proper crossing,' he recalled. As a young man, he thought that was pretty good. But with hindsight, he was also painfully aware of how close we all are to finding ourselves on the wrong side of the law. He could identify with certain offenders because he realised that with different life circumstances and pressures, it could be him in trouble. Jubelin spoke of his view that a good police officer should have empathy for both victims and offenders. But, he added, 'I have empathy with the bad guy – until we reach a certain level of offence. Then that goes out the window.'

Jana Wendt steered the conversation to the homicide detective's infamous obsessiveness. He readily admitted to it, saying checks and balances are in place to mitigate against it. He never made promises to catch killers, having learned that it's unwise to do so. Throughout the interview, I gauged the audience's response every now and then. He had them in the palm of his hand.

'I make the commitment to do everything humanly possible to solve the case,' Jubelin said, expressing the belief that law enforcement professionals can maintain a scientific approach by looking at the facts. But having tunnel vision in a case has its uses too, and he freely admitted that he had aggressively bullied certain suspects.

'I don't discount it because it could lead to a person being proven innocent. I make no excuses. When I'm involved in a murder case, I go hard on a suspect.' He added, cheekily, 'And I don't want that to be misconstrued, since I'm currently facing criminal charges.' The audience laughed and he shot back, 'Oh yeah – laugh about it! I'm doing everything I can to stay out of jail.'

Inviting his listeners to picture his first day in the lock-up, he said, 'If I go to jail, I'm sure I'm going to be very popular in there.' He role-played greeting the men he put there with a friendly wave. 'Hi guys! Remember me?' The audience were entirely under Jubelin's spell, laughing and cheering uproariously, and I joined them whole-heartedly.

When the laughter died down, he changed tack. He told of a case in which the husband of the victim had to be asked the hard questions. He put the grieving man through a gruelling interrogation session, and some time later, came to the realisation that he was innocent, as he'd always maintained. Instead of unleashing on the detective, the man said the thuggish grilling in the interview room from Gary Jubelin filled him with confidence the right person was on the job to find his wife's killer.

'The dignified behaviour of victims' families in the midst of tragedy always inspires me. Families of victims want hard-arsed detectives going after killers, not social workers. If you're going to be a homicide detective, you have to be prepared to bleed for the case. I don't think it's fair on the victims to treat it as a nine to five job,' he said.

Jubelin said he had strong thoughts on who took William Tyrrell but qualified that, saying he couldn't be one hundred per cent certain. You could've heard a pin drop in the auditorium as people mentally worked through their own suspect lists. But we all knew he'd never give us a name, not during an active investigation. I wondered whether he was the 'senior detective' quoted in *Woman's Day* magazine in 2018 who said he knew who took William Tyrrell. I strongly doubted he'd take such a risk, but could it have been a strategic play to unnerve the culprit?

'It's not just gut instinct,' he said, meaning that evidence exists to support his views. For Gary Jubelin, the interview room represents what he calls 'the sharp end of policing'. He spoke of the tendency for guilty people to confess because they want to unburden themselves.

'I find a vulnerability, a need for the suspect to talk about it and I see the weight of guilt and shame lift when they confess,' he said. He noted that taking denials into account cannot factor into his investigative strategy because criminals operate under the belief that if they simply repeat their denials enough, people will believe them. 'In some cases, people actually convince themselves that they haven't done it.'

When asked about his on-screen role models, Jubelin sheepishly admitted to binge-watching the detective television show *Bosch* after someone likened him to the titular character. He also cited *Luther* and the classic British series *The Bill* as being on the more realistic side of dramatised police work.

Of course, when pressed, we discovered he most closely identifies with DCI Frank Burnside (played by Chris Ellison). Ellison has credited the memorable Cockney character as solely responsible for ruining his acting career, such was the realism of his portrayal of the hard-as-nails London detective.

But tough-nut Burnside might not think much of Gary's soft side. When it came to extracting information from people, for Jubelin it was all about relationships. He compared dealing with an informant to marriage – very intense.

'If I bullshit to them, they know. They have rat cunning from being in the prison system and they can smell it a mile away.' He told of some very charismatic informants he'd worked with over the years, and noted the value of empathy, respect, and 'even a little bit of love'. I thought about how I'd go making an effort to love that murdering child rapist Jeffrey Hillsley. Then, like someone had thrown an electrical safety switch, the cognitive processing part of my brain shut down on me altogether.

'I find some very inspirational people in the police force,' Jubelin said. But it's clear from his humiliatingly public stoush with NSW Police in 2018, and the subsequent charges of misconduct, that he also found some enemies. He had the charges of breaching the Surveillance Devices Act on 22 January 2019 and was given a court date of 24 September.

Eight months later and just three weeks out from his court date, Jubelin still hadn't had a brief of evidence served on him. But the detective was looking on the bright side, and spoke of the support that had been most important to him. Families of homicide victims from his past cases publicly threw their support behind him.

'I'm looking at the positives. It's shown what respect the victims' families hold me in,' Jubelin said. NSW Police Commissioner Mick Fuller spoke of Jubelin in 2019, saying that his opinion of him as 'a quality police officer' was undiminished by the charges. A public petition circulated online gathered more than 13,000 signatures calling for the immediate withdrawal of the criminal charges against him.

On stage, Jubelin repeated the statement he'd consistently said in front of television news cameras. 'Within the scope of investigating the William Tyrrell matter, I had lawful and operational reasons to record those conversations.' Then he added, 'I wasn't pushed out of the police.'

From his words, I gathered that the way things were managed after the allegations arose made his position untenable. But he wasn't blaming the police and said there was no animosity between him and the police who took over the Tyrrell case. When asked about being sidelined at the inquest, Jubelin said it was a hard pill to swallow, being taken off the investigation. But he'd felt confident in how he directed Strike Force Rosann.

'I put my faith in the coronial process and the Coroner. I've made them aware that I'm available if required to give evidence. I'm more than confident with the decisions I made in running the investigation.'

Jana Wendt concluded the interview with Gary Jubelin by questioning the cop who never took a sick day in thirty-four years about his life as a retired detective.

'What do you do with your time these days?'

'I'm an unemployed accused criminal. But I've got things to do. My life's not meaningless,' he joked. Then, he went on to talk about his desire to champion the cause of particularly disadvantaged victims of crime.

'Bowraville turned me into who I am. If I'm proud of anything, it's that.' It's telling that he didn't cite bringing in the infamous Rooster Perish as his greatest career achievement. The detective was immortalised on the small screen in Channel Nine's *Underbelly: Badness* series. Perish and his associates plied their drugs and weapons trade on the Mid North Coast and famously cut up the body of criminal informant Terry Falconer, dumping it in the Hastings River. It was fished out by some locals near Wauchope, west of Port Macquarie. Jubelin was portrayed as Dirty Harry – the good cop who's prepared to do whatever it takes to catch any punks that pull out their handguns and make his day.

But for the real Gary Jubelin, his successful capture and prosecution of criminal underworld figures paled into insignificance. It was his work on the Bowraville murders that had stood out to him – because it demonstrated the power of love for the victims' families, not just raw tenacity. In Bowraville, he wasn't even able to secure a conviction.

'I will push against my organisation if I feel things aren't going in the right direction,' he asserted. 'I want the families of victims to know that I'm working for them. I'm not working for the cops. Some people are critical of that approach. But I don't accept that the organisation will necessarily do the right thing. We have to push them to do it,' he said, smiling. I wanted to ask him one question about the court proceedings he would face later that year: 'Do you feel lucky?'

14

SHARKS

The twin towns of Laurieton and North Haven are big on fishing. My father and uncle would take the boat up the river. I recall being in it when they turned it over more than once at the choppy bar. Folk from the Dunghutti, Gumbaynggirr or Birpai mobs will tell you that when the white moths hover over the mangroves, the tailor are running. Flathead are best caught at the end of the run-out; whiting follow the opposite pattern. My grandmother taught me to look for mutton birds circling and diving just past the surf break, a dead giveaway that bait fish are fleeing schools of sea bream.

If these predictions failed to yield fish, we'd go get beach worms. The little suckers are notoriously difficult to catch. They'll coil up their still-buried bodies and pull themselves in half rather than be pulled out of the sand. So you tempt them with a pipi – a mollusc with a triangular shell. When the worm shows its whiskery head, you've got half a second to grab it. You must pull without hesitating. If you've done it right, a metre of juicy wormflesh will streak out of the sand – a small miracle that extracts profuse praise from tourists and grudging nods from the local fishos.

As kids, we knew never to dip a toe in at dawn or dusk – 'shark time', my grandmother called it. She told me once that a group of sharks was called a 'shiver'. A shiver of sharks. It gave me goosebumps. At sunset, we'd watch the bull sharks creep upriver like stealth bombers, right into our favourite daytime swimming waters. After frying up the day's catch, we'd sit in the caravan annexe and play cards. I was Dad's preferred partner for Five Hundred. We had worked out a system to avoid open table-talk. If he played a small trump, it signalled I was to take the lead. I knew this meant he wasn't confident in his hand. The fun of interpreting my father's glances, gazes and decoy tells became my only reason for playing cards.

I digress into my holiday memories here to paint a picture of the Camden Haven as a quaint little spot populated by salt-of-the-earth types in love with traditions that are quintessentially Australian. There's a nice closeness between Indigenous locals and us whitefellas, founded on mutual connections to the natural world. Many of us know, and some of us suspect, that we spring from the same Indigenous bloodlines. Apart from fishing and farming, there's our shared history working in timber cutting, agriculture and finding ways to survive and thrive after floods and bushfires. And now, pandemics and economic meltdown.

To comprehend the impact of William Tyrrell's disappearance on the people here, you must perceive the 'eternal holiday' vibe of this place. There are no race riots, no great crimewaves beyond the occasional pilfered wheelie bin. We see our stomping ground as friendly, relaxed, quiet, family-orientated and, above all, safe.

But William's disappearance would expose a shiver of sharks in the Camden Haven – the most treacherous species of predator. We learned that paedophiles lurked everywhere. Residents were horrified to find out just how many registered sex offenders had opted for a life in the country. With around eighty names listed on the Child Protection Register in 2014, the place was quickly losing its shine. I guess paedophiles like fishing too.

*

Journalists covering the William Tyrrell story weren't in need of sensational angles, but the theory that we were looking for a paedophile ring gave them one anyway. Almost immediately after William disappeared, it seemed that something truly sinister had led to the disappearance of this little boy in that impossibly short timeframe. A cabin at a seedy local caravan park was searched after the park's owner reported hearing a child crying in the weeks after William went missing. The couple who'd hired the cabin in question were from Victoria. Police contacted them and ruled them out as suspects. The sound of the crying child has never been explained. Perhaps it was a catbird.

News producers were poised to seize upon any new detail that would justify pointing out the misdemeanours of locals who may be child killers in disguise. And there were shivers of candidates. A parade of suspected and convicted felons graced the news headlines. Dirty laundry hung alongside the weekend washing in Kendall's backyards. It seemed no one was immune to scrutiny. Some persons of interest found themselves in the wrong place at the wrong time. Others deserved to be caught in the searchlights.

One such person was Derek Nichols, a distinguished-looking gentleman who had a love for music and children, particularly twelve-year-old boys. Tall with white hair, spectacles above a genial smile and pale musician's hands, Nichols looks harmless enough. A music teacher and former choir master, Nichols lived a literal stone's throw from Kendall Community Preschool, and for most of his sojourn there, not a soul knew he was a registered child sex offender. Convicted in Tasmania in 1987, Nichols was an Anglican priest with a penchant for pornography depicting horrific child sex abuse. He had also worked as a school chaplain and a religious education teacher.

Tasmania's *Mercury* newspaper uncovered the shocking revelation that despite his first conviction as a sex offender in 1987, he was never de-frocked by the Anglican church. Sometime after he was caught offending, Nichols' wife had divorced him. He fled Tasmania after a bishop refused to authorise him to officiate at Anglican church events because of his criminal record. He passed Nichols' name around, effectively ending his career with the church, but only unofficially. In 2016, his name came up at the Royal Commission into Institutional Responses to Child Sex Abuse.

Undeterred, Nichols landed in Kendall. He continued in his wicked ways, being convicted of possessing child pornography in 2007. Strike Force Rosann detectives looked closely at Nichols and searched his house, but no evidence of his involvement in William's disappearance was ever uncovered. The year William went missing, Nichols quietly moved away from Kendall and hasn't resurfaced since.

The next candidate in our paedophile parade would not be named publicly until 2019, at the inquest. In a shocking twist, the public would hear the name of Robert Donohoe (pronounced 'Donohue') for the first time. He was an itinerant worker who had held a number of temporary jobs, including a sales assistant position at Lakewood's Woolworths Caltex service station.

Robert Donohoe was called to the stand in August 2019 to be questioned about his possible involvement in the William Tyrrell matter. At court, Donohoe was aided by an advocate. Anna Wyndham had refused to look at him when she entered the courtroom. Throughout his testimony, she kept touching her face, a hand resting lightly under her chin. I wondered if she was self-comforting.

Moments after taking the stand, Robert Donohoe pointedly reminded Mr Craddock that he has special needs.

'I have a cognitive impairment, so could you take it very slow?' Mr Craddock didn't get time to answer before Deputy State Coroner Harriet Grahame shot back, unflinchingly.

'Mr Donohoe, if you have any difficulty understanding something, you speak directly to me.' But Donohoe persisted in seeking to win the court's sympathy, which – given the nature of his offences – was in short supply. Donohoe ignored the Coroner and continued, 'I've been bashed in jail and everything so my memory is not a hundred per cent.'

Donohoe confirmed he had involved himself in the search for William Tyrrell but had no recollection of the SES briefing he attended, nor their group's call sign, Taree 56.

'The place was like a football match, the amount of people that were there.' Donohoe's shift finished late that night. 'I had to go to work the next day. I was exhausted,' he complained to Mr Craddock insipidly.

Donohoe had been arrested on the Mid North Coast just four days after William Tyrrell's disappearance. He had perpetrated sex crimes on two young, intellectually disabled men whom he'd met through the SES. He had befriended and groomed them to accept his sexual advances, meticulously planning each step until he finally raped them both multiple times. Donohoe was convicted of five charges, three counts of aggravated sexual assault and two of sexual assault involving taking advantage of impairment. He was sentenced to five-and-a-half years' imprisonment and would serve a three-year non-parole period. Having served his sentence, Donohoe was released from prison in November 2018.

One of Donohoe's victims in 2014 was a severely disabled man with the cognitive aptitude of a seven- to eight-year-old. In a display of predatory forward planning, Donohoe set about weaving a trap in which to catch his prey. He purposefully befriended the man and invited him over to his house. Donohoe would coax him into baths, saying it would help the man 'relax his muscles', which were sore after playing cricket – and repeatedly raped him.

When Robert's brother, Tim, gave evidence, we heard that the siblings were very close. Strangely though, Tim said he had no idea where his brother was working between 2011 and 2014. He did recall Robert working with the SES and knew he had certification to work on building sites. Tim said he didn't know Robert had been arrested and gone to prison until a year after he was incarcerated. At this time, Tim lived on a rural property in Wagga Wagga with their parents. He recalled their father bringing Donohoe's white Suzuki van to the property in September 2014, after Donohoe was arrested.

Detectives Dukes and Lonegan from the Homicide Squad executed a search warrant there in August 2018. Some effort had been made at concealing the van in the shed. Storage boxes and junk was packed around it, making it impossible to access. The inquest's faithful watched on video as police cleared it all away – boxes, plastic coverings, woollen blankets. Tim Donohoe appeared hostile on the stand. He made a point of leaving the courtroom without the customary bow to the Coroner when he was dismissed. Robert Donohoe smirked as his brother exited.

At the second sitting of the inquest in Sydney, I overheard Donohoe telling his disability advocate that he'd had to lie about what he was doing in Sydney to the person covering his shifts at work. He spoke of his anxiety at having to give evidence and how his expression freezes when he gets paranoid. 'When anyone asks me a question, I just clam up. I feel it come across my face.' I studied him during a break in proceedings. There were only four of us still in the courtroom.

Donohoe looks pasty. He speaks loudly. He has a baby-face, its roundness accentuated by the fact that he is balding. I thought of Donohoe as Captain Smirk. He mentioned his annoyance at having to spend a night in a police cell, then launched into a discourse about a television series on taxidermy. When court resumed that day, the Coroner announced that she would hear the remainder of Donohoe's evidence in a closed court session.

Because of what I'd just overheard, I knew Donohoe was facing fresh charges originating from Port Macquarie police, which explained the need for a closed court. Another shark cruising in local waters. The Coroner also set an interim non-publication order in place, so it remains unclear whether these charges pertained to the William Tyrrell investigation.

Sharon Starr, the store manager of the Woolworths Caltex service station at Lakewood, made a statement to police on 14 February 2019. Starr's evidence riveted the court. Her appearance on the stand had the instant effect of wiping the smirk off Robert Donohoe's face. Periodically, he would laugh. Perhaps it was for no reason, or perhaps he was releasing nervous energy. Sharon Starr described Donohoe as 'creepy' and 'embarrassing', scaring local schoolgirls to the point where they wouldn't enter the shop when he was on shift. I didn't see her look at Donohoe once.

Donohoe worked between three and five shifts each week, including Friday evenings. He'd stay overnight rather than drive home to Taree, sleeping in his van. The vehicle was stationed in the carpark of Kendall swimming pool or at the Kendall Showground, just a stone's throw from Benaroon Drive. At the August inquest session in 2019, we did not hear whether Donohoe had been working on the Friday William disappeared. But one thing is certain – he took part in the SES search on that Friday. The Coroner issued a request for photos taken during the search period to be submitted to police sometime in 2018. No doubt she was looking for images that showed what Robert Donohoe was up to during that time.

Donohoe's antics at work greatly entertained the public gallery at the inquest. Starr spoke of occasions when Donohoe would bring a lighted candle in to fragrance the back room of the service station – an area packed with fuel dispensing equipment. 'There are signs warning people not to use naked flames,' Starr said. But when she raised the danger of explosion with Donohoe, he replied, 'I like the smell of candles.' She also told of his peculiar habit of stamping children's hands with a star-shaped ink stamp. She'd had to stop him, saying, 'We don't do that. It's not part of something we do. Parents might not like it.' Donohoe reluctantly put his stamp away. Starr also testified that Donohoe brought live chickens to the petrol station. He told Starr he had hoped to sell their eggs. She told him, 'We don't sell eggs.'

At the service station, staff sign on and off using an electronic finger scanner. When the scanner isn't working, they revert to paper sheets. Starr said when police inquired about Donohoe's whereabouts on 12 September 2014, she couldn't find the sign-on sheets. They weren't in their usual place at the office. Hearing Starr recall this, Donohoe's expression froze. He knew Starr was suggesting he took them. His expression darkened in an effort to intimidate the witness, but she refused to look at him.

'Anyway, Head Office will have them,' Starr recalled thinking. When she left the stand, Sharon Starr looked frazzled. Donohoe glared at her with pointed hostility, and his trademark smirk skipped across his face as she fled the room. I caught up with her outside to let her know that I thought she'd been courageous to give evidence.

'Well done. It's a brave thing you did. Are you getting support?' I asked.

She thanked me and replied, 'I'm fine. I'm going for a cigarette.' After Starr's evidence, the inquest collectively held its breath as they waited for Donohoe to make his appearance.

*

Detective Senior Sergeant Mark Dukes recorded an electronic interview of Donohoe at Wagga Wagga police station in November 2018. We were shown the footage. Donohoe wore prison greens and his customary smirk. He was not cooperating, refusing even to confirm his name and date of birth for the record. A disability advocate was also present, although Donohoe ignored her. He was steering his own ship.

Dukes began, in a firm but polite voice.

'I'm going to ask you some questions about the disappearance and suspected murder of William Tyrrell on the twelfth day of September 2014. Do you understand that?' Donohoe remained silent. At this, his disability advocate interrupted. 'The solicitor advised that this recording would just be to ask if he consented to this recording.'

'I appreciate that,' Dukes replied, through gritted teeth. He left the interview room and arranged for a local policeman to take the particulars. Once the detectives had departed, Donohoe cooperated like a submissive lamb.

Donohoe looked very different in person. In the video, he'd looked almost tough. I wondered whether he'd purposely chosen to wear calmative pink to the inquest to emphasise his harmlessness. It only had the effect of intensifying Sharon Starr's assessment of him, in my view. I wondered whether he'd mentioned his keen interest in taxidermy for the benefit of eavesdroppers. Or is it only me who finds a hobby stuffing dead animals a tad weird? And I also wondered, if he happened past Benaroon Drive and saw a small boy in a Spiderman suit wandering there, would he stop his van and snatch him?

When Donohoe had worked briefly as a contractor installing National Broadband Network (NBN) connections, Troy Brown worked with him. Donohoe's timesheet indicated that he was working on an NBN job near Taree on 12 September. It was signed off – the signatory being Brown. But the witness surprised the inquest – while the document bore his name, the signature was not his. He wasn't authorised to sign off workers' timesheets at that time. 'That was above my pay grade,' he said. The question of why his signature had been forged was for Donohoe to answer – but he exercised his right to remain silent.

I did some more digging on Donohoe. He completed his Higher School Certificate, passing all but one subject. He holds a Diploma of Community Studies from Canberra Institute of Technology and a Certificate III in Mental Health Studies. Interestingly, his area of specialisation is working with clients who have mental disabilities and complex special needs. In 2017, Donohoe proved capable of representing himself at his appeal against thirteen counts of sexual assault. Not bad for a mentally impaired man, but not effective – he lost. Yet he couldn't remember a thing about what he was up to on the day William Tyrrell disappeared.

*

The treatment of William Tyrrell's abduction as a targeted one meant that, although both sets of parents were excluded, their associates could not be ruled out. Statistics overwhelmingly predict that a family member is responsible in most cases involving missing children. At the inquest, Gerard Craddock said the same. But the list of people who knew of the family's movements on that Thursday and Friday was pretty short. It included William's foster grandmother and possibly a few tradesmen or neighbours who knew her, his childcare supervisors, perhaps a few of the foster parents' work colleagues, the staff at the cattery and the house-sitters Anna called to see if they were available that weekend.

'Police have not drawn the positive conclusion that a known relative or associate was not involved in William's disappearance,' Craddock asserted in 2019. But The Boss himself had deftly steered us away from this conclusion by the close of the August sittings, instead sketching a profile that fed into parents' fears about opportunistic abductors. He wanted us to see that this was a very unusual case. In many ways, it defied the statistics. Although at that time, no one, including Mr Craddock, knew for certain who took William, The Boss was impressively confident in his prediction.

'The offender is a sneaky, complex offender who has hidden their desires for some time and has chosen to act on those desires,' said Mr Craddock. If the abduction was random, perpetrated by an opportunistic stranger, it could have been anybody. But to get away with it, the perpetrator would need to have a genuine reason for being there. And there's not too many people with reason to be in the area of Benaroon Drive on a Friday morning.

Mr Craddock's view was buttressed by an assessment from professional criminal profiler Dr Sarah Yule.[28] Her report showed detectives why she believed an opportunistic criminal abducted William. Dr Yule argued that William was a random target, saying that the unique facts made a premeditated kidnapping unlikely.

According to Yule, the window of opportunity was small, so in all likelihood the person had a legitimate reason to be in the street that day. Since few people knew the children would be at the house, the boy couldn't have been targeted in advance, although the house could have been watched earlier that morning if the perp had formulated a plan when they'd first seen the children playing.

There was no evidence the foster family was followed on their trip north. And, as we've noted, had a stranger been haunting the area, chances are they would have been spotted and known to be out of place. This further strengthens the theory that our random opportunist had a legitimate reason to be in that quiet, dead-end street. But this was a high-risk crime, if it was random. The perpetrator ran the real risk of being seen from the verandah of Nancy's house, as well as being observed by neighbours. Still, if the offender was known to William, perhaps he went voluntarily to the perp. What if all they had to do was open the car door for him? They could plausibly deny any wrong-doing if they were caught. All they needed to say was, 'I found him wandering out here. I was just taking him to find his mum.'

Dr Yule stressed the importance of looking for the mistakes one invariably makes when they commit an impulsive, opportunistic crime. The likelihood of a resident of Benaroon Drive, Ellendale Crescent or even of Batar Creek Road taking William that day was low. The opportunity must be taken decisively, the instant it presents itself. There could be no delay, no noise, no kerfuffle that could attract someone's attention. And by definition, the perpetrator could not have been expecting such an opportunity to arise, being a random act. So there could be little planning, just swift, decisive action. And if that was the perp's modus operandi, it wasn't their first rodeo.

Jubelin put the scenario together for us in a media interview, placing us inside the mind of the perpetrator.

'You cross the Camden Haven River and nobody notices young William with the seatbelt over him. You bypass the police station in Laurieton and you just keep driving. By the time William's mother calls 000 you are 30 km away. There are tens of thousands of hectares of dense bushland between you and Kendall. William is strapped in beside you, dressed in his Spiderman suit.'

Another means of reducing the potential for failure or capture in abducting a child is to have help. But your helpers need to be experienced. For the first two years of the investigation, Strike Force Rosann consistently sent a very public message – they believed they could be dealing with an organised paedophile ring. In 2014, not long before William vanished, Operation Twigg uncovered a secret paedophile ring on the Mid North Coast. The police prosecuted more than thirty people, some of whom had international links. Police have never revealed whether there was a connection between Operation Twigg and the Tyrrell investigation. But we can be certain that whether they worked together or separately, we were dealing with a sizable shiver of sharks.

15

HIGH ROLLERS

With no eyewitnesses and no forensic evidence, solving the William Tyrrell case would rest heavily on alibis. It was difficult to rule out one suspect in particular, because he'd given an unverifiable alibi for 12 September 2014. He said he was alone in bushland in the Bago State Forest, east of Wauchope and not far from Kendall. That person was Anthony Jones.

Jones was a violent thug of significant interest to the boys in blue. His rap sheet was long, but I reckon he'd like it to be even longer. At the time of William's disappearance he had ninety convictions stretching over forty years, a point he bragged about in the lock-up. He'd been imprisoned for assaulting women and children, intimidating police officers, breaking and entering, and numerous drug offences.

Photos of Jones had circulated in media reports after William's disappearance, and going by these, he appeared much-altered since prison. He'd started as a macho, moustachioed lumberjack and dissolved into a long-haired, half-crazed wraith. When Jones turned up to Taree courthouse in March 2020 he was wearing a sweater emblazoned 'Harvard'.

As Tony Jones came forward to take the stand, he turned and stared right at me. He had a slighter frame than I'd imagined.

His dark grey hair was long, pulled back in a straggly ponytail with shorter strands falling over his left eye. Jones mentioned he has a lung problem that makes it difficult for him to breathe and speak at the same time. He would tilt his head right back to look at the ceiling when Mr Craddock spoke, mouth hanging open to emphasise the fact that he was not listening and was perilously close to asphyxiation. When it was his turn to speak, he over-enunciated his 'esses', like a menacing serpent. Mercifully, he forgot to keep it up after a while. In a sharp, too-loud voice, he also repeatedly interrupted The Boss. The Boss was not amused.

We learned that Jones lived in Wauchope in 2014 and had associates in Kendall and Dunbogan. His live-in partner eventually disowned him. Jones was involved with the community support group Grandparents As Parents Again (GAPA). Formed by Uniting Care Burnside and the Country Women's Association, the organisation provides a social network for grandparents raising their grandchildren either informally or under a foster care arrangement.

Keeping it in the family, Jones' ex-partner was the niece of GAPA's former president, a woman whom I won't name here. There's no indication that these two ladies had any untoward intentions in their work with GAPA. But the same cannot be said for Jones. His association with the group was flimsy. He rarely attended meetings. But it gave him access to kids. The naivety of certain GAPA members enabled him to perpetrate his sick crimes without fear of detection. Incredibly, the Wauchope chapter once appointed him treasurer.

Tony Jones was convicted in 2015 of molesting a young intellectually disabled girl. His modus operandi was to overdose her with medication for autism. Once rendered semi-conscious, she was defenceless against his perverted activities. He kept the abuse up for some time. The child was just eleven when Jones was finally caught.

He was charged with aggravated child sexual assault and handed a woefully inadequate prison sentence of just three years. He was paroled in two.

Unrepentant while in the clink, he bragged about his exploits. Nevertheless, before sentencing his lawyer said that Jones was 'deeply ashamed of his behaviour'. When Jones was kicked out of the family home, relatives said the decision to remove him was an easy one. They said they hadn't known the extent of his criminal record. His partner and children described him as a 'cretin', a 'mutt' and a 'dog' with no respect for other people or for the law. They accused him in open court of drugging his partner with sleeping pills, thieving money, burning out cars to collect insurance money and associating with known paedophiles.

Another despicable creature, also associated with the GAPA group, was Paul Bickford. 'Bickies' was once named Port Macquarie Senior Volunteer of the Year. A former president of GAPA, he enjoyed the community's respect until he was ignominiously dethroned amid a series of child sex charges in 2011.

When he was nominated for his award in 2009, Paul Bickford was described to a local journalist as 'a very special person who has changed many people's lives'. That would become an unexpectedly apt description. Bickford was instrumental in organising meetings, social days and respite camps for grandparents and children. He also expanded GAPA by founding additional chapters on the Mid North Coast. The truth is, Bickford's antics split the group. The Port Macquarie News reported that Mr Bickford was shocked to win the award.

'I just don't believe it,' he said. Reading this in the paper, I had to concur.[29]

My tuition business had dealings with GAPA in 2011–2012. We offered twelve-month scholarships of free tuition to two local children fostered by their grandparents. In 2011, we met with

Paul Bickford's deputy. I'm grateful I never had the misfortune to meet the president.

Bickford's sexual predilection for children became public knowledge during his court case, revealing his true motives as a volunteer. He had molested a young girl while driving to the shop to buy lollies. Like Jones' victim, the girl had an intellectual disability. She resorted to self-harming behaviour before finally gathering the courage to report him.

Bickford's comments to reporters secured a conviction in the court of public opinion even before the Port Macquarie District Court could dish out a sentence.

'I'm just an ordinary guy, really,' Bickford replied when asked in 2015 if he was a paedophile. 'I'm just being what I always am.' He laughed at suggestions that he was part of a ring, despite being convicted of indecent assault. He argued that he couldn't be considered part of a paedophile ring since he'd been found guilty of only 'harming one child, not *children*'. Bickford denied knowing anything about William Tyrrell's disappearance. While Tony Jones admitted he was friends with Bickford, Paul wasn't returning the favour. He told reporters that Jones was no more than an acquaintance and denied knowing anything about his activities.

'I haven't got the faintest idea what Tony has done or hasn't done,' he said. But a relative of Jones, Katrina Cherry, told police that Tony and Paul sometimes went fishing together. She asserted they were close friends. Six weeks before William went missing, Paul Bickford was having a birthday. He received a message on his Facebook page wishing him many happy returns. The sender was none other than his old 'acquaintance', Tony Jones.

Other family members would testify at the inquest's third sitting in Taree. Testimony from two witnesses put Bickford at the Jones house frequently. One of them was Duane, Tony's son. He told Mr Craddock that Bickford and his father were best mates. 'Mum wouldn't let him in because of the kids,' the inquest heard. 'He'd come to the front of the house and call out, and Tony would go outside to meet him.' Jones arranged mates rates accommodation at a local hotel for his pal when Bickford was kicked out of home. They drank together frequently, united by their 'common interests'.

Our anti-hero had a lengthy relationship with a woman called Debbie. They lived together on and off while Tony steadily worked on lengthening his rap sheet. The two fought like ferrets in a bag and, given Jones' penchant for drink driving and injecting speed, or 'goey' as he called it, this is unsurprising. His adult daughter and her live-in partner Katrina Cherry were staying at Jones' house in Wauchope on 12 September 2014.

Debbie testified that Tony Jones left the house early that Friday, telling family he was going to collect scrap metal with his son. When Debbie's son was discovered at home, unaware he was supposed to be with Tony, they waited for him to arrive home and confronted him about the lie. The inquest heard that Tony Jones came home sozzled at around two, saying he'd been drinking with Paul Bickford. Bickford claimed he was having lunch with people in Port Macquarie, although he couldn't recall who joined him or where they ate.

But Jones told police a different story. He said he'd been out bush collecting scrap metal – alone. On a different occasion during a second police interview, he said he'd been cutting up wood with a chainsaw he'd borrowed from the local council – until he realised council records could quickly dissolve that fabrication.

Jones changed his alibi again in 2018. This time he told police he'd gone to pick up a hot water system at a neighbour's house. But he had his days mixed up – an honest mistake, he told us. The thing with alibis is they work best when you stick with just the one.

Media reports portrayed Jones and Bickford as key figures in a suspected paedophile network operating on the Mid North Coast.

There is limited evidence supporting this claim. If past form is any indicator, it seems Jones preferred acting as a lone wolf when preying on children. Sharing secrets is a dangerous practice for a child sex offender. It's equally likely that Bickies too erred on the side of caution by keeping his filthy deeds to himself.

Still, the men's vehicles added a layer of suspicion. Bickford's car was a white Holden Commodore, while Jones has been linked to another vehicle – a car found upturned and burnt out in bushland near Kendall. Detectives were led to the site by the informant, only to find that the car had been flipped onto its roof and set alight. It's highly likely that police were able to recover the vehicle identification number from the wreck, but we've never heard any further reports about what they discovered. Police were also very interested in another car in Jones' circle.

Jones sometimes drove a white Toyota Camry station wagon in 2014, although he strenuously denies it. He told the court his partner wouldn't allow him to drive it – as if that would stop him – and in case we didn't swallow that, it had blown a welch plug and was undrivable at the time. At first, Jones told police he'd disposed of the car and didn't know where it was. It was later found garaged at a neighbour's house after an informant squealed. When asked in March 2020 about the car, Jones held up both hands and leaned back in his seat.

'Oh, don't ask me about that again,' he said to Mr Craddock. 'If you ask me about the Camry again, I'm not going to answer.'

Jones isn't one to control his impulses. When confronted by a Channel Nine crew on a Sydney street after reporting to his parole officer in 2018, he blew up and raged like a lunatic, threatening to break the recording equipment and reporter Steve Marshall's face. Screaming violent threats and hissing like a hellcat, nose to nose, he gave the impression of a man completely unhinged. When Marshall asked him whether he was in Kendall that day, Jones spat venom.

'Piss off, idiot, I wasn't even questioned on it. Where I was on the day he disappeared was with my next-door neighbour, getting her hot water system. You got your answers.' Marshall persisted, asking Jones how he could confirm his alibi if he was drunk that day by lunchtime, as he'd previously said.

'I just told you where I was, fool!' Jones shouted back, right in the reporter's face.[30] Katrina Cherry has said she'd never heard the tale about the hot water system. She was prompted to contact police because she said she 'never felt right about it from day one', meaning William's disappearance and Jones' strange behaviour on that day and afterward. It was Cherry who tipped off police that Jones used his ex-wife's white Toyota Camry station wagon, without her knowledge and against her express wishes.

In 2020, the inquest heard that Tony Jones had shown an interest in the William Tyrrell disappearance. He announced at a family dinner that he'd decided to join the search. Puzzled at this display of community spirit, his son readied two trail bikes for the trip to Kendall. Jones said the Wauchope Community Centre was handing out free fuel vouchers to volunteers, so he went and obtained some. When he returned home, he told his son he'd changed his mind about going on the search. Jones had cashed in the vouchers. He shamelessly told the inquest what he did with the money.

'I bought some longnecks with it.' According to his son, Jones said he took the beers to his mate Paul Bickford and spent the afternoon drinking with him. If using charitable funds to get drunk wasn't bad enough, he proceeded to further taunt the court with the jubilant confession that he was most likely next door sleeping with Debbie's best friend when William went missing. 'That's where I was most of the time,' he volunteered, clearly pleased with himself. Like so many others blinded by conceit, Jones clearly fancied himself a lady-killer.

As he was escorted from his last court appearance, Jones remarked to Detective Dukes that he'd taken a shine to a certain bookish female sitting in the back row. Dukes gleefully passed that intel on to me, the target of his affections. I told Dukes that I'd be open to all offers if there was an interview in it for me. When I told my husband that night, he reminded me that prison has the effect of lowering a guy's standards. So much for flattery.

In February 2018, the media had gone into a froth over a connection between Jones and Bill Spedding. Katrina Cherry described certain connections between the two men in a media interview as 'insane' and 'almost inexplicable'. The fact is that both men had been named persons of interest by Strike Force Rosann – Bill because he had visited the house the same week William disappeared, and Tony because he had form as a child sex offender and no provable alibi for the day in question.

Timing was everything. Bill wouldn't be cleared of all child sex allegations until March 2018, so the moment a tenuous link was discovered between the two, Bill Spedding was dragged back into the fray. But Bill's reply to all this was simple – you can't choose your neighbours. In Wellington, he'd had the misfortune to live across the road from an unpleasant character by the name of Jones. It's a common surname. Unfortunately for Bill, this bloke's first name was Anthony.

Throughout the William Tyrrell investigation, Jones kept showing up like a bad penny. The house across the street from Bill and Margaret was a hub of activity, all of it negative. Police would frequently be called to quell various disturbances of the Wellington peace. Bill's enduring memory of Tony and Debbie was of them huddled under a blanket Marg gave them, watching their house burn to the ground. Bill put it down to faulty electrical wiring, which he'd warned Tony about after a maintenance check. Debbie had dealt with Bill too, previously buying a washing machine from him. But Wello is a small place and full of connections with the Camden Haven area.

A more telling coincidence was remarked upon by the Coroner when she heard evidence about random fires, including Tony's house, at least three of Tony's cars and his friend's garage going up in smoke. There are no less than six burnt out cars connected to this investigation, including a white ute that Jones had resprayed blue.

'It seems a lot of vehicles are burning out around the place. I never knew this was such a common problem,' she remarked drily. Like me, she must've noticed that it's a stroke of good fortune that Jones is in the scrap metal business. I was amused to see the Coroner stare wordlessly into space when Jones informed the court why he was so certain he'd not been in the Kendall forest on the day William vanished.

'I wouldn't have been there because I didn't have a scrapping permit for that area.' It was reassuring to hear that Mr Jones has such a healthy respect for this area of the law.

While I was digging up material about Tony Jones, I unearthed a story so bizarre that it had the unmistakable ring of truth. It demonstrates in technicolour three of Jones' irksome attributes: his utter disregard for the law, his lack of respect for basic human decency and, perhaps most telling, his tendency to write his own rules.

In 2004, Debbie's pet chihuahua died. Wanting to secure a permanent resting place for her beloved Kia, Debbie got Tony to bury the dog in the grave occupied by her parents in Wellington cemetery. When questioned by her brothers about the legality of this move, she insisted that she had the right – being the executor of her parents' will and because she'd paid for their funeral and burial plot.

'As far as I'm concerned it's my land and I have the right to bury the dog there.' But her brothers didn't see things her way. One told a reporter that he couldn't sleep knowing that a dead dog was lying on top of his parents.

'I couldn't believe it. Tony buried their dog in Mum and Dad's grave. Tony came up and told us not to worry about the grass being disturbed on Mum and Dad's grave because he'd just buried the dog there.' Tony had thoughtfully added a small cross and some flowers to the grave in memory of Kia. The journo who interviewed one of the brothers couldn't resist the obvious headline: 'Son won't let sleeping dog lie'.[31]

After the lively spectacle of the house fire, the next time Bill saw Tony Jones was when the police put him into his cell at Cessnock Correctional Centre. With Jones' long, scraggly hair and wispy beard, Bill didn't recognise him. But Tony sure recognised Bill. Primarily, he recognised Bill as his ticket to a reduced sentence. This was no random pairing of cell mates. Tony had been offered a deal – or so he believed – to get Bill to confide in him. Police hoped one of them might spill something they knew about William Tyrrell's disappearance. They shared a cell for a month. It wasn't until after Bill was released that he discovered Tony Jones had been named a person of interest in the William Tyrrell case. For years, Bill and I thought it was the detectives' design to trap Bill into revealing something to Tony. On reflection, I think we had it the wrong way around.

The powerful influence of family grievances cannot be ignored in the Cherry–Jones dispute. Katrina, her partner (Tony's daughter), Tony's ex and his children all detest him. Throw in drugs, alcohol, habitual lying, infidelity, child abuse and a shady criminal background and you have a cesspool in which anything can be hidden. Lying is a way of life for Jones. But still, could his family and associates really have been ignorant of his extensive rap sheet? I tried to assess Tony's capabilities from a safe distance, until the final sitting of the inquest in March 2020. Could Tony Jones be William Tyrrell's abductor? For most of the investigation, I would have answered in the affirmative.

*

By August 2019, my pink paper sheaf had outgrown the largest bulldog clip I could find. I moved it to a cardboard box. It was time to bring the wider picture into focus. I began to assemble the big parade.

First, there was Bill Spedding, whose connection with the Benaroon Drive house rang alarm bells with Gary Jubelin, especially after the difficulties establishing his school assembly alibi. Galvanised into action by an apparently coincidental Crime Stoppers tip-off, investigators took the unusual gamble of naming their star POI and going through his house, yard and office like a dose of salts – but, most embarrassingly, they came up empty-handed. With his alibi firmed up by revelations at the 2019 inquest, Bill Spedding seemed in the clear.

While police were looking at the neighbours, a few other names were mentioned – the Beanie Man, the Night Owl, the Tennis Player and Brer Rabbit – who all lived within cooee of the abduction site. It seemed quiet little Benaroon Drive was a hive of suspicion and the heat applied by investigators smoked out some stinging accusations. Habits once considered merely 'odd' were reinterpreted as sinister. Neighbours named each other as potential suspects. The police haven't turned up anything incriminating on any of these men to date in regard to William Tyrrell's disappearance.

At the commencement of the inquest, we met a new frontrunner – Robert Donohoe, whose work van was hidden in a remote shed and once was home to a brood of chickens. His boss told us he had bizarre habits and police told us he had serious form preying sexually upon intellectually disabled men. Donohoe wisely chose to clam up at interview.

For the defence, Donohoe had no foreknowledge that William would be in Kendall that day; police never revealed whether they recovered forensic evidence from Donohoe's vehicle, so presumably they didn't. He had no obvious connection to the house in Benaroon Drive. And Donohoe had no history abusing children.

For the prosecution, Donohoe had to overcome a big problem: an alibi underpinned by a forged work sign-off document. His silence was more leaden than golden in court and during police interviews. He was known to lurk around Kendall swimming pool and the Kendall Showground, places that could give him ready access to children. And, his connection with the Showground may have put him within an interesting circle of friends. Actually, a ring of friends might be a more apt description. More on that later.

Next came Tony Jones, who had form as a child predator and ably demonstrated to viewers, throughout his highly publicised television appearances, that he wasn't always in perfect control of his aggression.

For the defence, Jones couldn't have known William would be at the house that day; no forensic evidence was ever found in the vehicle he drove; he had no history of snatching children, just drugging young girls and – if he wanted to borrow the car – his wife. Moreover, his record of offending didn't appear to fit the profile of a boy-attracted paedophile; and, like anyone else in the frame, he would've been hard pressed to lure, snatch and transport a toddler without being seen or heard.

For the prosecution, we had the significant issue of an unsubstantiated alibi – one that went through several changes, in fact. We had his close association with local paedo Bickford, and the possibility that they met up that very day. If they did, Jones lied about it, giving further cause for suspicion. Jones also misled police about the fate of the vehicle hidden in an associate's shed. He knew the bush, being a scrapper. And finally, a point that couldn't be ignored was that he knew Kendall like the back of his hand. These facts would have troubled his defenders, if he'd had any.

Then there was Paul Savage, the next subject of Jubelin's undivided attention and the focus of some questionable investigative strategies that were to land the Strike Force leader in hot water.

Savage's unwanted interest in a female postie threw a shadow over him, and he certainly had the home-ground advantage. His house was in close proximity to the house from which William was taken. And he may have nursed a grudge against Nancy Wyndham for rejecting his unwanted visits.

For Savage, his alibi – being at home – was not helpful because it put him at ground zero. But did he have a motive and the means to carry the boy away unnoticed? In February 2020, the court issued a statement saying Paul Savage was no longer considered a person of interest. I wasn't sure what to make of that statement.

In 2019 at the August inquest, Ron Chapman swore he'd seen William Tyrrell being spirited away in a fawn-coloured Toyota Land Cruiser, with a mid-blue sedan following closely behind. We wondered why Chapman hadn't come forward earlier. So did he, it turns out. What might we make of this development? By 2019, the sea of suspicion was already heaving with interesting vehicles and, although Chapman's revelations made a splash with the public, for the police, two more were just irrelevant flotsam.

Indeed, as if the list of POIs wasn't extensive enough, the addition of VOIs made things even more unwieldy. Vehicles of interest to police included a four-wheel drive seen speeding in the area, but not the one Ron Chapman saw turning into Laurel Street. Many other cars were mentioned – a white Holden Commodore sedan, the same in a station wagon and a black Camry hatchback seen at Kendall shops.

A year into the investigation, there was also the bombshell announcement: police revealed that Anna had seen two vehicles that had seemed to be casing the house that morning. They were old, dirty and parked very close together with the drivers' windows down – an old, white station wagon and a grey sedan. Where were the drivers? To this day, nobody knows. Why did no one else in the street see them? Ditto. By the end of this book, we'll also have among our VOI list an entire fleet of Toyota Camrys.

*

On Monday 9 March 2020, the Taree inquest had just adjourned for lunch. As I walked outside, the media gaggle was abuzz with a rumour. A witness might be able to place Tony Jones closer to the crime scene. I discussed this over coffee with a journalist, then we returned to court to hear evidence from the mystery witness. Max Jones – a sixty-two-year-old man who is unrelated to Tony as far as he knows – took the stand. His wispy white beard and diminutive height gave him the appearance of a tiny wizard. He wore a hearing loop device that almost entirely covered his face. It gave him some trouble until the Coroner told him where to position it.

Max Jones said he used to take his dog for walks by Queens Lake, in Laurieton. On 12 September 2014, he'd set off from Henry Kendall Reserve, driving down the bush track to the water's edge and parking his car. Mr Jones told police about a man he'd seen in a parked car. To him, the man looked suspicious. Mr Jones had waved as he'd approached, and in response, the other driver quickly rolled up his window. Mr Jones couldn't see inside the vehicle because it was all fogged up. The driver looked hostile, frightened even, he felt. When Mr Jones returned from the bushwalk with his dog, the car was gone.

This testimony was unremarkable until we heard the key fact: the car was a beaten-up white Toyota Camry station wagon.

The Camry's occupant behaved suspiciously enough that Mr Jones remembered physical details about him, including a moustache that he would later recognise as adorning the face of Tony Jones when he saw his picture in a newspaper eight months later

'How confident are you that it was him?' Mr Craddock asked the witness.

'I'm one hundred per cent sure it was him,' he replied. So far, so good. But then, he swatted a fly into the ointment. 'It was definitely the car I seen in the paper and on the news.' The confounding influence of the media on memory strikes again.

Mr Craddock tried to separate the witness's memories of the car from those of its occupant. We heard that he was a slightly tanned man in his mid-fifties, middling in height and weight. Mr Jones recalled a dark moustache, but 'not a handlebar moustache'. He'd worn it differently from how it appeared in the later photo. He wore a cap over collar-length hair.

The witness estimated that he saw Tony Jones at the reserve around lunchtime that Friday. If true, this gives the lie to Jones' first alibi – that he was in the Bago State Forest collecting scrap metal all day. Having become accustomed to hearing bogus testimony and tangles of recollections that end up proving false, I dismissed this evidence and tuned out as Mr Jones drawled on about going to the local club and neglecting to tell his friends what he'd seen.

But then, a noise caught my attention, coming from the foster family's camp. Anna Wyndham was crying. Biting her lip and swallowing hard, she fought to regain control, but tears flowed and her faithful Bridesmaid was at the ready with the tissues. Was she crying at the terrible coincidence of a meeting of two Joneses – one, the abductor of her child and the other an observer who may have had the power to intervene before it was too late? Or was she crying at the misery of enduring yet another red herring?

Another thought crossed my mind. Whatever this man saw that day, perhaps it brought to mind the decision not to reveal Anna's sighting of the white station wagon to the people of Kendall in September 2014. That move might have made all the difference. And that is a thought worth crying about.

16

LUCKY DIP

In response to the mystery of what happened to William Tyrrell, many opportunists crept out of the woodwork, bringing with them their crazy ideas. Some folks took it upon themselves to exploit the secrecy surrounding the foster family's identities, weighing in on public opinion with some truly bizarre theories. Social media exploded with stories that turn speculation into a science. They started with the reasonable (outlaw bikie gangs) then moved to the dubious (wealthy, child-selling adoption agents) and the truly spurious (a top-secret espionage organisation). Many suggested William was never in Kendall at all that day.

From there, things quickly descended to the lunatic fringe – Satanists, witches, shadow people, reptilian shape-shifting aliens and, my particular favourite, yowies. Some of the commentators I ran into had checked out of the Hotel Reality well before 12 September 2014.

These stories make me think of a writing exercise I used to set in English exams. You give the student a prompt sentence, then let them run with it to create their own narrative: 'William Tyrrell wandered away from his foster mother and … Now, you make up the rest of the story. Pay close attention to your spelling and punctuation. You have forty minutes.' But with a lot more time than

247

forty minutes to invent their tales, and absolutely no attention to spelling and punctuation, the speculators went to work. Soon, the online environment was awash with intricate theories that defied all logic and reason.

The more sedate tales told of shadowy figures they'd seen reflected in the house's windows. 'Have you seen those photos? They say his foster mother took them. But who's he *really* looking at? Someone else is behind the camera. And, what about the three people and the car you can see in the windows? If you enlarge it to ten times its size, you can just make out their shapes ...' This is one comment I encountered online, reproduced verbatim.

There are two noxious ideas here. The first is the Imposter Photographer, which I won't even dignify with a comment. The second theory is the Shadowy Stranger. It informs us that we can see (insert your preferred person of interest here) lurking around the perimeter of the house. Incredibly, people actually took the advice to enlarge the photos to see if they could spot the stranger. Discussion forums were replete with reproductions, enlarged and marked with texta outlines to help us make out the shapes. After four additional pictures were released, the Shadowy Stranger theory really took flight. Before long, the shapes were not humans at all, but spirits. Shadow People from the nearby Kendall Cemetery. 'Nuff said.

We now turn to the protagonist of my favourite bush yarns: the yowie. Yowies are the Australian cousins of the cryptid Big Foot and his alpine brother, the Abominable Snowman or Yeti. Some cryptozoologists believe the Bunyip legends of Indigenous Australian folklore are forerunners to this hirsute beast. Pictures of dark, hairy sasquatches concealed in the bushes around the yards of Benaroon Drive have circulated the internet, and there are a few sites wholly dedicated to the Yowie Snatch theory. They feature entertaining anecdotes of campers and hunters encountering yowies in remote forests.

Locals from Comboyne have even joined the fray, with some ripping yarns about sighting the Big Fella in bushland so frequently cleared by fires that any yowies would've been burnt to a crisp by 2014. I've reluctantly corresponded with a woman who is convinced she can see a yowie lurking in the side garden of Nancy's house. It's in the shadows, but if you look really, really close, you can just make out a pair of whitish eyes …

Failing to convince us of the existence of big, hairy men, stories of little green men became the order of the day. The Alien Abduction theory took root when other explanations were in short supply. These people wonder whether a child could be teleported to Planet X, or Nibiru, for those in the know. That September, its orbit brought it closer to the Earth than at any time in the past, according to secret calculations from NASA and, before them, the creators of the Mayan Calendar. We were also warned not to rule out intervention by reptilian, shape-shifting aliens. According to proponents of the Alien Abduction theory, the reptilians have connections in the White House.

Numerology enthusiasts have helpfully crunched some numbers for us and uncovered patterns that they say – and I concur – are truly mind-blowing. I can't run all the numbers for you here. I just can't. But I will say this: if you add up all the digits in the foster mother's birthdate, multiply that by the digits on the numberplate of Chris Rowley's police car, divide the product by the number of Pull-Ups the average toddler goes through in a week, then turn that into an improper fraction, you end up with … the lowest common denominator.

One inventive fellow hoping to garner himself an online following put forth a complicated argument that William Tyrrell didn't actually exist. This one certainly scored points for originality. He worked really hard to show that William was a fictional figure created to throw the public off an inconvenient scent that cadaver dogs picked up in a certain resort unit in Portugal. This guy would have us believe William Tyrrell was invented as a decoy to distract us from seeing flaws in the Madeleine McCann investigation. And how did he come to this startling conclusion? Well, the foster carers and the McCanns have something in common, he told us. They both hired public relations firms. It's open and shut.

Others got on the bandwagon with the news that we've all been duped. William Tyrrell died years before 2014. Well, that is probably true. Various William Tyrrells have, in fact. One who died in 1968 was an Air Vice Marshall who played rugby union for Ireland. He didn't die playing footy though. He just got old, as have lots of other William Tyrrells over the centuries. Lots of others, apart from our little guy.

*

One warm, fuzzy theory that was not ruled out for years – even by police – was a little outlandish in its optimism, but it continued to attract us anyway. Could it be that some childless person had taken William with hopes to raise him as their own son? A woman I met at the inquest certainly thought this one had staying power.

She had been collecting school photos from the internet – probably not with parental permission – which she compared with William's age-altered picture, using a highly sophisticated method. She overlaid the pictures with tracing paper and marked with her texta all the points of similarity. She theorised that a person who once lost a child called William to FACS themselves, and who is mentally unwell, believes William Tyrrell is really their son.

According to this woman, that individual mounted what they saw as a rescue in Kendall, nabbed the child and is now raising them at home. So adept were they in their master plan that they fearlessly sent William off to public school to be photographed. If such a parent does exist, I would like to meet them.

One ordinary day in Queensland, a young man told his friends he could be William Tyrrell's real father. He'd had a relationship with Karlie Tyrrell in 2010, around the time she became pregnant. In 2014, he reportedly rekindled a friendship with Karlie, to help her deal with William's disappearance. The man's mother, Sue, has stated publicly her belief that William is alive and living in an Aboriginal community somewhere in outback Australia. Sue never met William, although she said she did meet Lindsay once. Sue's son has convictions for assault, stalking, destroying property and driving while under the influence of drugs. He wouldn't comment and I wasn't prepared to force the issue, frankly.

I've seen video footage of women purporting to have the Gift, tracing William's presumed last steps through Kendall's bush tracks. I heard one asking William's restless spirit to point out where his bones are, so she can confirm his death. But the spirit didn't comply that particular day.

Another woman told of a vision, to anyone who'd listen, that William was taken by container ship to Bangkok, where he now works as a child sex slave. She 'tuned into his aura' or something. She named his birth mother (incorrectly) and presented all manner of other inaccurate facts to lend weight to her theory. Another – they keep on coming – drew a picture of a 'thick-lipped man with curly hair and bulging eyes', who she just knows was involved. I can't stop myself from wondering what her ex-husband looks like.

Still another woman says William talks to her through a radio. When she tunes it just right to the remote listening channel, he speaks to her through snippets of seemingly random songs. He's in the river, he tells her, although when I listened I couldn't make out the words. I had to rely on her convenient subtitles for that. Going by the videos posted online, it seems she's employed the assistance of some skinny teenage YouTuber who likes messing about with crude audio sampling software.

A woman who calls herself a 'psychic detective' says she's had a vision of William in a private school playground in Western Australia. When she saw him, he was with a man on a motorbike who looked like a grown-up version of William. The boy appeared to be happy and settled and was eating a sandwich. The woman is not a detective, for the record.

Meanwhile, real detectives were inundated with dreamers and visionaries, seers and spooks who purported to know something about where William went. Police asked, then begged, then warned, then flat out ordered these people to stop. Some serial pests were eventually prosecuted and spent a stretch cooling their heels in jail.

*

A particularly resourceful storyteller merged the William Tyrrell case with the famous narrative of the novel *Picnic at Hanging Rock*. The story goes that in the year 1900, a group of young girls went on a picnic at Hanging Rock, an isolated spot in Victoria. It's a real place, where a mysterious tragedy occurred – at least according to the initial popular understanding.

The girls' attention was attracted by something beyond a distinctive, tall rock formation. Hanging Rock derives its name from that monolith. One by one, three of them squeezed through the narrow cleft, into oblivion. Witnesses heard a brief scream, but they were never seen again, author Joan Lindsay told us. Speculation centred on the possibility of an electromagnetic confluence in the area. Hanging Rock became the Bermuda Triangle of the bush – and pseudo-scientific theories abounded.

After Joan Lindsay's death in 1984, Australia discovered the mind-bending truth. The story was a work of fiction. A final chapter never published in the first edition gave us Joan Lindsay's explanation, which moved the tale into the realm of science fiction – the rock was located at the entrance to a space-time wormhole. It seems the publishers had made a good decision to excise that part from the book. Instead, they framed it as a true story right from its first release. Visitors to Hanging Rock have been spooked ever since. And more than once, I've encountered people on the internet who claim that William Tyrrell's disappearance is another 'Hanging Rock incident' attributable to a unique convergence of mysterious 'energies' in the area. These folk remain blissfully unaware that this particular myth was exploded forty years ago.

Now that I've finished mocking this ship of fools, it's important I make one thing clear: all of these efforts to bring the supernatural or spurious into the frame make detectives' work more difficult. They clog valid information channels, distract the public from ways in which they could genuinely help, cast unwarranted suspicion on innocent people, and most toxic of all, they insult the bravery of William's loved ones.

With this in mind, we turn to the satanic ritual abuse cults as the final hypothesis. I have purposely separated this theory from the others because I don't feel it's a topic that can be dismissed quite as summarily. It's a knotty one. These stories were given legs by a growing online trend attributing genuine child abuse cases to cults and secretive clubs. Believers hope to convince us there exists a vast network of paedophilic Satan worshippers who procure children for nefarious purposes. And that government departments, such as FACS, are involved.

The exposure of senior politicians, cardinals, Hollywood producers and onscreen celebrities as abusers in recent years has poured rocket fuel on speculations about organised sex cults. Perhaps they exist, in some quarters, although how organised they really are is another question.

If satanic sex cults do exist, they don't account for the vast majority of cases of child abuse. Statistics tell us that the average victim is perpetrated against by their own family members or their close associates, for no higher aim than their own gratification. Perhaps theories such as the satanic cult one help people to imagine there was a greater purpose to their suffering. Perhaps it is a strange romanticising of an ugly truth that enables people to garner the peer support they desperately need.

I've read and heard many stories that point to institutionalised child abuse. It is a horrible reality, and if you find yourself reluctant to believe it, a read through reports from Strike Force Tuno and the Royal Commission into Institutional Responses to Child Sex Abuse is an excellent cure for ignorance. But, when a child goes missing, as an isolated case, it's hasty and unwise to conclude they're the victim of a global conspiracy involving shadowy elites. What we have, at best, is a string of unrelated anecdotes without any hard evidence to link them.

*

Social media has not been the only repository for salacious gossip. Its inky ancestor has sold enough papers to soak up Bass Strait on the strength of this case. But, not content with reporting on the investigation, which had stalled, and because facts about the three-year-old's background were off-limits, they needed a sideline. All seasoned journos know that if you want to sell stories about people, make them either victims or villains. So they went for the villains. There was a good deal of entirely justifiable reporting, much of it thoroughly researched, about the parade of predators labelled persons of interest. But there was a lot of crud too.

A case in point is the fiasco surrounding the sign-writing on Bill Spedding's van. On 3 January 2015, a picture of that vehicle graced *The Daily Telegraph's* front page. It could've turned out to be an expensive pic if not for some fancy footwork. Bill Spedding was depicted standing beside the van, with its blue vinyl reverse lettering spelling out a worthy catch-phrase. It would soon enter the vernacular of sleuths everywhere: 'Peddo's Hire'. Bill was unimpressed, to put it mildly. I wondered if the picture researcher had opportunely spilled their coffee on the 'S', because it had been mysteriously expunged from the image.

Bill inadvertently destroyed his chances of receiving compensation by hastily peeling off the letters when a friend alerted him that he now had a nation-wide nickname. Bill told me later he kicked himself for not snapping a pic of the lettering in situ that day, which would have proven beyond doubt that the 'S' had been clearly visible on the date the photo was created. Despite claims about colour saturation and the finer details of print resolution, few doubted there'd been digital jiggery pokery.

That admittedly epic front page shot couldn't be compared to the original signage, because by the time Bill's lawyer tried, the van had no lettering on the front. And it couldn't be compared to the original photo, which clearly showed the phantom 'S'. Although I spent weeks trying, I could not locate a single copy – digital or otherwise – of the photo. It had been purchased by persons unknown – lock, stock, barrel and negatives – from the local photographer who'd taken it.

In this unsavoury episode, the question of why a person hoping to conceal their proclivities for child sex would emblazon their van with such a message was ignored. Bill received more death threats after this incident. People didn't want to consider that the name 'Speddo' has always been his nickname. Rather than seeing a missing blue letter, they just saw red. Do media professionals not see how they are insulting their nation's intelligence? Do they really hold us in such contempt? Are Australians that suggestible? Well, newspaper and magazine sales figures suggest that yes, we are.

I recall seeing a quote from US *60 Minutes* contributor Andy Rooney on someone's Websleuths account. It goes like this:

'People will generally accept facts as truth only if the facts agree with what they already believe.' This is true, and there's a term for it – confirmation bias. It was very kind of an American media man to exhort us in this area. It's ironic that Websleuths is infamous for shutting down any threads and censoring any comments that suggest a narrative the admin doesn't accept. Many users have found themselves banned or blocked for pointing fingers in the 'wrong' direction.

I ask you to test my own confirmation bias as I take you through the reasons I didn't believe William Tyrrell's birth family perpetrated a second abduction in 2014. When the abduction theory was first put on the table, William's foster parents told police that they suspected the birth family. The motive was simple – the 'bios' (a terrible term now in common use) wanted their kids back. They may have even wanted revenge on FACS or the 'fosters' (the terrible term's opposite). We knew they had form.

Some felt that although police had surveillance footage of both parents that proved they were elsewhere at the time of the disappearance, perhaps they organised someone else to take William from Kendall. It's a fair theory, considering the hobbies of some of their associates. Facebook sleuthers were salivating at the photo gallery they'd collected of rebellious, tattooed youths holding up their bongs, their weapons and both middle fingers. One finger is cheeky, but two is downright hard-arsed.

To perpetrate this bold abduction, the birth family would need foreknowledge of William's trip north. But the trip was a surprise, we were told. An important question arises at this juncture: why take only William? Didn't they want Lindsay back too? Perhaps that was the plot, but the second abduction failed.

Despite what they had said publicly, the police still weren't ruling out the birth family – or at least their associates – as suspects. A close relative of Brendan Collins had made a phone call to a Port

Macquarie newspaper that left a nasty taste in the mouth of the journalist on the other end. Police looked into his history and found he was associated with a number of different addresses and seven different vehicles. As late as May 2015, surveillance operations continued on the bios and co. And in the operations logs I've seen, the names of the officers tasked with the job have been redacted. That can only mean one thing – they were working undercover.

With covert operatives on their trail, you would think police would have soon busted Karlie and Brendan if they'd had anything to do with William's disappearance. If the person arranged to take the toddler had fled overseas or hidden with an extended family member, for example, it's hard to explain how the bio parents would ever get to see him. He'd have to hide out, waiting for the time when he could live with his birth parents somewhere so remote that they wouldn't be recognised.

One element of the bio angle that did give me pause for thought is the idea that William might have known his kidnapper. Otherwise, as Nathan points out, he would likely have screamed and run away from them. That's assuming he was startled by the person who approached him and that he didn't voluntarily engage in dialogue with them.

Natalie Collins told me that Brendan wouldn't have stolen William because he is not capable of pulling it off. She said that, when the child vanished, Brendan wanted to go and search for him, but he felt the police would suspect him. He eventually did ask to join the search. Brendan told me he was turned away to avoid unwanted publicity. He blamed himself for the whole situation, believing he should have left Karlie years ago and taken the kids off her.

In October of 2014, Anna Wyndham sent a handwritten letter expressing her condolences to Karlie and Brendan. Included in the envelope were photos of William. The letter confirms Anna knew Karlie was due to give birth within a week. At that stage, the Tyrrells had not been cleared of involvement, although police publicly stated they had. We know this because police records reveal Karlie Tyrrell's phone was tapped. Surveillance crews continued to watch her from a building across the road.

At the inquest, Mr Craddock revealed that CCTV footage places Karlie and Brendan in Sydney on 12 September. Watching that vision of Brendan in Macca's and Karlie at the shops, I toyed with an idea. Could they have purposely set up their CCTV alibis to rule them out as suspects? It would be a masterstroke to use digital means to timestamp yourself away from suspicion.

It's easy to assume that two parents desperate to bring their children home had nothing to lose. But, in fact, the bio family did have four valuable chips on number 48 at the roulette table: if they got caught, they risked never seeing any of their children again.

At the inquest, Mr Craddock bossed us around until we had one particular idea clear in our minds – William's foster care status had nothing to do with his disappearance. It seemed to be his mantra. It was good news in triplicate: it exonerated Anna and Nathan; it took the heat off FACS. But by extension, it also excluded Karlie and Brendan and their associates. The message I got was that Mr Craddock was satisfied William wasn't abducted by the birth family, but that he was abducted by someone. His opening address assured us, 'William was taken and removed from the vicinity in a car.'

*

With William still missing, local police were under immense pressure to get a result. Hope for recovering him alive was all but extinguished, although social media gurus continued to keep the faith, as did the foster parents' public relations reps. Working with Anna and Nathan, they created an official campaign, 'Where's William? Bring Him Home.' Their brief was to lobby for more police resources to stop the case from going cold. Always working from the premise that William was still alive and being held somewhere, the firm worked pro bono.

The firm offset their costs through donations and through the sale of merchandise designed to keep the little boy's face before the public. But the sale of posters, stickers and t-shirts, and their calls for donations soon got people's backs up. From the armchair, it might have appeared the firm was trying to cash in on the tragedy. People didn't understand the money was being used to try to bring William home.

At first, online groups and pages seemed great tools that could really help find William. Each night, thousands of Australians, including me, would stay up late, scouring pages such as 'Let's Find Little William Tyrrell', 'Bring Little Spiderman William Tyrrell Home' and every other conceivable variation. But instead of working together for a result, the various groups quickly separated into factions.

Among the unofficial groups was W4W Walking Warriors Australia. Photos of children who looked like William were circulated without approval, hampering police work with a flood of information about false sightings. They also released a poster featuring a Crime Stoppers phone number that was incorrect. False information about the foster family was disseminated through this site and other rogue groups.

Whoever you think should have had full control over what was published about William, it wasn't a bunch of strangers online. The problem was, it was almost irresistible to join the mob. Early on, before I had any access to information, I too waded waist-deep in the waters of unsubstantiated rumour, online gossip and ignorant speculation.

I developed friendships – of sorts – with strangers on Websleuths, which attracts people from all over the world. Many of them are seeking to inject some intrigue into their lives. Websleuthing becomes addictive, serving something inside us more than serving the cause of finding the little boy in whose name we'd first gathered.

Here's the trajectory: first you read Websleuths threads as a guest, hiding in the background. You're a harmless little fly who's landed temporarily, and suddenly you're surrounded by sticky threads of web. You resist making comments, because that requires setting up an account. Certain commentators and particularly juicy theories attract your interest. These thin silken threads have been spun by unknown spiders, lurking in the dark recesses online. They have each of their eight legs spinning different threads.

Soon, you get the idea you know some things others don't. Questions are posed that you can answer. You flap your little fly wings. And with the movement, the threads wind around you, drawing you further in. You can't help yourself. You must join in and be heard. You tell yourself it might help find the boy or at least find the perpetrator.

Abandoning caution, you crawl right into the middle of the web. You progress from making comments on threads to starting new discussions. You've forgotten you're a fly. You toy with the idea of getting the admins to verify you as an expert. That really adds weight to your posts. Your wings grow heavy and stiffen. Your body changes.

Then, in the ultimate validation of your expertise, other sleuths ask you questions publicly and tell you to personally message them your replies. You get a bigger and bigger head. Now, your intel is solid gold, shared privately with just a select few. You court them, inviting them into your parlour. They share information back, and because it has become so personal you lend it credibility. And before long, you are the amateur expert on the case. You've become the spider. Time to spin some threads of your own.

Many Websleuthers claimed to be best friends with William's family members, day care mates and case workers. People become competitive over the strangest things. One member wrote a different 'Good Night' message to William every night for years. She wore her tenacious belief that he was still alive, it seemed to me, as a badge of honour. And anyone who didn't speak to William in the present tense was branded faithless – a traitor.

The psychics we met in the rogues' gallery earlier brought their pestilence to Websleuths, making all sorts of bogus claims to cosy up to members who might have some intel. They could then fossick for facts to reverse engineer their predictions. The singular purpose of these creatures from the internet's darker recesses was to elevate themselves. The lure of cash, ego, cash, notoriety, cash, power ... and cash can induce people to say and do almost anything to garner a following. All sorts of people can surprisingly elevate themselves above the teeming masses through shameless self-promotion. Amusingly, many of the psychics I've seen plying their trade online have no idea how to spell the name of their profession. Strange that people who can look into the future can't be bothered to look into a dictionary.

*

One of Bill Spedding's customers from Wellington – whom I'm calling Dotty – inserted herself into the Tyrrell investigation when she discovered that an old workmate from a western Sydney RSL Club was involved in the Tyrrell matter. That workmate was Natalie Collins, William's biological grandmother. The two had worked together at the club, but otherwise had no connection. Years before William went missing, Dotty suddenly left the club for reasons not made clear.

When she heard the name Tyrrell, Dotty realised the missing boy was Natalie Collins' grandson. Keen to see if she could get something out of it, Dotty tried to ingratiate herself with Natalie, but was ignored. Early in 2016, she upped the ante. Dotty made much of a few photos she'd had someone take of her with her 'best friend' Natalie, which she used as evidence on Facebook of their 'rekindled friendship'.

What Natalie didn't know when she agreed to be photographed with her was that Dotty would soon go to the Department of Housing to apply for a three-bedroom house, citing Natalie as her intended housemate. The moment the application appeared on the system with Natalie's name attached to it, police flagged it as suspicious. Three bedrooms had them wondering: could the third room be intended for William? They placed Dotty under surveillance and tightened their attention on Natalie Collins.

Appearing on television in 2016, Dotty told the interviewer that she and Natalie were close friends, her story implying they were setting up house together. Natalie and Dotty were former work associates, nothing more. The two women would have nothing to do with each other after this time. Determined to milk her flimsy connection to William Tyrrell's grandmother, Dotty promptly sued the television network for payment she said was due for the interview she gave them. The case was thrown out of court.

Television producers didn't need spider silk to weave a web of spurious connections. In a bizarre coincidence, Dotty had once lived with Tony Jones' brother-in-law in a share house in Wellington. Life does sometimes throw up those 'six degrees of separation' anomalies, by chance. But we don't usually notice them because no one's drawing lines to connect them into a compelling image for television viewers. And because Tony Jones and Dotty are both from Wellington, producers couldn't resist cutting and pasting Bill Spedding into one corner of their feature graphic – a spider's web.

17

DOUBLE OR NOTHING

On 13 June 13 2018, Gary Jubelin mounted a fresh forensic search for evidence in the bushland around Benaroon Drive and at other nearby sites in Kendall. The intention was to rule out any answer other than human intervention to the question of what happened to William Tyrrell in 2014. Named Operation Noland, the forensic search was conducted over four weeks in 2018. Four square kilometres of bushland was covered.

When the inquest resumed in August the following year, the court heard from Detective Sergeant Laura Beacroft, who was tasked with organising what she dubbed 'the re-search' of the area around Benaroon Drive and the Kendall State Forest in June 2018. Once again, police tasked personnel from the State Emergency Service and the Rural Fire Service. Volunteers from the Salvation Army provided meals for searchers back at what police called the 'stand down area' at the Kendall Showground. This is the place from which teams are assembled, dispatched and recalled for shift changes, meals and rest.

The search was conducted at the surface and sub-surface soil strata. To this end, tangled lantana and other vegetation had to be cleared. For a time, a chorus of brush cutters and chainsaws outsang the local throng of cockatoos and king parrots.

GPS-tracked officers walked in a straight line at a spacing of two metres either side. The data was downloaded each afternoon and fed into the police's central database to create visual 'breadcrumb trails' left by each searcher. Searchers were equipped with McLeod tools – double-headed instruments with rake and hoe functions. Every inch of soil was carefully turned over and any leaf litter or other matter hand-searched. Officers picked their way forward, each find being carefully photographed, bagged as evidence and logged. Searchers were attuned to anything out of place in the natural environment.

Senior Constables Daniel Dring and Kris Rattenbury were specially trained Police Search Advisors who gave evidence, describing their role, which involved directing forty officers over four weeks. Rattenbury spoke of the motivation and enthusiasm of the searchers: 'The highest I've ever seen. Media attention on the case was unprecedented, making everyone very keen to find out what happened.'

A forensic anthropologist was on call should any bones – human or animal – be found. Onsite detectives would determine the relevance of other finds. Cadaver dogs assisted. Ground obstructed by fallen trees and branches, animal burrows and areas deemed impenetrable were sniffed over by dogs. Soil was probed to allow for odour release. Sites that looked recently disturbed were combed over and marked for closer inspection. When a searcher made a discovery, the call would go up and down the line: 'Find!' And the entire group would halt until the item had been assessed.

A local man informed police about some disturbed headstones in the cemetery, but the search there yielded unremarkable results: an uprooted cross, the lovingly sheathed bones of a fox terrier, another expired pet, a tree marked with an 'X'. It seems various locals had sneakily availed themselves of little doggy plots there over the years. No harm done; no progress either.

A child's board-and-rope play house was discovered, a sign declared it was 'Cooper's Cubby', but clearly, young Cooper had abandoned it to the lantana some time ago. A second structure was found, this one a handmade doll mansion of cardboard, toilet tubes, sticks and glittery treasures.

Filling out the find list were animal bones, two shovels, a crowbar, bags and backpacks, toys, clothing, plastic and paper household rubbish and a bonus spear gun. One searcher found number plates and a service book that came from a vehicle reported as stolen. But ultimately, all of these finds and all of the drudgery led nowhere. The evidence concluded with a statement from Dring: he was confident that William Tyrrell's remains were not in the area.

A child's shoe sole was uncovered. Even viewing it enlarged onscreen in the courtroom, I couldn't tell it apart from its surroundings. The leather had taken on the colour of leaf matter, bleached pale by exposure to the elements. It wasn't William's. Nothing was. Not a molecule of pertinent forensic evidence was detected. Mr Craddock cited the shoe sole to demonstrate the agonising exactitude with which searchers combed that green tangle of bushland, and I've just given you a taste of it here. This painstaking process is the reason why police have remained confident that no physical evidence was missed.

*

At the start of this narrative, I took you back to the 2013 rescue of little Tyler Kennedy. The two-year-old went missing from Johns River, a whistle-stop on the North Coast railway line just south of Kendall. It happened at 10.30 on a Friday morning, which is eerie. But although you know we found him, you haven't heard the whole story.

That Friday, Amanda Kennedy had booked her car in for 10.30. The workshop was on a rural property. While the mechanic did his safety checks, her daughter sat down in the shade of a mandarin tree and picked clover and dandelions, singing to herself. Tyler toddled off around the side of the shed, exploring. His mother put on her sunglasses. Two hundred metres distant, a white-pebbled drive led to the farmhouse, cutting through a green sweep of lawn. A profusion of bougainvillea draped over the lattice of a shady verandah, a splash of red against the green.

Amanda walked with the little girl around the shed's corner. Tyler wasn't in sight. To the rear of the farmhouse lay a few outbuildings, a chicken yard and a giant, spreading fig tree. Then, hanging from a low branch, she saw what must've attracted him – a swing. Eyes scanning along the neatly painted fence, she returned to the swing with its red plastic seat – built just for a toddler of Tyler's size.

But she still couldn't see his white t-shirt among the green. Amanda reached the fence that separated the yard from the unslashed paddocks beyond. Her throat tightened and that peculiar dance began, energised by adrenaline. *How could I not have noticed? It was just a few seconds.* She tried to count them but they were outnumbered by sharp arrows of conscience.

Tyler Kennedy had crept off out of sight in just a few short minutes. He was in a place entirely unfamiliar to him – a riverfront property stretching across forty-two acres. Rough paddocks, a pine forest verging on a marshy wetland and dense bush that merges with thirteen hundred hectares of that old nemesis, the state forest.

As in William's case, I first heard about Tyler on my car radio. It was the image of my own child wandering panic-stricken that first captured my attention. But then I heard a detail that fell on me like a hammer blow in slow motion.

'… a mechanical workshop on a rural property at Johns River.' I realised with shock where that was. It was the farm: our family's home-base. We'd lived there for years until our relatives Elaine and Nigel Braun bought it. Yes – the same Elaine Braun whose birth mother and siblings I was to search for and find a year later.

My family and I know that place like the backs of our hands, every twig. And we know the well-holes, dangerously obscured and not fitted with covers. Images of these death-traps, the deep dams my father had excavated, and the steeply banked Stewarts River fuelled my sense of urgency to get down to the farm.

Back in 2013, home for me was in Laurieton. I prepared myself, dressing warmly and grabbing my water bottle. I stopped at Woolworths at Lakewood to buy a few torches and batteries. When I arrived at the farmhouse the mechanic, Nigel, and his wife were very quiet. Elaine hugged me tearfully. Cups of tea sat undisturbed on the table. The hushed, respectful vocal tones clued me in – the child's mother was in the next room. On the couch, Amanda sat staring vacantly at her smartphone. She was in pieces, a quivering wreck. Little Tyler had been missing for eight hours and nightfall was already upon us.

I loaded batteries into one of the new torches and headed outside. I could hear vehicles being driven off the property behind me and saw a few pairs of red tail-lights receding from view. It looked like the search teams were changing shifts. I approached a police constable stationed near the farmhouse. I was surprised to find him alone. He shone a beam into my face.

'Do you realise you're trespassing?' I laughed, explaining I was a member of the property owners' family come to help with the search.

'The search has been called off for the night,' he informed me.

'Called off?'

'Yes. We can't put teams on the ground in the dark. And in this mist. It's a safety issue. I'm here to inform any members of the public who may show up that they're not permitted on the property.' I shone my torch into his face to see if he was serious. He was.

He told me the official search for little Tyler was called off at 5.30. They'd already spent hours deploying tracker dogs, a PolAir helicopter and highly trained ground searchers from the Manning Great Lakes Local Area Command police. They'd found no sign of Tyler, not even a scent to track. They planned to bring in divers at first light. I hoped they hadn't told his mother this piece of news.

I asked the constable whether he knew about the well shafts on the property. He didn't. I asked him if he realised Tyler was lightly dressed in shorts and a flimsy cotton t-shirt and was barefoot. I could see the concern on his face, but he had his orders. The time was seven o'clock and it was five degrees.

'So, we can't do any more searching tonight, officially?'

'Nope. Sorry. We can't risk it.' He shook his head gravely. 'But rest assured, the search will re-commence at first light.'

'You've got to be kidding me!' I said, walking past him to the front of the property, accessed by a dirt road. It runs parallel to the fast-flowing Stewarts River. It was empty except for a single patrol car parked on the dusty verge. Everyone else had gone home.

I returned to the officer, still standing there, guarding nothing. I gave his face another blast with my torch. He squinted and said he wouldn't stop me from continuing my own search, as it was my family's property. So I left him there and headed out to the furthest boundary fence alone.

In the ten-acre pine forest, I worked methodically from the southern fence line. I walked a series of straightish lines parallel to the fence, moving a little further north on each pass.

Nothing stirred in the forest, except mosquitoes. My voice sounded unnaturally loud as I called out the little boy's name. On the thick carpet of brown pine needles, my feet hardly made a sound. The dark green foliage felt oppressive. It closed in places, denying me access through the trees.

A thought gradually settled on me, an explanation for Tyler's disappearance that hadn't occurred to me until that moment. Perhaps I wasn't alone in the pine forest. What if there was a perpetrator?

And could they be watching me, even now? All I had with me was a torch and a plastic water bottle. I suddenly felt vulnerable out there alone. I needed to find a search buddy.

As I emerged from the pines, the green flash of an aircraft's starboard lights caught my eye. Now I fancy they were pointing me westwards, but then, I was oblivious, and headed back to the house like a startled rabbit.

Before I reached it, my brother-in-law Jake met me. He steered me in a different direction, eastwards to the edge of the state forest. I was relieved to see him so I didn't argue, for once. For three hours, we tramped through thick scrub, crossing fences and trail bike tracks, only stopping where the forest was rendered impassable by thickets of lantana.

West of the pine forest was a swamp. The water was perhaps half a metre deep in some places, interspersed with patches of muddy bog. Beyond it ran the railway line. Well after midnight, a familiar ding ding ding of bells rang out. In the distance flashed the red warning lights of the level crossing. Jake and I watched as the Brisbane to Sydney Trainlink service thundered through, its single headlight blazing in the darkness. It was the same train that would one day take me to an inquest in Sydney. I hoped Tyler's mother hadn't heard it from the house.

We decided to head back to the farmhouse to see if we could marshal some help. The night was growing colder by the minute and we were freezing. Inside, we stood by the woodstove, its warmth spreading through us like whisky. Tyler's mother was in much the same state as we'd left her. Fixated trance-like, staring at her thumb as it buzzed over her smartphone. Her plump young face wore a wounded look that only grief can create. Her brunette hair was pulled up tightly into a messy bun, as if the strands were holding her together somehow.

Elaine and Nigel conversed in low tones in the kitchen. No one else was inside. There wasn't anyone else to help. I stared in despair at the woman on the couch and a mean thought occurred to me. Why isn't she out there searching? But I never saw the silken, spidery threads shooting out of her wrist as she held that phone. What I didn't know was that this determined mother was quietly mobilising an army.

I wanted to know how Tyler had become lost. Nigel filled me in on the events leading up to his disappearance.

'Do the police suspect human intervention?'

'They're not ruling it out,' he said. But they had no suspects in view. They'd eliminated the boy's parents now; they'd initially been top of the list. The isolated setting made a random abduction improbable.

We discussed distances. Nigel's mechanical workshop was three hundred metres away from the pine forest. This meant Tyler would've needed to traverse five acres of yard, two barbed wire fences and a huge, unslashed paddock to get there. And that's precisely what that resourceful toddler did. His departure from the workshop wasn't noticed for about five minutes – not long, but long enough.

Nigel and the searchers had concentrated their earliest efforts on the riverbank, the dams, creek, fields and the rugged scrub to the east. Nigel shook his head. 'He wouldn't have gone into the pine forest, and he definitely wouldn't be in the swamp. I mean, why would a two-year-old go there? He's barely walking!' Why indeed?

Elaine offered me a hot drink, a tempting diversion, but the urgency of the situation compelled us back outside to search. I swallowed a gulp of milky coffee before I stepped outside and the milky fog swallowed me. Jake and I checked the well-holes, the waterholes, the creek again – nothing. But when we emerged from the bushes a while later – something. Something extraordinary.

More than a hundred people had materialised out of nowhere. They were assembling on the dirt road at the gates, ready to search en masse. There were people dressed in outdoor gear, kitted up with backpacks, wielding torches, hatchets and walking sticks. We were thrilled, but puzzled. Where had they come from? We hadn't heard any cars approaching. There still weren't any vehicles visible on the roadway.

As she digitally spun the story of her missing boy across the web, Tyler's determined mother had forewarned them all to park further up the road, outside the police's exclusion zone. It was an invasion by stealth. Today, I think of Amanda Kennedy as Spiderwoman.

'Walk up to the fence,' she'd texted to them. 'We'll send someone to let you in.'

The constable was there, still keeping vigil – and the volunteers were refusing to leave. It was a heartening sight – a display of community.

Men, women and children had come in response to desperate calls on social media and, incredibly, some were already en route before the official search was shut down. Folks came from Coffs Harbour, Macksville and Kempsey in the north to Newcastle, Sydney and Wollongong in the south.

We went to welcome the troops and let them in through the fence furthest from the good officer on duty. Rather than trying to hold the line, he wisely turned a blind eye. Many had already organised themselves into parties to do both ad hoc and organised line searches. They pushed on through the night, covering and re-covering every square inch of the property.

Among those volunteers were Kay and her family. They'd driven up from Forster when they heard the search had been suspended. In fact, her son had pestered Kay for an hour to take them up there. On one pass through a dark paddock, Kay came face to face with a bull. She backed off and from then on stayed with her group.

Enlisting the help of a young man and his retired army dog, they concentrated their efforts in the swamp. It was hard going, furrowed, muddy and thick with thorny scrub. Police had already tramped all

271

around that area with tracker dogs. I too had searched in that marsh and had written it off as impenetrable. But Kay was a determined woman. She and her son pushed on that night an hour after I left the scene and happened to hear a small cry.

*

According to a large study carried out by the United States Department of Justice in 1999, 74 per cent of abducted children who don't come home are murdered within three hours.[32] I quote this American source because there have been few such studies done in Australia. More encouragingly, in all but 4.5 per cent of cases, missing children turn up again unharmed. In some cases, as in Tyler's, the deciding factor is people power.

Promise me if you're ever in a situation where you can help look for someone who's lost, you won't hesitate like I did when William Tyrrell went missing. I deeply regret it, even though I know now that we couldn't have saved him. When you get the chance, get out there and search. Show your neighbours the Aussie spirit is alive and well, even in the face of certain death. It could be the last throw of the dice. Even if an abduction can't be ruled out, keep looking. Because the stakes are far higher than double or nothing.

18

LOSING STREAK

In 2014, Kendall had been enjoying some good times. The village was a hive of activity, with the Kendall Community Trust, the Men's Shed, the Kendall National Violin Competition, the Country Women's Association and all manner of volunteer groups staging events. The humble delights of country life made the annual Camden Haven Show a popular event that year. The Kendall Showground on Batar Creek Road hosted equestrian events, prize poultry competitions, displays of art and craft, jams and baked goods, plants, flowers, vegetables and a baby animal nursery. In 2014, the most eagerly awaited events were the lawnmower races and the crowd-pleasing Demolition Derby.

In a May 2014 issue of the *Kendall Chronicle*, we heard from a local wag who invites residents to dob in some vandals and a couple of rev heads.

We all have noticed that some idiot has acquired a can of paint and decided the town should see his 'art'. Someone in the community knows who this dope is, so we embark on the Kendall Men's Shed Rewards Programme – give a name to the police, and on conviction we will pay the reporter $200. Do the right thing by the community and let the police know who this fool is.

The writer went on to report on a recent heritage day, describing it as 'an absolute pearler.' He wrote:

273

The weather was perfect, the sausages well cooked, until a white Commodore and a green Holden ute felt the need to prove to all and sundry that they cared not for road rules or pedestrian safety. Despite our age, all the folk in the Kendall Green area can read, and can also recognise numerals. Registration plates are relatively easy. If you drive a bright green ute with blue registration plates and a loud exhaust, it makes no sense that you want to keep proving to the community that you don't want your licence to drive. Why don't you just hand it in and save us all some trouble?[33]

In 2014, at nearby Herons Creek, a heritage conservation project had made a little splash. A local minister who'd found himself churchless had refurbished an old Anglican chapel with hopes of turning it into a hub for community gatherings. Incorporating a walking trail sign-posting other heritage sites of interest, the project attracted council grant money and donations from supporters, enabling Pastor Martin Parish to realise what he called his 'dream'. Services were held at the tiny wooden church every second Sunday of the month.

The aptly named Pastor Parish told the local paper that the Heritage Trail and chapel restoration initiative would well and truly put Herons Creek on the map. His words proved prophetic, but not for the reasons he'd hoped. Parish enlisted the help of volunteer workers to restore the Herons Creek chapel to its former modesty. Among them was a man whose infamy would soon eclipse the meagre fame of the heritage project.

In 2018, a person named Frank Abbott came to be of interest to detectives investigating William Tyrrell's disappearance. In September 2014, Abbott was living on a property at Herons Creek owned by Martin Parish's father. Since 2007, Abbott had done odd jobs there, off and on. He'd first worked with brothers Martin and Danny Parish in Johns River. He was invited to live in a caravan at their property by Martin's father, Kevin, in 2012. Abbott had apparently known Kevin for many years and called him Pop.

The Parish property at Herons Creek was used for a number of enterprises. Danny Parish would buy old buses and strip them down for conversion into mobile homes. A shed on the property accommodated up to ten buses. Also on the place was a bush timber mill, quite a few cars and a scattering of ramshackle buildings, including an old demountable school classroom and a barely liveable house which Martin was hoping to convert to a family history museum. An historic tramway line ran through the property, which was of interest to Herons Creek's heritage enthusiasts.

According to inquest testimony from the property's other occupant, Danny Parish, handyman Frank Abbott soon wore out his welcome and Pop wanted him to leave. But he declined. When challenged by Danny Parish, his response was menacing. He threatened Danny with a machete, telling him with a grin, 'You'll never get rid of me!' And with his next statement, Abbott gave Danny Parish genuine reason to fear what he might do if pressed. 'I've been up before court twice for murder ... If I go to jail, I don't care. I'll get three square meals a day,' Frank Abbott gloated.

*

Frank Abbott first came to police attention in 1968 in connection with a murder investigation. I spent some time researching the case of Helen Harrison who, at just seventeen, was found dead in a shallow grave in the bushland of East Kurrajong, north of Sydney. Helen's body was found near an isolated timber cutters' road. Detectives found she'd been stripped to the waist, raped and robbed of $20 in cash. Reward money and the promise of a pardon was offered to any accomplice who came forward with information. But with scant evidence to work with, the case went cold.

Twenty-three years later, two people came forward with new evidence. They claimed that back in 1977 Frank Abbott had told them he'd killed Helen Harrison and bragged that he'd gotten away with it. A third witness, a fellow prisoner whom police called Mr X, claimed he too had heard Abbott admit to the killing. Abbott denied any involvement but the case went to trial. His defence rested on the idea that the witnesses were motivated by money. They hoped to collect the $5000 reward, his lawyer argued. Abbott's trial resulted in a hung jury.

But the evidence was compelling enough to convince the state to re-try Abbott some years later. This time, everything hinged on a technicality. Abbott's alibi rested on the testimony of his parents, who'd said he was home with them at the critical period. Abbott's parents had died in the interval between the two trials. His defence team argued that the situation involved an unacceptable delay which compromised his ability to get a fair trial.

In 1991, a permanent stay of proceedings was granted. But that victory would unfortunately not mark the end of Abbott's association with crime. He would go on to notch up a string of despicable acts that he wouldn't pay for until his senior years.

The Helen Harrison case bothered me a good deal. How do you beat a murder rap twice? I did some further digging and found that in 1991 the jury deliberated for twenty-one hours after the first three-week trial. The Crown maintained that Abbott, by this time aged fifty-three, had admitted to three people that he'd 'knocked' the girl. But the witnesses refused to come forward because Abbott had threatened their families.

The witness known as Mr X said he'd been forced at gunpoint to help Abbott and an accomplice push the vehicle involved into the Hawkesbury River. 'You're now involved in the murder of that girl,' Frank Abbott had told him. Abbott went on to gloat about how he'd followed Helen Harrison on her bike, forced her into his car and drove her into bushland where he raped and murdered her. He showed the witness a pair of blue panties he said were Helen's. Mr X was convinced that Abbott had indeed managed to get away with murder.[34]

When the defence asked the witness why Abbott wouldn't have just killed him too, he said that he did some fast-talking. He convinced Abbott that he'd already told someone else about the involvement of the vehicle and that they'd tell the police if he disappeared. Abbott already had a long criminal history, including breaking, entering and stealing, firearms offences and escaping from custody.

After being acquitted in his second murder trial in 1994, Abbott fell off the radar for a couple of years until he turned up in Johns River.

*

In November 2019, Frank Abbott was transferred from prison into police custody for an interview while serving a sentence for child sexual assault in Cessnock Correctional Centre. No charges would be laid in 2019, but he would be required to give evidence at the William Tyrrell inquest.

Taree courthouse was the stage on which a farce was to play out via video link from Cessnock. By 2020, Frank Abbott's ample frame had shrunk considerably. I'd seen pictures of him with a gigantic belly. Prison life seemed to have been hard on Abbott (or kind, depending on how you see weight loss). He was once a redhead, but his hair had faded to white fuzz. He had small, round eyes and a ruddy complexion. Another candidate for the driver of the teal car seen cruising the street by Anna Wyndham the morning William disappeared, I thought.

In March 2020, Abbott made the laughable decision to represent himself at the inquest. It made a mockery of the proceedings, but I sensed the Coroner was simply giving him enough rope. Abbott seemed to be perpetually testing his microphone – and the Coroner's patience – with a string of burps, farts, throaty phlegm-hocks and, yes, snores. Abbott's emissions certainly exceeded his admissions that week.

More seriously, Abbott's presence created a predicament for the Coroner. She had to respectfully afford him the same right to question each witness as the rest of the bar table. But because the man had clearly resigned himself to dying in prison, he was intent on milking the situation for every ounce of attention he could get. On the final day of evidence, Abbott feigned an attack of deafness, delaying the start of proceedings for half an hour. He looked positively gleeful as technicians scurried about. But his hearing acuity magically picked up at just the right moments to refute the testimony of his opponents. And he had quite a few that day.

Over the course of two days, Mr Craddock piggy-backed us through a quagmire of facts about Frank Abbott that left us all in need of a good bath. I present them here, in a rapid torrent, and invite you to pull on your gumboots.

*

At the Taree inquest, an elderly local woman, Iris Northam, testified that Frank Abbott had once worked for her husband, known as Dooley. He did odd jobs on cars and maintenance work around the house. He also collected scrap metal.

In 1996, thirty-four-year-old Margaret Cox was found dead in suspicious circumstances in a riverbed not far from the seaside hamlet of Old Bar, east of Taree.[35] Abbott was known to have been in the area at the time, but so had lots of people. The next day, at an antique auction in Johns River, Mrs Northam recalled seeing Frank Abbott with some strange, bloody marks on his arms. Mrs Northam's husband asked him about the injuries and he simply replied, 'Oysters.' But Mrs Northam wasn't satisfied with that explanation. She'd been oystering all her life and knew they make marks that are thin and irregular. As Mrs Northam said to her husband later that day, the wounds were not like oyster cuts. They were deep scratches.

'There were probably seven or eight marks on the arm,' she told the Taree inquest. 'They looked like finger marks. Something had gouged skin out.' Mrs Northam described the marks as long and straight and a few days old. 'They had a certain look,' she added, 'like wounds get before they start to heal. Police wouldn't comment on whether Abbott had been a person of interest in that investigation. Margaret Cox's murder eventually became filed as a cold case.

Just before the Coroner excused Mrs Northam, Mr Craddock presented the woman with a home phone number written on a piece of paper. He asked her if she knew whose number that was, explaining that the phone connected to that number was in contact with Abbott's phone at least a dozen times from 15 September 2014. She said that number belonged to her husband, Dooley Northam. Unfortunately, Mr Northam had developed dementia and could not be called upon to testify.

Former Johns River resident Patrick Teeling added some further detail about Frank Abbott's life. Mr Teeling had bought the Johns River store in 1989. He met Frank Abbott around that time and recalled seeing him at the shop, pushing his way into conversations and invading personal space. Teeling felt Abbott was purposely driving customers away from his shop. After hearing local gossip about more than one suspected murder involving Abbott, Teeling was wary. People warned the shopkeeper not to let his kids anywhere near Abbott.

Frank Abbott was living across the Pacific Highway from Teeling's shop, now called Rosie's Café. He drove an early model Holden, a square, light blue monstrosity. Teeling often heard a car engine revving at night, so once he went outside to investigate. He observed Abbott driving out of his place without any headlights or parkers on. When he was further down the highway, he turned on the lights. This mysterious 'blind driving' behaviour was a frequent occurrence.

Patrick Teeling sold the Johns River shop to another man. Then, it was sold again, this time to a local couple, Colin and Jan Anderson. Mr Teeling got a cleaning contract at the Royal Hotel at Kew, and would see Frank Abbott knocking about with a local man called Ray Porter. Frank and Ray went to Kew together a lot. They would hang out with a few mates outside the shops. Frank Abbott, Ray Porter and his old mate Dooley Northam were horse racing enthusiasts and liked playing the one-armed bandits – poker machines. Porter was easily spotted out and about in Kendall and Kew because he had an old Jack Russell terrier that followed him around like a shadow.

One day in 2014, after William Tyrrell went missing, Patrick Teeling saw Abbott and Porter at the Kew shops. Mr Teeling said Abbott breathlessly blurted out, 'I knew they'd get him, that Jones chap. They took his cars last night.'

'He decided he just had to tell you?" Mr Craddock asked Mr Teeling.

'Yeah, for some unknown reason,' Mr Teeling said. He recalled walking away wondering why on earth Frank would tell him such a thing. That night, he saw television news reporting on a man called Tony Jones being named a person of interest. Mr Teeling suspected Abbott was trying to cover his tracks by implicating Jones.

Colin and Jan Anderson didn't do much to improve Abbott's public image when they testified at the 2020 inquest. They had first met Abbott in connection with Patrick Teeling's old store at Johns River. They had a few suspicions about Abbott. He'd been caught thieving off them. But they decided to give him another chance and put him to work in their new venture in Wauchope – a takeaway shop.

The inquest heard from the Andersons that, around Wauchope, Abbott was considered a 'dirty old man', and a man not to be trusted around children. Abbott apparently had them downright worried when he told the Andersons that in searching Bill Spedding's place, police were looking in the wrong spot for William Tyrrell. Colin Anderson said he thought it a very strange thing to say.

Colin and Jan's son Dean testified against Abbott as well. He said Abbott would boast about 'beating a murder charge in Sydney like it was a badge of honour'. Abbott had told him of 'a bad smell he'd noticed around the Logans Crossing area'. Anderson told the inquest that he assumed it was probably a dead kangaroo, and he told Abbott so. But Abbott was insistent that he knew the difference between a dead kangaroo and a dead human.

Dean Anderson told him to either report the smell to police or shut up about it. Abbott demurred, saying he would probably get the blame for it if there was something up there. Aside from questioning how Abbott knew what a dead body smelt like, I couldn't help wondering about his use of the preposition 'up'. Considering the land is very flat over that way, it sounded like he was referring to a location uphill. Somewhere like the foothills of Logans Crossing.

*

Frank Abbott liked to spread himself around. He particularly liked to ingratiate himself with Christian groups. In 2010, Abbott secured some odd job work at a local drug and alcohol rehabilitation centre. A bush acreage, it incorporated a lake and a collection of private cabins to accommodate guests. It was a privately owned and operated Christian facility where recovering addicts could obtain support, accommodation and employment.

Frank Abbott lent a hand around the campground. He possessed some handy practical skills and made himself useful. But when his skill set was found to include theft and supply of drugs to recovering addicts, he was given a stern talking-to. Eventually, the owner became fed up after he caught Abbott brokering deals trading narcotics for sex with vulnerable single mothers, and in 2011 he was given the boot.

The owner had another property a little further north in Johns River. Abbott moved between the two properties doing various jobs in return for food and lodging. Strangely, during Abbott's association with the property, an accountant was found there, murdered. He was a mild-mannered person with no known enemies. No one was ever charged in relation to the killing.

By 2011, Abbott was homeless. He moved in with his fishing mate Ray Porter. Porter lived on a property beside the Johns River pub. The yard was filled with old public bus carcasses. Abbott lived there, promising work in return for food and lodging. Nobody knows how that deal worked out for Ray Porter, but I could hazard a guess. According to testimony from his associates, Abbott liked to bum lifts, overcharge his most vulnerable elderly clients and live at other people's places rent-free.

Ray's brother Ron was an administrator of the Kendall Showground, and had appointed Ray as caretaker. After he moved from Johns River, Ray Porter lived in a caravan at the Kendall Showground. When I heard this evidence, I wondered whether the Porters ever crossed paths with a balding, scented-candle-toting man travelling with a van full of chickens.

*

Frank Abbott had a bad run with vehicles, particularly for a man who claimed that he didn't drive. He owned a number of old bangers which were bought and sold with abandon, mostly among Abbott's few friends. Once, back in 2007, when Dooley Northam asked what had happened to Frank's latest car, Abbott said some young fellows from next door stole the vehicle and burnt it. Mrs Northam told the court Abbott didn't seem too concerned about this. I found it a fortunate coincidence that he had an interest in collecting scrap metal.

A friend gave me an interesting scrap to ponder about the behaviours of paedophiles who work cooperatively. They often go to the trouble of purchasing a number of identical vehicles – usually old, cheap cars. They have individual registration plates, of course. But the same makes and models work well in confounding eye-witnesses. And if someone does happen to recall a licence plate, they can be easily switched before the vehicle is seized for forensic testing.

If the exact makes and models can't be procured, similar-looking cars of the same vintage are good substitutes. I couldn't help but think about all those old-model white station wagons that had been mentioned in the search for answers to William's disappearance.

Diagonally opposite the coffee shop at Kew was the Royal Hotel. On the other corner was an antique dealership. Elizabeth Rowley, antique dealer and wife of Senior Constable Chris Rowley, told the inquest that she frequently saw Abbott being driven around Kew in an old white station wagon. She didn't see who was driving that particular day. Sometimes Abbott hung around with Ray Porter; sometimes Dooley Northam. Mrs Rowley once heard Dooley loudly warning Abbott not to get caught driving without a licence because the antique shop was owned by 'the copper's wife'. It was intended to get a rise out of Abbott, who liked to tell people he never drove without a licence.

Mrs Rowley recalled that Abbott tried to flog a rare 1930s penny to her one day. But there were scratch marks around the altered date. It was a fake. I wondered whether Abbott had ever knocked about with another man who I recall was interested in collecting and trading coins. A person who lived in Benaroon Drive who may have had visitors in the early morning of 12 September 2014.

After Dooley Northam saw how Abbott acted when he got angry with someone, he became worried. He spoke to Elizabeth Rowley about his concerns and asked her to pass some information on to her husband. Mrs Rowley told the court that Northam spoke to her about Abbott's past. He told her Abbott may have 'got off a murder' once, and that he may be responsible for someone going missing. He added that his suspicions related to William Tyrrell's disappearance.

When the inquest heard testimony from Mrs Rowley that Ray Porter drove an old white Commodore station wagon, I noticed Anna Wyndham whisper to the Bridesmaid, her constant companion. Anna had a terracotta-coloured cardigan although it wasn't cold. She put it on backwards over her arms and chest, like a blanket. I noticed Anna always brought what a psychologist might call 'a self-comforting item' to court – a soft shawl, a quilted fabric wrap, a cosy knit and, once, a padded jacket with a neckline made of possum-coloured fur.

19

BURN AND TURN

Throughout 2018, the Mid North Coast, along with much of the nation, found itself in the grip of drought. Nothing new there. But in the spring of 2019, we gradually became aware of a new crisis – a significant portion of Australia was ablaze. Locally, multiple bushfires had broken through containment lines and the situation was deteriorating rapidly. Volunteers from the Rural Fire Service stepped up, and locals swamped their headquarters with home-baked goods to keep the firies going. Donations of labour, food, fuel, firefighting equipment, generators and vehicles enabled crews to do their work.

Port Macquarie was under serious threat – hard to believe for a coastal town. There were huge blazes at Lake Cathie and Bonny Hills, and flames licked at the feet of Laurieton's North Brother mountain, sweeping unchecked up the coast. The firefront decimated bushland and properties east of the highway at Johns River. In fact, the staging ground for the Rural Fire Service's Johns River units was our old family farm – where Tyler Kennedy had been lost and found in 2013. The Wharf Road property was saved, but many neighbouring farms were not.

In a bid to stop the Johns River blaze from spreading north, the Rural Fire Service deployed multiple units from the coastal villages of Forster, Tuncurry, Harrington and Old Bar, east of Taree. But resources were stretched to the limit. In preparation for the worst, residents from Laurieton, North Haven and Dunbogan were evacuated, but there wasn't really anywhere safe to go, only 'safer places'. People congregated on the beaches. The destruction was unprecedented.

Inland, a small fire broke out at Upsalls Creek, on Kendall's doorstep, but air crews extinguished it before it could take hold and enter the Middle Brother State Forest. The big worry in Kendall was that Middle Brother would go up in flames. It had happened before, many decades ago, and it had been devastating. Another firefront threatened us from the west. This one would provide dramatic fodder for television news for months. It destroyed entire townships in the area southwest of Taree. Hillville and Rainbow Flat were the hardest hit. Homes, farms, schools and, tragically, lives were lost.

Yet another massive fire was raging uncontained in the northwest, around Mount Seaview, Yarras and Long Flat. More fires were spreading west of Kempsey. Eventually, two of these would merge into a firefront of apocalyptic proportions. Firies switched to protecting properties, rather than trying to hold containment lines. Some of us manned the emergency radio scanner, passing on the latest reports through social media, night and day. My involvement in the drama eventually ended when my family had to evacuate from Comboyne.

I recall posting updated maps from the Rural Fire Service's 'Fires Near Me' app and seeing tiny Comboyne sitting right in the path of four enormous fires that were devouring thousands of hectares of bushland at speed. We never came within reach of the flames, but columns of smoke kilometres wide loomed over us on all sides and made breathing difficult. We stayed with friends of ours, a family of seven. These folk had recently emigrated from Scotland and were remarkably composed under the circumstances. Australia had given them a baptism of fire – far too warm a welcome.

When we returned home to the farm, we set about patrolling for spot fires caused by flying embers. They were difficult days, but we managed because of the generosity of others. The measure of a community's spirit is how it responds in times of crisis. The way locals weathered the 2019 fires proved that Kendall is undeniably resilient.

Not only did the bushfire disaster result in heartening revelations about the area, it also laid it bare. Literally. Countless acres of land, practically impenetrable in the initial sweeps for evidence related to William, were now bereft of all obstacles, both natural and constructed. The barbed and knotted undergrowth that had refused to yield its secrets to searchers had now dematerialised, exposing vast reaches of blackened, naked earth.

*

In September 2019 and again in March 2020, two fresh forensic searches were made at a new site in Logans Crossing – a log dump, which was just up the road from Herons Creek. Police were tight-lipped about what they found, telling one reporter they were 'just tying up some loose ends'. But considering the level of activity out there, some of us weren't buying that story. At the time of writing, the finds made at the site were yet to be announced.

In 2019, when the heat was turned on him, Frank Abbott made every effort to place Tony Jones at the Logans Crossing log dump. He'd made previous attempts to link Jones to William's disappearance. Following the airing of a segment on *A Current Affair* in October 2018, Abbott approached police from his prison cell in Nowra. He wanted to make a statement, and was adamant that Tony Jones should be investigated. Abbott went so far as to speak with Detective Robert Dingle about it.

At the Taree inquest, Abbott used a series of sneaky 'questions', which the Coroner pointed out were actually statements, to tell the court he recalled meeting Jones at Logans Crossing in July 2015. Ray Porter took Abbott along on a ride with a property owner at Logans Crossing. The site is graced by a mountain, which is in turn disgraced by an old, disused radio tower. A little further on from the tower is a log dump. Abbott claimed to have met two men there. They were driving an old white station wagon. One of the men was aged in his forties and was with a boy of about seven. Abbott insisted the other man told him his name was Jones and that he was from 'out west'.

I watched Abbott closely as Mr Craddock asked for the tower photo to be displayed onscreen. I noticed Abbott suddenly became very still. The fact that Abbott has taken such pains to connect Jones with the log dump site at Logans Crossing is very telling. It suggested to me that something significant had been found at that location – and Abbott knew it was incriminating.

*

When Tony Jones was questioned about his connection with Frank Abbott in March 2020, he reacted angrily. He only has one setting, it seems. Jones wanted us to believe that he met Abbott for the first time in 2019 when they were both in Grafton prison. Apparently, Jones didn't like what Abbott was saying about the Tyrrell investigation when he was knocking about in Kew and Kendall with his buddies. He had heard talk through the lively lock-up grapevine. Abbott told the inquest that he spoke about it with Jones – saying he hadn't given him up. Frank Abbott said he was locked in his room for weeks because word was he was going to be shivved (prison lingo for being stabbed with a makeshift blade). But Tony Jones flatly denied all of this, saying he'd never met Frank Abbott until their altercation in prison.

But now, it was truth time. Mr Craddock wanted Jones to admit that he'd actually known Abbott since at least 2014. Jones grudgingly admitted he knew Abbott lurked at the house across the road from his and Debbie's place in Wauchope. He conceded that he knew Abbott was his neighbour's father.

When The Boss asked Jones about Max Jones' claim to have seen him at Henry Kendall Reserve in Laurieton on the day William went missing, Tony Jones threw a little tantrum.

'Well that person who recognised me needs to go to an optometrist.' Then, Jones reminded Mr Craddock that he suffered greatly with emphysema. At first we couldn't see the connection. Mr Craddock looked as puzzled as the public gallery. But he was faking. When The Boss wants to regain control of the courtroom, I've noticed he uses long, unsettling pauses. He laid one on Jones and it worked a treat.

'How is it you are so sure that Max Jones is mistaken about seeing you in the fogged-up car that day?' he asked mildly. Jones took the bait.

'I couldn't have been there because with my emphysema, I couldn't have sat in a car with the windows wound up.' Then Tony Jones coughed – emphatically. What he should've said was that he couldn't have been out there because he'd already told them he was out collecting scrap metal.

*

Frank Abbott had been working as a hired hand on Martin Parish's property in Herons Creek for some years before the pastor began his heritage chapel project in 2011. Abbott volunteered at the church build, having moved from Ray Porter's digs in Johns River. Although Ray Porter was not a church member, he'd sometimes drop in to the Herons Creek chapel for morning tea.

In 2012, Abbott set up a temporary bedroom in Bay Three of Danny Parish's bus shed, again managing to live rent-free. He would end up living in two caravans with an annexe set up between them. In 2014, Abbott was charged with sex offences against an eight-year-old girl. At first, he was refused bail. Martin Parish and his wife supported his bail application.

After Abbott's unfortunate troubles with the law, and a stint in prison, Martin Parish asked his flock to help Frank by offering him somewhere to live. Someone obliged. A drifting, odd-jobs man, Geoffrey Owen lived on a property at Misty Way, Logans Crossing. Owen had a caravan he'd recently vacated and said that Abbott could use it. No one warned the family in Misty Way that they would soon be living next door to a person who'd been charged with a sex offence against a child.

Abbott's bail conditions stipulated that he wouldn't be permitted to attend the church. Martin Parish chauffeured him around during this time. The pastor admitted in court that he already knew of Abbott's criminal record and other allegations originating in Taree and Johns River.

Early in 2015, when he'd invited Abbott to use the van, Owen had gone to live with his girlfriend. But things fizzled out and Owen soon moved back in. Fortunately for Abbott, there was another caravan available owned by a neighbour – a woman named Gretel. She invited Abbott to use her caravan, which was located near the fence line bordering the two acreages.

Owen was in poor health and relied on his kindly neighbour, Gretel, to take care of his medications and help him with other small tasks. Owen is a gnome-like man, stooped and sporting a white Santa beard. But his eyes are alert and full of a quality that I suspect Gary Jubelin would describe as 'rat cunning'.

People living in Misty Way were told to be careful around Geoff Owen. One neighbour said Owen was schizophrenic and liked to be left alone. He'd gone off his meds one time and inexplicably killed a neighbour's dog. He'd reportedly been involved in the Kendall

Men's Shed but had been asked to leave. He also had a drink driving conviction under his belt. Owen drove a white Holden Rodeo dual cab in 2014. His girlfriend at the time was a woman with blonde hair. She drove a light blue car. I vaguely wondered whether Ronald Chapman could've mistaken a Rodeo for a Land Cruiser.

Owen told police he went to the Kendall Community Centre to pay his advertising account on Friday 12 September. Then he drove to Port Macquarie and ran some errands. Owen said he heard the news about a boy going missing from Kendall on a radio news bulletin. When he returned to Logans Crossing that afternoon, he drove through Herons Creek, rather than Kendall. He told police he stayed home all day and night.

Detectives from Strike Force Rosann were interested in Owen for a simple reason: he was Nancy Wyndham's handyman. She had booked him to complete some repair work on her decking, but a hospital stay had forced Owen to postpone the job until sometime after 12 September 2014. So it seems he wasn't expected at the house on the day William Tyrrell disappeared.

Geoffrey Owen appeared at the August 2019 leg of the inquest in Taree. He and Frank Abbott had reportedly been seen sitting around a campfire together on the Parish property. They had been seen in cars together. And we discovered that – both being handymen – Owen and Abbott had worked on jobs together. They had certainly worked on Martin Parish's little chapel.

But under the spotlight at the Coroner's Court, Owen made every effort to distance himself from Frank Abbott, saying that he was never happy with the quality of work Abbott did. I fancied we were all wondering the same thing. Did Owen handball Nancy's simple deck repair job at 48 Benaroon Drive to Frank Abbott when he realised he couldn't attend? And what might've happened had Mr Abbott seen a small boy momentarily unsupervised in the vicinity of that house?

Interestingly, Geoffrey Owen celebrated nuptials at the beginning of 2020. The wedding was held the Saturday before Owen expected to be subpoenaed to testify at the March 2020 inquest. I wondered if he thought he might be 'going away' for a while after his court appearance. And, of course, Martin Parish officiated over the service at the Herons Creek chapel.

*

Next door to the property on Misty Way at Logans Crossing, where Owen and Abbott were living, lived a family with two young daughters. In 2014, Abbott went to the neighbours' house in the middle of the night, uninvited. The neighbours weren't pleased to see him at their door. He wanted to tell them some news, he said excitedly. Abbott told them that police were questioning Geoffrey Owen over the William Tyrrell matter.

The neighbours were puzzled. Why was Abbott so keen to share this information, and so urgently? He'd never mentioned the case to them before. In court at Taree, Abbott flatly denied going to the neighbours' house that night, despite both the man and his wife testifying emphatically and convincingly.

Abbott's neighbours – who deserve to remain unnamed after all they've endured – took the stand, and I could see they were very uncomfortable. The woman, petite and tanned, looked positively fearful. She refused to look at the video screen where Abbott sat crouching in prison. She managed a small smile directed at her husband, who tried to reassure her from a distance. In my view, they were exceptionally brave.

The neighbours said they often saw Frank Abbott, Ray Porter with his little dog and another man sitting at the Kew shops, having coffee together. I wondered who that man could've been. Abbott used to unnerve his neighbours, particularly the woman.

Once, he stood in the middle of the road blocking her way and forcing her to stop the vehicle. He wanted her to give him a ride. Abbott tried to open the car's back door and, in a panic, the neighbour drove off.

During her testimony, the brown-eyed woman kept touching her blonde hair and gesticulating nervously as she struggled to find the right words. She had some particularly awkward news to share with the court. She discovered one day, to her horror, that her neighbour, Frank Abbott, was a dog lover.

Abbott used to lure her chocolate labrador over to his place with bones, and Buddy couldn't resist. The neighbours didn't like him going over there. He was often gone for hours. One particular day, they were having afternoon tea on the verandah when Buddy showed up. Someone noticed something wrong with his rear end. It was red and swollen, and had a greasy substance clinging to the fur under his tail. It was Vaseline.

The neighbour told the court that one afternoon his wife burst through the door in a panic. She told her husband she'd gone looking for Buddy, who had wandered off. She saw Abbott's caravan door ajar and looked inside. Then immediately wished she hadn't. Poor Buddy was backed up to the bed, tail up. And Abbott was proving himself the ultimate dog. The portrait painted in court of Frank Abbott made everyone's stomach churn. I wondered how Martin Parish was feeling.

*

Martin Parish is in his mid-fifties. He's tall, bespectacled and grey-haired and has a resting facial expression that could be misread as smug. A Roger Ramjet chin that implies a stubborn temperament is his most notable feature. During his excruciating court appearance in March 2020, Parish fumbled for excuses as he confessed that, yes, he did know about Abbott's sexual proclivities for children and dogs, and that, yes, he also knew of Abbott's criminal record, and no, he did not feel it his duty to warn his vulnerable neighbours – a family with two children.

But Mr Craddock was only just getting warmed up. He would go on to elicit gasps from the assembly as he effortlessly pulled apart Parish's weak defence of his actions – and inaction. We were to discover that Parish had been Abbott's greatest advocate for the better part of a decade. He'd stood up for him in court. He'd attended his appeal hearings. He'd been there for his sentencing – just outside the room, he took pains to add, as if that made him less culpable. And just weeks before Parish was due to testify to the Coroner, he'd been visiting 'poor Frank' in prison.

Stories had been circulating about the goings-on at the Herons Creek chapel. People were being asked to support 'poor Frank'. His picture would be displayed during church services, accompanied by prayer requests. At one event, Parish went to the lengths of amplifying Frank's live phone call from prison and passing the receiver around so everyone could offer him their encouragement personally. One church member revealed on the local grapevine that the pastor had been challenged at times by parishioners who didn't think he should be supporting Abbott. Parish groped for some justification he could put before the court, 'Nobody's perfect.'

It is clear that church members were unaware of the full extent of Martin Parish's advocacy for Frank Abbott. He reluctantly admitted as much in court. Parish covered his own backside administratively by lodging a single report about Abbott's conviction on child sex charges in April 2015. As a minister, he was legally obliged to do so.

But any other reports Parish made were delivered via personal conversations with his supporters, not his congregation. The Herons Creek chapel is home to a lovely group of people who have good hearts and motives. They have been victimised since the inquest's revelations. Mr Craddock pointed out that this was essentially a failure of a shepherd to protect his sheep from a wolf, whom he encouraged to worship among them.

Martin Parish periodically interrupted Mr Craddock during questioning. I could see it irritated The Boss. His facial expressions at times failed to conceal it. Parish had worked in the juvenile justice system as a chaplain, he told the inquest. Presumably, this explained his sympathy for Frank Abbott. A decade too late, Martin Parish finally attempted to distance himself from Abbott.

'Were you friends?' Mr Craddock asked Parish.

'I would say I'm actually Frank's pastor, if that makes sense. I regard him as one of the sheep of my flock.' Mr Craddock's eyes lit up at this. He and the Coroner exchanged confused glances, then he went in for the kill.

'Could you explain to the court the difference between those two roles?' he asked quietly. 'I mean, did you give him advice in your pastoral role?'

'Yes. Frank would download on me sometimes and I'd listen.'

'How would you define what happens in a friendship?' Craddock persisted. 'Was it only at church services you saw Frank Abbott?'

'No. We did community barbecues, heritage events, movies under the stars. And we had other contact. I'd bump into him at the Kew shops. I'd drive him places a fair bit, you know, drop him off at Wauchope or at Ray Porter's house. And he'd visit the property.' Mr Craddock feigned confusion, indicating that he didn't understand why all of this didn't count as a friendship.

'Throughout his prison sentence, you've maintained telephone contact weekly.'

'I don't ring him; he rings me,' Parish protested. You could've heard a pin drop in the courtroom. Not a sound came from the video link.

Parish went on to tell the court his wife got to know Abbott as well. I grew positively mirthful at his next statement. Parish mentioned that Abbott would sometimes visit their home.

'He looked after our dogs while we were away.'

*

Eventually, Abbott returned to church at Herons Creek until, late in 2016, he was arrested again. This time, he faced a raft of child rape charges against three boys and a girl. The case went to trial and, incredibly, Martin Parish supported his bail application again. This time, he was bailed under the condition that he'd live at the Parish property in Herons Creek.

Mr Craddock sensed the mood in court. He demonstrated that by asking an awkward question that Parish clearly didn't want to answer.

'Did you accept the jury's verdict as properly reflective of guilt on his part of those sex offences against young children?'

'He certainly was convicted,' he said. Then he added, 'He was denied the chance to appeal. I had difficulty with that, yes.'

'You didn't wish to accept the jury's verdict?'

'That's true, yes. I have spoken to Frank Abbott, and he has said there were mitigating circumstances.' At this juncture, I saw Nathan Thomas shake his head in disbelief. There were audible gasps.

Craddock pressed on.

'Do you know where Frank Abbott was on 12 September 2014?'

Parish replied. 'Only from the questions I've asked Frank. He told me he was in Wauchope the day William went missing.' He went on, trying to convince the court that because he'd observed some regularity in Abbott's patterns, he had a good read on his daily habits to scratch Abbott as a person of interest.

The court was played a series of phone conversations between Abbott and Parish. They were recorded in August 2019. In the first,

Parish told Abbott that his old mate Ray Porter had passed away. Abbott didn't seem too shocked. 'Me best mate. We used to go fishing all the time,' he replied. To me, it sounded like he'd already heard the news. At the mention of Ray Porter, the conversation immediately turned to cars. I found that a bit odd.

'That car. I never drove that. I drove the red one,' Abbott said in the recording. He was referring to a blue-green coloured 1995 model Camry sedan that was mentioned more than once that day in court. We saw an image of it, captured by point-to-point road cameras. The teal-coloured car was being driven by an unidentified someone with a bulky frame, sitting a fair way back from the steering wheel.

A little later in the prison phone call, the court heard Martin Parish revising what he called his 'homework'. In short, he was doing Abbott's legwork for an appeal they hoped to launch against his hefty sixteen-year sentence.

Mr Craddock asked a pointed question about volunteering to find things out for Abbott.

'Would you accept that was something a bit more than just the pastoral role of a minister of religion?' Then he turned his attention to another nugget captured in the recorded phone calls.

'How are we going to get the court to realise that Danny is a pathological liar?' Parish asked Abbott. I thought about his choice of words. Although they certainly would have known the call was recorded, I felt this was a bit of a slip-up. Had he said, 'I wish they'd realise …' he could have preserved the illusion but, to my mind, asking 'How are *we* going to …' signalled intentional deceit.

Then Martin Parish said something else I found an odd thing to say while under overt monitoring. He said he felt his brother Danny was likely involved in William Tyrrell's disappearance. If that was true, I wondered why it needed saying at all, since Abbott was already onboard with that theory. Second, if Parish really thought his brother Danny was involved, then, like you must be doing right now, I wondered why Martin might have kept this from the police.

Apparently, so did Parish's wife, whose expression turned stony. She didn't know where to look. Parish took a nervous sip of water. He reminded the court – for the third time – that he has an acquired brain injury. Then, he tried to invoke the teachings of Jesus regarding lost and found lambs to explain his complex shepherding relationship with Abbott. Just when I began to wonder whether The Boss was going to let Parish slip through his fingers, he brought his line of questioning to its pointy end.

'Mr Parish, why did you ask Mr Abbott questions about his whereabouts on the day William Tyrrell went missing?'

*

Parish next had to endure barrister Michelle Swift's questions on behalf of William's birth family. She wanted to know what protections Parish had put in place at the church when Abbott returned, having been charged with a child sex offence. Parish gave a stilted discourse on protocols churches are required to follow in advising parents of young children, and how he appointed himself and his wife to monitor Abbott closely whenever children were around at church. He said, 'We certainly go out of our way to make sure sex abuse of children doesn't happen.' But, I thought to myself, hadn't Parish previously affirmed Abbott's innocence? Swift's questions highlighted a dismal failure to warn people about the danger posed by a person whom he'd actively assisted to get bail. Parish had no answer. Then Swift asked about the role of pastoral privilege should Abbott or someone else make a confession to a crime.

'What would you do in such an instance?'

'I would stop the conversation and say that this is reportable,' Parish replied, evidently pleased with himself that he'd given a good answer.

'Don't you think it would be better to listen to the confession, then tell the police?' Now, that's what I would call a Swift counter-attack, I thought to myself, watching Parish freeze in his seat.

*

Danny Parish is a very large man, both in height and width. His slightly stooped posture makes me suspect he has back problems. With his long ginger hair swept back in a ponytail, the effect is undeniably effeminate. His hair is greying at the forehead and sides. He has ruddy cheeks, small, round eyes and a double chin.

Danny Parish's evidence flatly contradicted his brother's.

'In your opinion, how did Frank and Martin get along?' Mr Craddock asked the witness.

'Best friends. I couldn't explain it any better than that,' Danny replied. He had a husky, breathy type of voice. He gave a history of his dealings with Abbott, mainly work history. He affirmed that Martin had known Abbott since 2007, if not before. He said that Martin always stood up for Frank.

Danny told the court that Abbott had threatened him and said he was afraid of what Abbott might do to him.

'I learned to stay away from him. You don't want to cross Frank. He's dangerous. He scares me when he loses his temper.' Danny Parish went on to talk about Ray Porter, a man he described as 'not very nice, withdrawn'. Porter was in his sixties in 2014, and by all accounts was not a well man. 'He looked like he was in a permanent depression,' Danny said.

On the witness stand, Danny mentioned that he'd seen a picture in the newspaper of a white station wagon connected to the abduction in Kendall that looked very familiar to him. Danny noticed it had been drawn with two driving lights set low on the front. He believed it looked just like Ray Porter's car. Danny went over and knocked on Frank's caravan door and told him about it.

'Frank told me it wasn't Ray's car,' Danny testified.

Danny Parish noted that Abbott was a physically active man who was able to get around easily. He walked everywhere, and was often seen on the roadside walking to and from Kendall and Kew. He always wore a brown jumper, in cold or hot weather. Some locals would remark that it looked a bit odd out of season.

I noticed Danny Parish had an excellent memory for facts. He was able to effortlessly recall specific names, dates, street addresses and past registration numbers of cars he'd owned. He came across as a credible witness. I wondered about Martin's comment that Danny was a pathological liar.

Through Danny's evidence the inquest heard about another timber mill worker at the Parish property. Steve Arter had stayed there for a while in 2014 and reportedly spent a lot of time with Frank Abbott, including on 11 September. Danny Parish testified that he had driven Arter to Port Macquarie airport about a week before the school holidays. I wondered why he was being so vague in court about the date. Later, I worked out the term break had started on Friday 19 September, so the date Arter left may have been 12 September. Pop Parish, Danny's father, paid for Arter's air ticket so he could fly to Melbourne to be with his wife.

According to their recorded phone conversations, Frank Abbott tasked Martin Parish with finding out from bank statements exactly when Steve Arter flew out that September. He suggested to the pastor that Steve could've been driving Danny Parish's 1994 maroon-red Camry around that time.

When Mr Craddock asked Danny Parish about this particular car, the witness was nonchalant.

'There were two or three red Camrys on the property during that time,' he said. He explained that he was a Camry fan, and that he would collect them to use for spare parts.

'How many Camry vehicles would you estimate were there in September 2014?' The Boss asked mildly, looking down at his notes as if distracted.

'Ten,' he replied. In the silence Craddock's pause threw over the court like a heavy blanket, Danny Parish started blinking involuntarily.

When Danny Parish began giving evidence, I was confused about his position on Frank Abbott's likely involvement in the abduction of William Tyrrell. Although he spoke of his fear of Abbott, I couldn't seriously imagine the older man overpowering the younger. Danny is a mountain of a man. Was he involved himself, and trying to deflect suspicion onto Abbott? Or was he genuinely suspicious of him? As enemies, there was no way of knowing whether the two men were intent on throwing each other under the bus, or whether just one of them was.

Danny seemed a savvy character. He knew the power of each tiny detail of testimony. He struck me as a bush lawyer, by habit. But was he just employing rhetoric this time, for the court's benefit? I couldn't tell. And to date, I still haven't decided.

Danny Parish testified that he never saw Abbott drink more than a single beer at a time. He was implying that this habit was Abbott's insurance against inadvertent ramblings that could give away his secrets.

Mr Craddock asked Danny Parish where he thought Frank Abbott was on 11 and 12 September 2014. The witness answered with impressive certitude.

'Frank had been working with me on Bus 726 in the morning on the eleventh. Ray Porter picked him up about lunchtime,' Parish said. He couldn't recall seeing Abbott for the rest of the day. 'He must have come home late that night because he was home early in the morning.'

Then Danny Parish made his most damning statement against Abbott. In 2016, Abbott allegedly said to Danny Parish, 'I know where William Tyrrell is. Why don't you check Geoff Owen's place?'

*

A protected witness fronted the inquest in 2020. He wore a yellow ribbon – the symbol of the hope of homecoming – in honour of William. It was a nice gesture. So I'll call him Mr Ribbon. The man used to employ Frank Abbott on and off and was connected with the bush timber mill on the Parish property at Herons Creek. The witness said he and Frank Abbott had been on friendly terms. But Mr Ribbon seemed to have thoughts about Abbott that he'd been keeping to himself. He described his former friend as 'a real tinkerer' who lived in 'appalling conditions'. He was 'wiry, very fit and strong, crafty and as sharp as a tack.' He also testified that Abbott and Danny Parish fought like cats and dogs.

Mr Ribbon once told Abbott he'd heard about his acquittal in the Helen Harrison murder case. Frank Abbott shocked him with an admission that his car was connected with the crime.

'Yeah. A couple of mates borrowed my car,' Abbott told the man. 'They took this girl for a drive and she had an epileptic fit and died. Twenty years later, I'm being charged with this murder.'

Like you, me and most of a certain jury, the witness must have struggled to believe that an epileptic seizure could result in a woman being stripped half-naked and raped. The seizure must've shaken that twenty bucks out of her wallet too. Mr Ribbon became very concerned about his friendship with Frank Abbott after that call.

The police recorded a number of phone calls between Abbott and the witness in 2019. Mr Ribbon can be heard asking Abbott why police were questioning him about the William Tyrrell case. Abbott's explanation was they were picking on him because of his previous unlucky brushes with the law. And because he lived in the vicinity. Mr Ribbon then asked Abbott where he was when William Tyrrell disappeared.

'I was in Wauchope.' Abbott answered. But he didn't say he knew nothing about William Tyrrell's disappearance. In fact, Abbott told the witness that he knew two people who were 'involved in taking Tyrrell', as he put it. That wording didn't sit well with me. What sort of person refers to a toddler by their surname?

Mr Ribbon wondered whether Abbott was using this claim to know the perpetrators for some kind of gain, or as a power play. Or did he really have inside knowledge? When Abbott asked the witness to come and visit him in prison so he could hand him the written names rather than saying them over the phone, Mr Ribbon immediately agreed to make that visit. Abbott gave him two scraps of paper with handwritten names on it. The witness took the papers straight to the police, who have not yet released their contents.

'By the way, did you win Lotto at some stage?' the witness asked Abbott during their phone call. Mr Ribbon was interested to find out how Abbott had come into some money back in 2014.

Abbott replied, 'No. I got $2000 at Grafton.' After this portion of the recording was played in the courtroom, the witness added an observation of his own.

'What I will say about Frank Abbott is that he would do anything for money – whether $5 or $500.'

Abbott also reportedly approached a child at Johns River once and was questioned by detectives about it. A white ute was identified as the vehicle in question. Abbott had told police he didn't know anyone with a white ute, then pulled up in Mr Ribbon's white ute – which he'd borrowed – right in front of police who were making an unexpected visit to the Herons Creek property. Mr Ribbon wondered why Abbott had lied to the police and started suspecting Abbott was a paedophile.

Then Abbott had another brush with the law. This time, he was accused of approaching a girl at Taree. By now, the witness said, his suspicion that Frank was a paedophile had grown very strong.

*

So, what are we to make of Frank Abbott? For the prosecution, we have these pieces of evidence. Frank Abbott has form as a predator of young boys. He has a dubious acquittal in his background. People seem afraid of him, and are uncertain of what he might be capable of doing if cornered. Frank's lifestyle is ideal for a man who needs to keep secrets.

Frank's alibi for 12 September 2014 is in question. Frank has lied about being able to drive. Frank has been proven to be a dog molester by an independent veterinarian's examination. Frank has been observed by neighbours to be strange, and is not trusted around children.

Frank was seen on numerous occasions to drive Ray Porter's car and a protected witness's ute, which fits a number of witness's descriptions of cars seen on Benaroon Drive and in Kendall on 12 September 2014. Frank was known to associate with Geoffrey Owen, who had a timely connection with Nancy Wyndham's house at 48 Benaroon Drive. (It seemed Mr Ribbon was a close associate of Frank Abbott. This person was no doubt feeling safer since Abbott received a prison sentence that would see him die in jail. The witness could be entirely innocent, or he could have been involved in Abbott's activities, and possibly cut a deal with police in exchange for turning on Abbott.)

By 2020, Frank Abbott had spun so many stories I can only describe him as a tornado of information. And always at the centre, in the calm eye, was Abbott's claim of innocence. He said that on

Friday 12 September 2014 his day had started at the takeaway shop in Wauchope. He never said how he got there from Herons Creek but he would've bummed a lift off someone.

After working at the shop, Abbott said he had lunch at the Uniting Church's charity kitchen, another Christian group he had joined. He cited a phone call he made from Wauchope to his brother as evidence of his whereabouts. Later that afternoon, he told police, he made a bank deposit, obviously hoping this would be conclusive proof of his alibi. But, in his recorded telephone conversation with Mr Ribbon, he said something different. He told the protected witness, 'Police have got proof I was in Wauchope. I withdrew money from the bank.'

Abbott had said that his work at the shop, a church lunch, a phone call and a bank transaction all place him at Wauchope that Friday, which is why he couldn't have committed the crime. But later, he said the police already knew someone in Kempsey did it. Kempsey is an hour's drive northward from Kendall. He tried a few different explanations to excuse himself when he spoke to police and, later, in his phone conversations with his minister.

I saw a pattern in Abbott's dealings with his pastor. Frank would bombard Martin Parish with information in an effort to bamboozle him. I speculated that Abbott might have been able to compel Parish to take his word for things and keep him onside, because with his acquired brain injury, Martin couldn't keep up cognitively with the chaotic storm that twisted around Frank Abbott. But the fact that Parish hasn't seemed to be labouring under duress in his relationship with Abbott raises some uncomfortable questions.

In other conversations going back some years, Abbott said he knew Tony Jones was involved and that William's remains would be found at Geoff Owen's place. He suggested that a last-minute flight on 12 September implicated Steven Arter. Frank also implied that Danny Parish might have been involved in the crime. Then, in his recorded prison phone call with Mr Ribbon, he claimed to know who took William Tyrrell and wrote their names down on paper, which he handed over to Mr Ribbon during a prison visit. But how would he know who the perpetrators were?

Abbott has whipped up an imperfect storm of 'evidence', but in the process has torn his own defence case to shreds. The only name he hasn't yet thrown up is that of Ray Porter. I think that fact is very telling. In fact, he seemed to make a statement by way of denial; he told Danny Parish that the car wanted in connection with William's disappearance definitely wasn't Ray's car. But how could he possibly know that?

Pesky 'false allegations' seemed to follow Frank Abbott around. By February 2019, Abbott had made no less than 64 court appearances in four years. And he was still on the loose. But Abbott's luck was running out. Eventually, in 2017, Abbott was convicted on ten counts of sexual misconduct against three children – two boys and a girl. His youngest victim was just seven. This brave little boy would be the undoing of Frank Abbott.

*

On Tuesday 17 March 2020, we heard evidence that would burn at least one person of interest and turn the nation's attention onto the William Tyrrell investigation like never before.

It would be an understatement to say that impending death can do funny things to people. That was certainly true in Ray Porter's experience. The elderly man had been a dialysis patient for some years. Terminal kidney disease had stolen his remaining fishing days and ultimately landed him in an aged care facility, Uniting Care's Mingaletta in Port Macquarie.

Although he wasn't a well man, by all accounts in April 2019, Porter still had good mental acuity. With nothing to look forward to but death, and nothing left to fear, Ray Porter made an explosive confession: he had picked up William Tyrrell in his car on 12 September 2014.

Kirston Okpegbue appeared at the inquest sporting dramatically long hair dyed bright lipstick red. But her appearance paled into insignificance when compared with what she revealed. The aged care nurse said she was working her way down a corridor dispensing medicine to patients when Porter approached her. He told her he was tired of getting visitors. He indicated that they were upsetting him, with all their questions. Then Porter confided in the nurse, whom he said he trusted because she had an honest face.

He said he had something he needed to get off his chest. He told Okpegbue that he had 'picked up his best mate with a cute little boy near a shed at Kendall school'.

'I asked him if he was talking about William Tyrrell and he said yes.' But Porter insisted that he didn't do anything wrong.

'All I did was give my best mate and a boy a lift.'

Mr Craddock respectfully questioned Ms Okpegbue, asking her about the specific location Ray Porter had mentioned.

'Ray said he had picked up his best mate at Kendall School. Behind the school was a shed. From there, they drove 300 kilometres north.' The nurse went on to say that Porter laid his head on her shoulder in a gesture of sorrowful distress. The impression I got from her testimony was that she believed Porter was telling the truth.

Another nurse came forward, adding a detail that she recalled Ms Okpegbue mention after she had the conversation with Porter. Apparently, Porter had mimed throwing something overboard from a boat.

Around the time of his unburdening to Ms Okpegbue, Porter had two visitors, his brother Tom and sister-in-law Irma. They had a conversation in the presence of another nurse, Renee Jenner. The visitors mentioned that they had to go to court. The nurse joked that Porter must be in trouble with the law. Porter then piped up.

'No,' he said seriously, 'it's about a little boy.'

'No it's not, Ray. Just leave it! I've told you so many times,' Irma snapped at him.

The nurse testified that she felt sure Porter's guest was trying to stop him talking to her. She got the feeling Ray had a lot more to say, and said she couldn't explain why, but she left the room feeling as if she wanted to vomit.

'It was just the way he said it to me and what happened in that room,' she told the court.

Ms Jenner made a statement to police without knowing about the disclosures Porter had already made to other nurses at the facility. This evidence yielded a new witness whom police had no idea about, who then came forward to speak to them.

Tom Porter told police that his brother Ray was a person who was easily influenced. People would take advantage of him, he said. He said that Ray had a good friend called Frank, who would sometimes take his car. Tom also claimed Ray had told him a bogus story about the reason police had interviewed and questioned him at the aged care home. Later, he confessed to Tom that he'd been telling police what he knew about Frank Abbott and the disappearance of the little boy in Kendall.

Tom Porter told police he formed the impression that Frank Abbott was not a very nice person. Apparently, one of his neighbours in Wauchope had told his brother Ray to stay away from Frank. Both Tom and Irma had the feeling that Ray was scared of Frank. Irma told police – in response to Renee Jenner's statements – that she only wanted to stop Ray talking about the little boy because it was so upsetting to him. She said she knew Ray was aware he was dying. Irma said she felt Ray was telling the truth because it was very unlikely that he would lie to his brother, particularly on his deathbed.

After Ray Porter died in 2019, Irma found a letter among his possessions. It was postmarked in such a way that she concluded it had been sent from jail. Not realising its possible significance, she threw the letter out. But she remembered what it had said. The letter instructed Ray Porter to pick up a boat and move it to a certain lady's place. It was signed 'From your good friend, Frank.'

20

HIGH STAKES

When the William Tyrrell inquest was adjourned indefinitely in 2020 due to the COVID-19 pandemic, Her Honour, Harriet Grahame, addressed the court with a heavy heart.

'I'm so sorry the world has done this. I wanted to finish the evidence this week. There's still work to be done. There's nothing in relation to this matter which I consider to be a cold case.' She gave a sympathetic nod to the representatives present from William's two families.

Counsel assisting Gerard Craddock reassured us that despite the adjournment, the police investigation would continue.

'There's no halt to that,' he said. Then he made an announcement that was welcomed by William Tyrrell's loved ones. 'As a consequence of evidence we have called here, there has already been a witness who we had no idea about who has come forward and will be speaking to police.'

Brendan Collins hadn't attended the third session of the inquest in 2020. We were told he wasn't well. I took that to mean he was suffering from an illness that was more than physical. Michelle Swift, his lawyer, requested that the media refrain from contacting her client while he was in a fragile state.

When I last saw Karlie Tyrrell, she'd grown her hair long again. She wore jeans and a black jacket to Taree courthouse, where she attended the last two days of the inquest with Brendan's mother, Natalie, and a few friends. I couldn't help but notice how much Natalie had aged since I'd last seen her just six months before. Her hair was dyed a darker blonde. Her eyes had dulled.

One of Natalie and Karlie's confidantes had kept me updated on Karlie's progress. She looked like she wasn't doing too well emotionally, and was sick with a chesty cough. In the foyer of Taree courthouse, Karlie spoke to Detective Senior Sergeant Mark Dukes.

'Oh, yous remember me, do yous?' she said with undisguised bitterness.

'Of course. You're a bit sick today?' Dukes asked brightly. He flashed the Jack Reacher smile at her.

'Yeah,' she retorted. 'It's not corona. 'Cause if it was I'd give it to all of yous – ha ha!' Dukes raised his hand, either in a wave or a signal of surrender – I wasn't sure which.

I've wrestled with my feelings about Karlie Tyrrell over the years. As mothers, we're tigresses. We will fight to the death for our children, even against ourselves. We fight to keep the worst of ourselves in check, putting our kids first. I had felt Karlie hadn't done that. I'd viewed it in stark black and white. But on Monday 16 March 2020, something happened that exposed my own hypocrisy.

After close to six years, Anna Wyndham brought an end to a cold war she hadn't started. She went over to the birth family camp in the courtroom and sought Karlie out. Then, taking out a shiny gold phone, Anna proceeded to show Karlie some recent photos of Lindsay. They smiled and laughed together. Karlie remarked on how big her daughter was now. Clearly, she hadn't seen her in a while. Then, the older tigress embraced the younger in a lasting hug that moved them both to tears – and everybody else as well.

*

The week of 4–10 August 2019 was National Missing Persons Week in Australia. The theme was 'Individuals, not statistics'. Anna Wyndham spoke about what the initiative meant to her. She said the expected things – the pain, the loss and suffering her family experienced. But I found it especially poignant to hear Anna speaking of how the family still grapples with the realisation that they've become members of a strange group: victims of crime. The question is, have they also become statistics?

'It's another knife in our hearts and a reminder that William and our family are now part of this tragic story surrounding a missing loved one. Being part of National Missing Persons Week is something we never expected would happen to us or our family. Our beautiful little boy needs to be home. He needs to be with us. But we don't know where he is. And we hope this campaign will put pressure on the people who took William from us. We hope it puts pressure on the people who know what happened to our little boy. Please, please, whoever you are. If you know something about William's disappearance, please help us. Please help the police bring William home to his family where he belongs.'[36]

Over the years, there has been a lot of talk about the possibility that William Tyrrell was still alive. I have admired people's optimism, but I haven't shared it. Supporters may have felt they'd be giving up on the little boy if they came to accept that he was dead. I understood that. But from the outset, it was most likely that he'd been killed within a few hours of the abduction. I've always hoped I'll be proven wrong.

I also appreciate entirely that a perennial hope, albeit a feeble one, should be maintained by William's family. They've lived in a state of suspended animation since 12 September 2014. We're so accustomed to closing a book and leaving its characters in stasis. They don't age or change. They don't live their lives. But in this case, we must remember that these are real people. The vast proportion of the public either gave them no further thought at all, pressing pause on the tragedy somehow, or asked them to get on with their lives, to get over it. But how could they?

A month before Missing Persons Week, in July 2019, Anna had told the media, 'I don't trust police. I can't, based on what they're doing with William's case.'[37] She and Nathan were featured on various media platforms, including podcasts, levelling allegations of infuriating indifference by NSW Police. They were very vocal in criticising the infighting and apathy that plagued the investigation, particularly after a number of phone calls and a long, emotional letter they penned to the Commissioner were comprehensively ignored.

'We got nothing,' lamented Anna to journalists. 'And I just find that absolutely unbelievable that there was nothing. That speaks volumes about the leadership of that organisation. It speaks volumes about the way they see what's important.'

The couple also had Scott Cook in their sights, saying the then-Homicide Commander was dishonest in his claims that Gary Jubelin and David Laidlaw were being afforded the support necessary to complete a proper handover of the case. Worse, they said, was Cook's astonishingly cold remark to the family that, 'You are not the only family that are victims of crime. William is not our only case.' Anna and Nathan seemed to be of the opinion that, to the upper echelons of NSW Police, they and the Tyrrells had indeed become statistics.

Their response to Commander Cook, which came when Anna gave evidence at Jubelin's court hearing, was: 'William is three years old. He was taken from his grandmother's house. It was a street with probably twenty houses on it. We were sitting just around the corner. I don't think you've got any other cases that describe that, and I don't think you can just give up on it.' They say that their pleas fell on deaf ears, that Cook made it patent to the couple that William's case would be moved to 'unsolved'.

During his court proceedings in 2019, Gary Jubelin's testimony included claims about Cook that were strikingly akin to Anna's. He said that, in 2017, Cook pointed to a photo of William and instructed Jubelin, 'No one cares about that little kid. Get him off the books. Get him to Unsolved Homicide.[38]

Cook, who has stridently denied making any such remarks, would soon rise to the rank of NSW Assistant Commissioner, while William's loved ones continued to languish in an unbearable limbo. The fact that Cook's legal team applied for a non-publication order on the statement in question speaks volumes.

But these people and their little boy are not mere statistics, and the people of the Mid North Coast have never perceived them thus. While the investigative team was disintegrating, the locals were rallying. Again.

We've already touched on the veritable army of concerned citizens that have appeared in the years since William's disappearance. But one initiative would prove a game-changer. A year after William disappeared, in collaboration with the *Where's William* website, musical theatre performer Simon Gleeson literally added his voice to the cause by recording the evocative anthem 'Bring Him Home' from *Les Misérables*.[39] This rendition was played and re-played on local radio around the Mid North Coast, in an effort to keep William at the forefront of people's minds and, more importantly, to elicit any information that might be of use in the investigation. The result, as we'll see shortly, should make it plain to us that this kind of good-hearted doggedness really can pay off.

*

Friday 13 March 2020 turned out to be most unlucky for Frank Abbott. On that day, we were told we'd be hearing sensitive testimony from two witnesses – a mother and daughter who must only be identified by the pseudonyms of 'Amy' and 'Tanya'. The Coroner welcomed the young girl with compassion.

'I'm so aware that coming to court can be very nerve-racking and stressful,' Coroner Harriet Grahame said. 'Take a deep breath, settle in and just answer the questions to the best of your knowledge, okay?' She nodded reassuringly to the girl, who looked to be around sixteen years of age.

Amy had opened her home to foster children in need of emergency care some years before. Tanya, her daughter, helped out by entertaining and babysitting the children at home. The women spoke of how they wanted to help at-risk kids. They told the court of their aims to make the children feel welcome, to put them at ease and to make them feel like they belonged somewhere.

In September 2017, they were hosting two brothers whom the court dubbed 'Jeffrey' and 'Matthew'. Jeffrey was a talkative seven-year-old. Matthew, who'd turned ten, was more reserved. They'd only been there for about a week, but were slowly warming to the foster family.

One afternoon, Tanya had the kids in her bedroom listening to music on her phone's music app. A refrain they knew as 'the William Tyrrell song' came on. This was Simon Gleeson's reworked version of 'Bring Him Home'. As they listened, out of the blue, the younger boy blurted out a stunning revelation.

'I know who killed William.' Tanya was curious as to what had prompted this.

'Who?' she asked. Ignoring the terrified expression on his brother's face at what he was about to reveal, Jeffrey told Tanya it was Frank Abbott.

'He had him in a suitcase.' Jeffrey went on to say he'd seen the suitcase. Matthew kept trying to 'shush' him. But Jeffrey continued, saying they knew William was dead but hadn't seen his body.

At this testimony, I saw Anna Wyndham's face crumple into a mess of grief. I'd never seen her this distraught throughout the inquest. The court was deathly quiet. No one looked at Frank Abbott onscreen. And we all watched the faces of poor Tanya and Amy.

Tanya testified that she told her mother, who questioned the boys further. Matthew was very angry with his little brother.

'You're not supposed to tell anyone,' he said. 'Stop telling her.'

'Why do you want Jeffrey to stop telling us?' Amy asked.

'Because he said if we told anyone, he'd snap our mum's neck.'

Tanya testified that she never believed the child was making it up. Jeffrey had seemed very serious, and very scared. But he wanted release from his terrible burden. As for Matthew, when gently questioned by Amy, he would signal his agreement by nodding his head. His only hesitation seemed to be coming from a desire to protect his little brother and his mum. He was petrified that something bad was going to happen.

On the same day that Tanya testified, we heard from the previously mentioned Mr Ribbon, who had in 2018 alerted police to his concerns about Abbott. On 1 February 2019, Abbott would be handed a sentence that he'd thoroughly earned: sixteen years in prison. After Abbott was incarcerated, the two had spoken on the telephone. Mr Ribbon told the court that during a phone call Abbott had placed to him from prison, they had spoken about the young boy's allegations. The witness said he was shocked to the core by what the children had said about Abbott killing William and putting his body in a suitcase. He pressed Abbott for an explanation.

'That must've come from somewhere. A little kid wouldn't have made that up,' he said to Abbott. Abbott calmly replied that he didn't know where it had come from.

'I never said that,' Abbott insisted.

After Jeffrey's disclosure, Amy called Crime Stoppers to make a report. I glanced across the courtroom at Anna. Her expression said it all. Rather than being frozen in shock or denial, her demeanour spoke of relief. Her brown eyes exuded sadness, yes, but her gaze was steady. I saw Anna and the Coroner share a long, unspoken exchange. When at last Anna broke the stare with a flutter of moistened eyelids, it gave me the impression of finality, if not of absolute closure. I sensed she had accepted that this was indeed what had happened to her little boy. It seemed we now had two separate confessions that implicated Abbott; one from an old mate on his deathbed and the other from a terrified child. On the face of it, neither had any reason to lie.

The Coroner excused the witness, then informed us that she would be hearing from a final witness in a closed court session later that day. I could only imagine how desperately Abbott wanted to know who that mystery person would be. Harriet Grahame's expression was grim. Abbott tried to interrupt as she stood and bowed before the adjournment. He was in mid-sentence when the Coroner swept from the chamber, completely ignoring him.

*

Frank Abbott's abuse was the reason for Matthew and Jeffrey going into respite foster care. I found it particularly poignant that the care and love shown to those children by a caring foster family led to the biggest break in the William Tyrrell case in six years. Amy, Tanya and their family were instrumental, if accidentally, in enabling the disclosure. Their kindness made the kids feel comfortable, loved and protected.

The ultimate goal of FACS is to save children. And the care provided to these two little boys did save them.

I've shed quite a few tears over William Tyrrell, the boy. And I've probably shed just as many over William Tyrrell, the investigation. But that day at Taree courthouse, I became so overwhelmed by the sense of poignancy that I fled the courtroom. I began to see the FACS organisation in a new light.

This story is a wonderful example of how the core ideals of the foster care system can be realised – when you have the right people on board. I realise that not all foster parents are created equal, and that some have wrong motives. There is terrible behaviour, abuse, cruelty, neglect and favouritism. But, as in the case of Amy's family, many of our nation's foster carers are motivated by decency, kindness and empathy for suffering children. And I think they deserve medals.

After the testimony of the babysitter who'd also heard Jeffrey's terrified claim about Frank Abbott, I saw tears streaming down the cheeks of the stoic woman I'd jokingly dubbed the Bridesmaid. As though for the first time, I saw her heart. I saw her care for William's foster parents, and fuelling that, her love for William Tyrrell. I saw her heartache for William's birth family, his mum and dad who she knew had been devastated by the need to surrender their children to safer homes. I have no doubt that Michelle White would've made William feel safe as she delivered him – a babe in arms – to a couple who she knew would protect him. Michelle White, I came to see, isn't an awkward bridesmaid at all. She's a guardian angel.

*

Although I was already suffering from information overload, when I wanted a writing break, I'd just read. I came across the story of Khandalyce Pearce, a two-year-old who was murdered in 2008. The killer, Daniel Holdom, had murdered her twenty-year-old mother, Karlie Pearce-Stevenson, four days earlier. He'd disposed of her remains in New South Wales's Belanglo State Forest, the hunting ground of notorious serial killer Ivan Milat.

The little girl's body was found in 2015, seven years after she died. She had been gagged with balls of dishcloth stuffed into her mouth and bound around the head with tape. Khandalyce was put inside a suitcase and dumped in a lonely spot by a South Australian highway. Crown prosecutor Mark Tedeschi QC told the Supreme Court that Holdom had killed Karlie by stomping on her neck and chest and her daughter by suffocation.

'This was a thrill kill, as evidenced by the taking, collecting and keeping of the trophy photographs he took of Karlie around the time of her death. Both murders fall within the worst case and can aptly be described as atrocious, detestable, hateful, gravely reprehensible and extremely wicked.'[40]

Tedeschi urged the court to impose two life sentences. Interestingly, at the time of the murders Holdom was involved with a gang of criminals who were moving drugs and weapons across state lines with the aid of two sets of identical cars – of the same make, model and colour.

I wondered whether Frank Abbott was referencing this case when he'd tried to scare his young victims. Was the suitcase just a convenient prop to use in frightening them into silence about his sexual assaults? Or did Holdom's method of disposing of a child's body strike a familiar chord?

It was getting late and this manuscript was due in three days. I'd been pulling all-nighters at my desk and calling in family favours to have my children taken care of while their dad was working. Everyone had become heartily sick of hearing about my submission deadline. Work became a cross between writing up my inquest notes each evening and shuffling through my collection of documents. My box of pink paper did indeed hold many answers to the mysteries of this case. But I never had a hope of working through everything in that bundle I'd collected. This was always going to be a job for an army, not an individual.

The revelations at the last inquest session had seen the case take a sharp, dog-leg turn. But, it didn't lead us to a little boy who was thriving somewhere in the care of others. Just as the dog-leg turn does in Benaroon Drive, it looked like it was leading to the cemetery.

At the 2020 inquest, I heard whispered speculations that William Tyrrell's body may have been buried in the ground or dumped at sea. These are not ghoulish preoccupations. It's vitally important that we bring little William home. From unofficial whispers I've heard, I am confident we will soon know the truth about his final resting place.

*

Silently growing in the Middle Brother State Forest are two gigantic blackbutt trees. They've been there for centuries. In fact, the national park was created to protect them. These *Eucalyptus pilularis* giants have the distinction of being among the few trees in the world with their own unique names. They are called Bird Tree and Benaroon.

At sixty-four metres high and fifteen metres in girth, Benaroon is the biggest blackbutt tree in the world. Its name comes from the Birpai language and it was borrowed to name the street from which William vanished. The contrast between the two figures is poignant ... an indomitable giant, flourishing untroubled for centuries, and a small seedling, uprooted so prematurely and so violently. We'll never really know either of them.

The evidence suggests there were a few people involved in the abduction and presumed murder of William Tyrrell from Benaroon Drive. I'm sure you can figure out the direction in which my accusing finger is pointing. The modus operandi of the actual snatch is still unclear. But it seems to have begun with people casing the house – just like Anna Wyndham always maintained. Let that awful truth sink in for a moment. Imagine the horror, the desperation and the outrage of seeing the cars that took your child away to be murdered – and not being believed.

I believe they would have needed a driver, a snatcher and a lookout. Perhaps they were there on innocent business the night before and had seen the family arrive. But what business? Visiting someone nearby? Or bushwhacking? Perhaps they installed themselves in a house onsite – with a neighbour or in a house they knew was empty that day. Perhaps a handyman had given them a heads-up about who was expected to be at 48 Benaroon Drive sometime that day. Or was it just opportunistic, with no foreknowledge, as police theorised?

Perhaps the cars left for a while, then one of those drivers ventured up Benaroon Drive again to the Millers' driveway, for a closer look. Perhaps he was tricky, using a different car. Or perhaps that was just the Crabbs checking the Millers' mailbox.

In any case, soon the opportune moment came, perhaps signalled by a lookout in communication with a snatcher. The lookout sees Dad leave, dressed up for work, laptop handy. He will be away for long enough …

They won't attempt the snatch unless certain they won't be seen. The lookout sees the perfect opportunity – the ladies make cups of tea. They sit down, sighing. Settling in. The lookout's line of sight allows the snatcher to come pretty close to the house. The women are still seated.

William runs around the side of the house. *Ah, a little bit of peace.*

Now!

The snatcher grabs William and puts his hand over his mouth. Two possibilities are open here. Perhaps he bundles the child into a vehicle that has done a U-turn. The driver stops briefly. A door quickly springs open, then closes. Risky. But no one's seen them. Or, perhaps the snatcher has operated on foot, using the bush tracks to deliver the child to others waiting on the other side. Via Albert Street, it's a snap to get to the primary school. No CCTV cameras to worry about. But there are bushwalkers around. Could also be risky.

When the snatcher has done his part, he sidles back home. By the time William's absence is noticed, the snatcher is back inside his house. It's the safest alibi – 'I was home alone.'

The snatcher snatched in under a minute. But to make all of this work, there had to be someone onsite, out of sight. A lookout in a house nearby – in their own house? Or both?

After William was driven away, perhaps they didn't go far. Perhaps they went past Ron Chapman's house, as he claimed. Perhaps he really did see a man and a woman, or perhaps he only thought it was a woman. Or perhaps Chapman was mistaken and they took the high road, avoiding the cameras. Or perhaps what Chapman saw was unrelated.

Perhaps they drove on and on, far away, or perhaps just to the rear of the public school about two kilometres west. There's a quiet little access road there that leads onto private property. The bush is thick there, and the green corrugated-iron machinery shed is isolated. I've been there snooping. It's a good spot to use if you don't want to be seen. There, perhaps the driver dropped off the man and the boy, then left.

Then Ray Porter picked them up. Was he a dupe whose station wagon they'd used earlier to watch the house? Or was he a co-conspirator? Porter can't tell us from the grave, but perhaps he already told us enough. From there, they drove away, perhaps up a nearby mountain road, or perhaps 300 kilometres north. Perhaps somewhere up around Grafton. I remember hearing that a certain person of interest often went up to his brother's place up that way. Nobody knows for sure. For now, we lose the trail. This is where the William Tyrrell inquest left us at the time of writing this book. But I'm confident that investigators know more than any of us about what happened next.

Here's a question to consider: why did we all think this scenario was so impossible? Anything's possible, as Anna Wyndham once told the inquest. And she, of all people, should know.

*

Child abductions by strangers are rare. And reformed perpetrators are scarce. Media interest is intense at first, stirring up hysteria. Coverage is widespread. But over time, if the offender isn't caught, the story slips into oblivion. The child victim's name evokes little more than a perfunctory sense of pathos and impotence. And so, we remain clueless about how to keep our children safe.

According to the Australian Institute of Criminology, around 40,000 people are reported missing in Australia each year. Of those, around half are children. The good news is that 99.5 per cent of missing persons are found within six months.[41] *The Wall Street Journal* tells us that, globally, we annually manage to lose eight million children, and these are only the ones that get reported to authorities.[42]

In light of these alarming statistics, people have asked me over the years what I think it is about William Tyrrell's story that so captured the public's attention. It's a fair question. What is so special about William Tyrrell's disappearance in comparison to others? Few missing children in Australia have dominated the social space like William Tyrrell. Internationally, the same is true for Madeleine McCann.

There are many factors that make William's story stand out. His tender age, his foster status, secrecy around his family, the rallying of the community and the Spiderman suit, an instantly recognisable symbol of heroism, have all built the story's impact. But it's the baffling circumstances in which he disappeared that are most compelling. The chances of a child going missing from a place like Benaroon Drive, Kendall, have to be no more than one in a million.

When police asked Australia to join them in searching for Spiderman, they gave us a picture taken literally minutes before he vanished. No doubt when Anna Wyndham approved the photo she took of William in his Spiderman costume for public release, she would have had no idea she'd likely grow to hate the image. His biological grandmother certainly did.

In the arena of law enforcement and justice, technology is creating changes so rapid we can barely keep up with them. Guilty people with internet and telephone access can persuade people to support them and innocent people can be judged from a distance by people who know nothing about them.

William Tyrrell's story reminds us that we're all in danger even while we're feeling safe. A murderous lunatic could be sitting in that unfamiliar car across the road from your place. Or it could be you – driving with too many beers onboard. Social media enables us to vicariously experience the tragedies of others. We observe mainly through imagery – all heavily manipulated, of course. Why bother reading when you can view and listen? Smugly, we then sit back and apportion blame. We feel righteous in our efforts to invent new laws, virtuous in our campaign to strengthen safeguards. And we feel entirely justified to tightly define parameters so we can measure, control and fix ills that frighten us.

But the real world's messier than we can handle and darker than we can fathom. We're all dealt a random hand of cards from a well-shuffled deck. I'd like to think that it's how we play them that makes the difference. Perhaps that will reduce our chance of being the family with a child who's unlucky enough to be one in a million.

EPILOGUE

For the people searching for Spiderman, the very first obstacle was lantana. This noxious, pretty weed invades grasslands, pastures and forests all around our stomping ground. It chokes waterways and prevents livestock from accessing drinking holes. It's hard to kill. It survives drought and grows in poor soil and even on steep, stony hillsides.

You can't burn the stuff because its oiliness fuels bushfires. It scratches and cuts up skin and triggers asthma attacks. It bleeds milk that irritates and burns. Its berries are lethal if ingested. The plant is toxic to birds, animals and humans and can shut down your organs and kill you. Australia spends $22 million a year trying to control it. Even so, the seeds will survive for half a century. I've become attuned to pulling out lantana wherever I see it growing. At my place, we had a variety with bright red flowers.

I went to work on a clump of red lantana the day after the inquest into William's disappearance was postponed indefinitely. An abrupt end to the proceedings came in response to the global pandemic of the COVID-19 coronavirus that first landed on Australian shores in January 2020. We were all devastated. We would have to wait for many months, perhaps many years, for the final answer to precisely what happened to William Tyrrell. But I have all the answers I need.

As I worked on the lantana, I thought about the ways in which life was changing. I wondered if those changes would be irrevocable.

I thought about my gratitude for the healthcare workers who risk their lives to draw a thin line of defence between us and COVID-19.

Then, I thought about the days before the virus. I thought back not so many years to those real-life superheroes who fought through the prickly scrub in their desperate search for a little boy in a Spiderman suit. And I thought about the tireless band of people who fought their way through other kinds of thickets to bring two grieving families closer to a sense of peace.

After that cursed red lantana was gone from my backyard, some wise soul advised me to plant a hedge of rosemary in its place. Rosemary – for remembrance. Now, there are no red flower heads to be seen, not a single one among a flourishing mass of fragrant green.

The William Tyrrell investigation remains ongoing at the time of publication. If you have any information relating to William's disappearance, please contact Crime Stoppers on 1800 333 000 or make a report at Crime Stoppers online at crimestoppers.com.au

It is never too late to speak up.

ENDNOTES

1   National Search and Rescue Council, 2010, *National Land Search operations manual*, Canberra, ACT: National Search and Rescue Council, p. 163.

2   Australian Institute of Health and Welfare, 2016, *Child protection Australia 2014–15*. Canberra, ACT: Australian Institute of Health and Welfare. Retrieved from www.aihw.gov.au/publication-detail/?id=60129554728.

3   Reddie, M, 2019, 'William Tyrrell abducted in a car by an offender who chose to "act on their desires", inquest hears', *ABC News*, 7 August. Retrieved from www.abc.net.au/news/2019-08-07/william-tyrrell-abducted-in-car-inquest-in-sydney-hears/11390346.

4   Browne, R, 2017, 'Missing boy William Tyrrell, in foster care when he vanished, is probably dead: court', *The Sydney Morning Herald*, 25 August.

5   *60 Minutes: Where is William?*, 2015, [TV program] Channel 9, 5 September.

6   *Sunday Night*, 2018, [TV program] Channel 7, 4 March.

7   Gusmaroli, D, 2018, '"He's dead": Distraught nan begs police to stop search for William', *The Daily Telegraph*, 15 June.

8   Wilkie, K, 2019, 'The unexplained 118 minutes: William Tyrrell investigation is thrown into turmoil after police admit confusion over when iconic last photograph of missing toddler in his Spider-Man suit was REALLY taken', *Daily Mail Australia*, 2 September.

9   'William Tyrell [sic] inquest told of terrifying high-pitched scream', (editorial), 2019, *WHO Weekly*, 26 March.

10 'William Tyrrell's final moments revealed at inquest into his disappearance' (editorial), 2019, *New Idea*, 26 March.

11   Coroners Act 2009 No 41 (NSW), Section 21.

12   see n5.

13   see n5.

14   see n5.

15   see n5.

16   Sutton, C, 2018, 'Mother of William Tyrrell's violent past of assaults and property destruction', news.com.au, 9 March.

17   'Let him come home: William Tyrrell's mother makes emotional plea to alleged abductor' (editorial), 2018, *The Guardian*, 4 March.

18   see n6.

19   'Witness against Bill Spedding described as "bizarre, obsessive" (editorial), 2015, *The Australian*, 27 June.

20   Duff, T, 2019, 'William Tyrrell's foster parents open up about enduring years of death threats and online abuse as people STILL believe they are to blame for the toddler's disappearance', *Daily Mail* Australia, 4 August.

21   see n5.

22   Hammer, H, Finkelhor, D, and Sedlak, AJ, 2002, *Children abducted by family members: National estimates and characteristics*, Washington, DC: Office of Juvenile Justice and Delinquency Prevention.

23   Rawsthorne, S, 2019, '"Keeps odd hours and lives alone": William Tyrrell's foster grandmother reveals her suspicions', *The Sydney Morning Herald*, 30 April.

24   Mitchell, G, 2020, 'Police seek to hold Gary Jubelin court hearing behind closed doors', *Sydney Morning Herald*, 3 February.

25   Mitchell, G, 2020, '"You're just a little boy": Tyrrell's neighbour recorded talking to himself, court hears', *Sydney Morning Herald*, 6 February.

26   Where's William?, 2020. Retrieved from www.whereswilliam.org.

27   Public online petition, 2019, 'The NSW DPP to withdraw all charges against Gary Jubelin. NOW: WE STAND WITH GARY JUBELIN', June 22. Retrieved from www.change.org

28   Damjanovic, D, 2015, 'William Tyrrell: Forensic profiler reveals details about three-year-old's suspected kidnapper', *ABC News*, 13 September.

29   'Paul Bickford's our No.1 senior volunteer' (editorial), 2009, *Port Macquarie News*, 17 November.

30   *A Current Affair*, 2018, [TV program] Channel 9, 13 February.

31   Hodder, S, 2004, 'Son won't let "sleeping" dog lie', *The Daily Liberal*, 14 October.

32   Johnson, JR and Girdner, LK, 1999, *Family abductors: Descriptive profiles and preventive interventions,* Juvenile Justice Bulletin, (January). Washington, DC: Office of Juvenile Justice and Delinquency Prevention. Retrieved from www.ncjrs.gov/pdffiles1/ojjdp/182788.pdf, pp 5–6.

33   Haldane, J, 2014, 'Kendall Mens Shed reward system', *Kendall Chronicle*, 24 May.

34   Cooke, J, 1994, 'Murder trial divides jurors', *The Sydney Morning Herald*, 8 July.

35   'NSW homicide squad reopening cold cases' (editorial), 2018, *Manning River Times*, 17 May.

36   Where's William?, 2019. Retrieved from www.whereswilliam.org/newsroom.

37   Harris, L, 2019, 'William Tyrrell's foster parents claim police are doing "nothing"', *10 News First*, 24 July. Retrieved from 10daily.com.au/news/crime/a190725ditex/william-tyrrells-foster-parents-claim-police-are-doing-nothing-20190725.

38   Mitchell, G, 2020, 'Tyrrell's foster-mother claims head of homicide told her she's "not the only victim of crime"', *The Sydney Morning Herald*, 13 February.

39   Fairhurst, T, 2015, 'Bring Him Home the call of Where's William campaign launch in Port Macquarie', *Port Macquarie News*, 4 August.

40   McPhee, S, 2018, '"Wicked" NSW murderer awaits jail sentence', *Illawarra Mercury*, 28 September.

41   Bricknell, S, and Renshaw, L, 2016, *Missing persons in Australia, 2008–2015*, Statistical Bulletin 01, Canberra, ACT: Australian Institute of Criminology, Canberra.

42   West, MG, 2012, 'Pooling resources to fight child abuse and abduction', *The Wall Street Journal*, 24 May.